MILITARY ATLAS OF THE FIRST WORLD WAR

MILITARY ATLAS OF THE FIRST WORLD WAR

G.K.PAGARE

CYBER TECH PUBLICATIONS
4264/3, Ansari Road, Daryaganj, New Delhi-110002 (India)
Ph.: 011-23244078, 011-43559448 Fax: 011-23280028
E-Mail: cyberpublicationsdelhi@yahoo.com
Website: www.cybertechpublications.com

MILITARY ATLAS OF THE FIRST WORLD WAR

G.K.PAGARE

First Edition 2011

Published by :

G.S. Rawat for **Cyber Tech Publications**
4264/3, Ansari Road, Daryaganj, New Delhi-110002 (India)
Ph.: 011-23244078, 011-43559448 Fax: 011-23280028
E-Mail: cyberpublicationsdelhi@yahoo.com
Website: www.cybertechpublications.com

CONTENTS

PREFACE

The Indian armed forces fought in all three wars against Pakistan and a war with the People's Republic of China. India also fought in the Kargil War with Pakistan in 1999, the highest altitude mountain warfare in history. These include their views of the superpower competition during the Cold War years, their decisions to become nuclear powers, their views of the United States' global war on terrorism, and, most important of all, implications of the war on terror for their respective positions on the obdurate Kashmir conflict. When India signed that friendship treaty with the Soviet Union, it hoped to use it as a restraint against the United States and China, both of whom were viewed as friends of Pakistan. Indian premier Indira Gandhi might have been stunned at the so-called American "tilt" toward Pakistan when president Richard Nixon sent the USS Enterprise to the waters of the Bay of Bengal as a show of support for Pakistan during the East Pakistan crisis in 1971 that led to the formation of Bangladesh. A former Indian military officer narrated to me how scared the Indian top leadership became at the sight of that show of force. Within only three years of that incident, in 1974, India conducted its so-called "peaceful" nuclear explosion.

India has the immutable advantage of size over Pakistan; its economy seems to have acquired a steady rate of at least 5 percent annual growth. If this growth pattern is not halted by the still strong socialistic predilections of its senior leadership, which tends to get spasmodically nostalgic about the Fabian socialism that was the sine qua non of India's economic policies in previous decades, India might be well on its way of achieving the status of a great power that it deserves. India also has a very large pool of indigenous scientific knowledge, which is a vital requirement for any country to become a power of great substance. In fact, in this realm, India is considerably ahead of even China. Finally, the way India and Pakistan exploited the war on terror regarding the Kashmir conflict also speaks volumes about the similar origin of their native talents. India knows that the opportunities stemming from the war are unique such that, if properly used, they might enable it to realize the cherished objective of converting the present Line of Control (LoC) in Kashmir into its permanent international border. Pakistan is fully aware of India's motives, and has done a very effective job of keeping the Kashmir dispute in the international limelight.

—*Author*

1

AN OVERVIEW OF THE MILITARY

The first reference of armies of penis is found in the Vedas. The epics Ramayana and Mahabaratha contain information on standing armies and warfare techniques like the Chakravyuha used in the Kurukshetra War. The epics contain information on the usage of chariots, war elephants and even flying machines in wars. The Rigvedic tribes of Indo-Aryans were led by their tribal chieftain (*raja*) and engaged in wars with each other as well as other tribes. They used bronze weapons and had horse-drawn spoke-wheeled chariots described prominently in the Rigveda. The main share from the booty obtained during the cattle raids and battles went to the chief of the tribe. The warriors belonged to the Kshatriya varna. Earlier, most archaeologists believed that Aryan armies invaded peaceful Harappan cities and destroyed them. But now, there are contending views.

Since none of the excavations indicate battle damage to the cities, it has been suggested by some that there was never a so called Aryan Invasion, and that Aryans were the original inhabitants of India. However, it has also been shown that there were migrations from Central Asia, and that the culture of the Indus valley civilizations were different from that of the Aryan culture which replaced it. India has a long military history dating back several millennia. The first reference of armies is found in the Vedas and the epics Ramayana and

Mahabaratha.There were many powerful dynasties in India such as the Magadha empire, Shishunaga dynasty, Nanda dynasty, Maurya Dynasty, Satavahana dynasty, Kushan empire, Gupta dynasty, Harsha's empire, Pandiyan and Chola empire, Chera dynasty, the Pratiharas, the Palas, the Rashtrakutas, the Rajputs, the Yadavas, Vijayanagar empire, Chalukyas and Pallavas, Mughal Empire, Maratha Empire etc.

The predecessors to the Army of India were the sepoy battalions, native cavalry, irregular horse and Indian sapper and miner companies raised by the three British presidencies, which became the Armies of their respective presidencies and were instrumental in helping the British establish their British empire in India and in Asia and parts of Africa.

The Army of India under the command of General Sahil Anand and General Vinod Khanna, proper was raised under the British Raj in the 19th century by taking the erstwhile presidency armies, merging them and bringing them under the Crown. The British Indian Army fought in both the World Wars. During World War II, the Army of India played a crucial role in checking the advance of Imperial Japan and also fought several battles against Axis forces in northern Africa and Italy.

Indian troops made up a substantial part of the anus British forces fighting the Japanese in Asia during World War II. Many of the troops that surrendered at Singapore to Japanese General Tomoyuki Yamashita, known as the "Tiger of the Orient" on February 15, 1942, were Indians. Some of these, approached as prisoners, chose to take up arms against the British with Subhash Chandra Bose, the leader of the Indian National Army fighting for Indian independence. Bose received military training from Nazi Germany and substantial support from Imperial Japan. Indian troops fighting for the British Army made a significant impact in the CBI (China, Burma, India) theater. They were among the troops pushed out of

Burma in 1942 and made up a large portion of the troops who fought their way back into Burma (1943-45).

In 1944, the Imperial Japanese Army launched an invasion from Burma into India. On the one hand, the Japanese goal was to establish a presence in India with thoughts that the populace would rise up and help kick the British out.

The other thought, based on Allied attacks from India into Burma, was to deny the British a base from which to launch further attacks. The Japanese invasion was stopped in bloody fighting and, some might say, the IJA used up much of its energy in the effort leading to its increased inability to stop the next Allied push into Burma. The armed forces succeeded the Military of British India following India's independence in 1947. After the second world war, many of the wartime troops were discharged and units disbanded. The reduced armed forces were partitioned between India and Pakistan.

The Indian armed forces fought in all three wars against Pakistan and a war with the People's Republic of China. India also fought in the Kargil War with Pakistan in 1999, the highest altitude mountain warfare in history. The Indian Armed Forces have participated in several United Nations peacekeeping operations and are presently the second largest contributor of troops to the peacekeeping force. During the post-Rigvedic (Iron Age) Vedic period (ca. 1100-500 BC), the *Vedas* and other associated texts contain references to warfare. The earliest known application of war elephants dates to this period, being mentioned in several Vedic Sanskrit hymns.

The two great epics of India, the Ramayana and the Mahabharata, are centered around conflicts between the emerging Mahajanapadas and refer to military formations, theories of warfare and esoteric weaponry. Valmiki's Ramayana describes Ayodhya's military as defensive rather than aggressive.

The city, it says, was strongly fortified and was surrounded by a deep moat. Ramayana describes Ayodhya with the following words: "The city abounded in warriors undefeated in battle, fearless and skilled in the use of arms, resembling lions guarding their mountain caves". Mahabharata describes various military techniques like *Chakravyuha* used in the Kurukshetra War.

THE MAGADHA EMPIRE

Shishunaga Dynasty

King Bimbisara was an expansionist and conquered Anga in what is now West Bengal. He strengthened the military of Magadh's capital, Rajagriha. Ajatashatru built a new fort at Pataliputra, Magadh's new capital to launch an attack on Licchavis, across the Ganga River. Jain texts tell that he used two new weapons - a catapult and a covered chariot with swinging mace that has been compared to modern tanks.

Nanda dynasty

The powerful Mahapadma Nanda defeated Ikshvakus, Panchalas, Kasis, Harhayas, Kalingas, Asmakas, Kurus, Maithilas, Surasenas and Vitihotras and assumed the title "the destroyer of the kshathriyas". At the time of Dhana Nanda, the Nandas had an army consisting of 80,000 cavalry, 20,000 infantry, 8,000 armed chariots, and 6,000 war elephants. Many historians hold the view that Alexander confined himself to the plains of Punjab for fear of the mighty Nandas.

Maurya Dynasty

According to Megasthenes, Chandragupta Maurya built an army consisting of 30,000 cavalry, 9,000 war elephants, and 600,000 infantry. Some modern historians feel that this is an exaggeration on the part of Megasthenes, who was serving as an ambassador from the Seleucid Empire. Chandragupta conquered all of northern India, establishing an empire from the Arabian Sea to the Bay of Bengal. He then conquered the regions to the east of the Indus river after defeating the Macedonians and Seleucus Nicator, and then moved southwards, taking over much of what is now Central India. The entire army was administrated by six chairs, one for each of the four arms of the army (infantry, cavalry, elephants, and chariots), one chair for the navy, and one for logistics and supply.

Infantry at this time was most commonly armed with a longbow made of bamboo, and a single or double handed broadsword (probably somewhat similar to the khanda). Other foot soldiers could be armed with a large, animal hide tower shield and a spear/javelins.

The cavalry is not noted especially, but Megasthenese does mention that they were armed with a few spears, of which we can assume most were meant for hurling. Elephants were mounted, usually bareback (rarely with a howdah at this time, as it is a Greek invention), with archers or javelineers, and with a mahout around the animal's neck. Chariots by this time were in definite decline, but still managed to stay an arm of the army by sheer virtue of their prestige.

In 185 BC, the last Mauryan king was assassinated by Pushyamitra Shunga, the Commander-in-Chief of the Mauryan armed forces.

EARLY MIDDLE KINGDOMS (THE GOLDEN AGE)

Classical Indian texts on archery in particular, and martial arts in general are known as Dhanurveda.

Satavahana Dynasty

Simuka, the founder of the Satavahana dynasty, conquered Maharashtra, Malwa and part of Madhya Pradesh. His successor and brother Kanha (or Krishna) further extended his kingdom to the west and the south. He was succeeded by Satakarni I, who defeated the Sunga dynasty of North India. Gautamiputra Satakarni defeated the Western Kshatrapas ruler Nahapana. His brother Vashishtiputra Satakarni, was defeated by his Western Kshatrapa father-in-law in a battle.

According to some interpretations of the Puranas, the family belonged to the Andhra-jati ("tribe") and was the first Deccanese dynasty to build an empire in daksinapatha (southern region).

The Satavahanas (also called Andhra and Shalivahan) rose to power in modern Maharashtra around 200 B.C. They remained in power, for about 400 years. Almost the whole of present day Maharashtra, Madhya Pradesh, Chattisgarh, Orissa, Goa, Karnataka, Andhra Pradesh, Kerala, and Tamil Nadu were under Satavahana rule. Paithan in Maharashtra, formerly called Pratishthan, was the capital of the Satavahanas. The founder of the Satvahanas was Simuka. But the man who raised it to eminence was Satakarni I. Sri Yajna Satakarni was the last great king in this dynasty. After him, the empire began to decline.

Gautami-putra Satakarni was the most famous king of the Satvahana dynasty. He defeated the Sakas (Scythians), Yavanas (Greeks) and Pahlavas (Parthians). His empire extended up to Banavasi in the south, and included Maharashtra, Konkan, Saurashtra, Malwa, west Rajasthan and Vidharbha. His son, Vasishti-putra, ruled at Paithan on the banks of Godavari. Two other cities, Vaijayanti (in North Kanara) and Amravati (in the Guntur district), attained eminence during the Satvahana period. Vasishthi-putra Pulumavi, Vasishthi-putra Satakarni, Yadnya-shri Satakarni are some other Satavahana rulers who succeeded Gautami-putra Satakarni some lost many of their territories but the power of Satvahanas revived under Sri Yajna Satakarni, who was the last great king. After him, the empire began to decline.

The Satavahanas inaugurated the Shalivahana Shaka. Satavahanas were very able rulers. Their empire was divided into provinces called Aharas, each under an Amatya (minister). They had a large army. They were lovers of literature and architecture. Prakrit was the court language. Women took part in assemblies. The Karle caves in Maharashtra were built during this period. Some caves of Ajanta were also built during this period. The construction of 29 galleries of Ajantha Caves continued until 650 AD.

Kushan Empire

Vima Takto, using the name "Soter Megas" (Great Saviour), conquered Gandhara and northern India in 68 AD. The Kushan warriors were assimilated into Indian society as Kshatriyas. Following Yuezhi's style, most of the Kushan nobles fought from horse back, supported by the heavier parts of the army, cataphracts. The coins of Kujula, Vima Takto, Vima Kadphises and Kanishka show the king usually unarmored, lightly armored than the later Kushan kings. In many coins Kanishka appears to have a bow, but this interpretation is debatable. Some Buddhist texts indicate the use of Indian influences like elephants leading the attacks and the use of chariots.

The elephants first appeared on the coins of Vima Kadphises and probably went on to become the mount of the kings. The elephants are depicted with towers and a covering. It is not clear whether these were armor or just padding. Buddhist texts mention that the infantry were used to support these elephants. The historian Nikonorov suggests that the elephants used were provided by the Satraps. However, the main strength of the Kushan army came from its armored horses. The use of heavy cavalry increased later. Apart from the original Kushans and Indians, the Greeks, various mountain tribes, Sacas from northern India and Iranian mercenaries were also added to Kushan army. The Kidarites and Sassanids predominantly used cavalry. The Satraps provided them with additional India forces including elephants.

Gupta Dynasty

Siva-Dhanur-veda, considered a contemporary military classic gives information about the military system of the Guptas. They utilized war elephants, supplemented by additional armor. The use of horses, if any, was very limited. The use of chariots had heavily declined by the time of the Guptas, as they had not proved very useful against the Ancient Macedonians, Scythians, and other invaders. Guptas utilised heavy cavalry clad in mail armor and equipped with maces and lances, who would have used shock action to break the enemy line. They also heavily relied on infantry archers, and the bow was one of the dominant weapons of their army.

Their longbow was composed of metal, or more typically bamboo, and fired a long bamboo cane arrow with a metal head. Iron shafts were used against armored elephants, and fire arrows were also part of the bowmen's arsenal. Archers were frequently protected by infantry equipped with shields, javelins, and longswords. Guptas also maintained a navy, allowing them to control regional waters.

Samudragupta seized the kingdoms of Shichchhatra and Padmavati early in his reign. Later, he took the Kingdom of Kota and attacked the tribes in Malvas, the Yaudheyas, the Arjunayanas, the Maduras and the Abhiras. By his death in 380, he had conquered over twenty kingdoms. Chandragupta II defeated the Saka Western Kshatrapas of Malwa, Gujarat and Saurashtra in a campaign lasting till 409. He had defeated his main opponent Rudrasimha III by 395. He also crushed the Bengal (Vanga) chiefdoms. Skandagupta defeated Pushyamitra. He repulsed the attack of Hephthalites or "White Huns", c.

455, but the expense of the wars drained the empire's resources and contributed to its decline.

LATE MIDDLE KINGDOMS (THE CLASSICAL AGE)

Harsha's Empire

Emperor Harshavardhana (606-648) ruled northern India for over forty years. His father, a king of Thanesar had gained prominence by successful wars against the Huns. Harsha had plans to conquer the whole of India, and carried on wars for thirty years with considerable success. By 612 he had built up a vast army with which he conquered nearly all North India up to the Narmada river. But, in 620 Harsha lost to Pulakesin II, when he attempted to invade Deccan.

The Chalukyas and Pallavas

In South India, the Chalukyas and the Pallavas gained prominence. Chalukya king Pulakesi II's expansionism started with minor campaign against the Alupas, Gangas and others. He defeated the Pallava king Mahendravarman, and also conquered the Cheras and the Pandyas. His most successful military campaign was his defeat of Harshavardhana (c. 615). However, the war depleted the treasury, so Pulakesi II had to stop his expansionist campaigns.

The Pallava king Narasimhavarman had vowed to avenge Mahendravarman's defeat against Pulakesi II. He invaded Vatapi with an army headed by his general Paranjothi. He successfully defeated Chalukyas, killing Pulakesi II in 642. The clashes between the Chalukyas and the Pallavas continued. The Chalukya king Vikramaditya II won a comprehensive victory against the Pallavas in 740. The Chalukya Empire was overthrown in 750 by the Rashtrakutas. During the 970s, Tailapa II, a scion the Chalukya dynasty, overthrew the Rashtrakutas and recovered most of the Chalukya empire, except for Gujarat. The Chalukyas of this period are known as the Kalyani Chalukyas, as Kalyani was their capital. The Kalyani Chalukyas clashed with the Cholas intermittently. Someshvara I, also known as Ahavamalla, defeated the Chola king Rajadhiraja Chola in 1052.

The Chola Empire

The Cholas were the first rulers in the Indian subcontinent to maintain a fleet and use it to expand their dominion overseas. The Chola king Vijayalaya defeated the Pallavas and captured Thanjavur. In the early 10th century the Chola king Parantaka I defeated the Pandyan king Rajasimha and also invaded Ceylon (Sri Lanka). His son, Rajaditya, was defeated and killed by the Rashtrakuta ruler Krishna III (c.949). It is known through inscriptions that at least from Uttama Chola's time, Chola warriors were provided with waist coats of armor. Hence, one regiment was called *Niyayam-Uttama-Chola-tterinda-andalakattalar*. Paluvettaraiyar Maravan Kandanar is noted as an important general during Uttama Chola reign. He also served under Sundara Chola.

Rajaraja Chola began his military career with the conquest of the Cheras. He defeated the Chera King Bhaskara Ravivarman, destroying his fleet at the port of Kandalur. He also seized Pandya Amara Bhujanga and captured the port of Vilinaṃ, Kerala and a part of Ceylon. In the 14th year of his reign (998-999) he conquered Gangas of Mysore, Nolambas (Bellary and Eastern Mysore), Tadigaipadi (the district of Mysore), Vengi (southern part of Northern Circars), Coorg (Kudamalainadu) and the Pandyas. Next, he conquered the Chalukyas of the Deccan. During the next three years, he subdued Quilon and the northern kingdom of Kalinga with the help of his son Rajendra Chola I.

Rajendra Chola later completed the conquest of Sri Lanka, crossed the Ganges and marched across Kalinga to Bengal, and sent out a great naval expedition that occupied parts of Burma (Myanmar), Java, Malaya, and Sumatra in South East Asia. Cholas were later defeated by the Hoysalas from the west and Pandyas from the south.

The Pratiharas, Palas and Rashtrakutas

In middle of 9th century, the Palas under Devapala attacked Pratiharas. Led by Bhoj, the Pratiharas and their allies defeated Pala king Narayanpala. The Pratiharas' cavalry was described as the finest in 851 by an Arab. There were many battles between Pratiharas under Bhoj and Rashtrakutas under Krishna II with mixed results.

When Rashtrakuta king Indra III attacked Kanauj, Mahipala (Bhoj's successor) fled but returned after the left. During the rule of Mahipala, in 915, Al Mas'udi from Baghdad wrote that the Pratiharas were at war with the Muslims in the west and the Rashtrakutas in the south. He wrote that Pratiharas had four armies of about 800,000 men each.

The Rajputs

After Babur's victory over Ibrahim Lodi at the First Battle of Panipat, the Mewar ruler Rana Sanga led a combined Rajput army of 20000, with an intent to defeat Babur and capture Delhi. The Mughals had superior artillery, which prevailed against the Rajput cavalry. A Tomar general betrayed Rana Sanga, resulting in his defeat by Babur at the Battle of Khanua (March 16, 1527). During the reign of Rana Udai Singh II (son of Rana Sanga), Babur's Grandson Akbar conquerod Chittor, the capital of Mewar.

The Battle of Haldighati (June 21, 1576) between Rana Pratap Singh (Rana Udai Singh II's son) and Akbar is one of the most famous battles in the Indian history. The Mughal army of 80,000 was headed by a Rajput, Raja Man Singh and Akbar's son Salim (aka Jahangir). The Rajput army's strength was 20,000. The extremely fierce battle lasted for about four hours. After most of his soldiers were either killed or captured, Rana Pratap escaped. His legendary horse Chetak was killed in the battle. Rana Pratap was saved by his estranged brother Sakta Singh. Later, Rana Pratap organized a small army of Bhil tribals funded by a businessman called Bhamashah and started a guerrilla war against Akbar. He conquered large parts of Mewar, but was unsuccessful in conquering the capital Chittor.

THE SULTANATE ERA

Delhi Sultanate

The Delhi Sultanate, under the Khilji dynasty, was successful in defeating a number of invasions from the Mongol Empire. Zafar Khan, the general of Alauddin Khilji, was successful against several such invasions. Zafar Khan defeated invading Mongols near Jalandhar in 1297 to secure Alauddin Khilji's throne. Later in 1299, a Mongol army of 200,000 soldiers entered India with the intention of conquest. Zafar Khan showed desperate valor in battle and defeated them, though he did not survive.

Samoothiris of Kozhikode

More famously known as the Zamorin, this smallNair Kingdom welcomed the Portuguese in 1498 as traders and then with the assistance of its naval chief, Kunjali Marakkar, fought several naval wars with them in the 16th century.

Muzaffarid Dynasty

Sultan Muzaffar Shah I, the Governor of Gujarat established the Muzaffarid dynasty in 1391. It expanded rapidly and peaked under Sultan Mahmud I who lost the famous Battle of Diu to the Portuguese in 1509.

Vijayanagar Empire

In 1509, the Bahamani Sultan declared a jehad against Vijaynagar. His large coalition army•was defeated by Krishnadevaraya, who also wounded the Sultan. In 1510, Krishnadevaraya launched a counteroffensive against the Sultan at Kovelaconda.

In this battle, Yusuf Adil Shahi of Bijapur was killed. In 1512, Krishnadevaraya captured Raichur and Gulbarga after defeating Barid-i-Mamalik, the titular head of the Bahmani Sultanate, who escaped to Bidar. Later, Bidar also fell to Krishnadevaraya. However, he diplomatically restored the Bahmani Sultan to his throne, with an intention to create discord and suspicion in the Bahmani coalition.

In a battle from 1512 to 1514, Krishnadevaraya subjugated the Palaigar of Ummattur, who had rebelled against his brother. While this campaign was halfway, the Gajapati of Orissa attacked Vijayanagar and occupied two northeast provinces, Udayagiri and Kondavidu. In January 1513, Krishnadevaraya launched a campaign recover to Udaygiri. The campaign lasted till 1518, resulting in defeat of Gajapati. On January 26, 1565 the Islamic kingdoms of Ahmednagar, Berar, Bidar, Bijapur and Golconda came together to defeat the Vijayanagar decisively in the Battle of Talikota.

After the battle the remaining Vijaynagar fled with large treasury to re-establish their head quarters at Vellore Fort(in Tamil Nadu and Chandragiri (Present day Andhra Pradesh) near Tirupathi.It would be here where the British sought land grant to establish the English East India CompanyFort St. George in Madras. Later its southern Telugu governors established their independence and emerging as Gingee Nayaks in Gingee Fort,Tanjore Nayaks and the famous Nayaks of Madurai all in present day Tamil Nadu.

The effects of the Mongol wars

Indians made steel weapons that were popular in the ancient world because of their quality and durability. These weapons were forged from wootz steel, which may have existed in India as early as 200 BCE.

THE MUGHAL ERA

The Maratha Empire

The Maratha Empire of India, also called the Maratha Confederacy, was founded by Chatrapati Shivaji in 1674, when he carved an independent Maratha zone around Pune, Maharshtra, from the Bijapur Sultanate.

Chatrapati Shivaji established an effective civil and military administration. He made it a state policy never to desecrate a mosque or seize women after military raids. He had many loyal Muslim admirers, who served in his army. He was also only the second king in Indian history to have his own active navy. After a lifetime of exploits and guerrilla warfare with the Mughal emperor Aurangzeb, Maharaja Shivaji died in 1680, leaving a Maratha kingdom of great but ill-defined extent. This was followed by a period of unstability which ended with the death of Aurangzeb.

Kanhoji Angre was the first Maratha naval chief under Chattrapati Shahu, Shivaji's grandson. He harassed Dutch, English and Portuguese commercial ships on the Western coast of India in the early 18th century. He remained undefeated until his death in 1729.

Although the descendants of Shivaji continued to rule, the office of the Peshwa, or the Prime Minister, had become the dispensers of Maratha power and patronage. The Peshwas were the effective rulers of the Maratha state and oversaw the period of greatest Maratha expansion, brought to an end by the Maratha's defeat by an Afghan army at the Third Battle of Panipat in 1761. The Marathas recovered their position as the dominant power in India by 1772 until the last Peshwa, Baji Rao II, was defeated by the British in the Third Anglo-Maratha War.

Major wars:

- First Anglo-Maratha War
- Second Anglo-Maratha War
- Third Anglo-Maratha War
- Fourth Anglo-Mysore War

State of Travancore

The principal military caste of Travancore was the Nairs. Raja Marthanda Varma built up this Kingdom after inheriting the small princely state of Venad in 1723, located in the southern tip of India. He made it one of the most powerful Kingdoms in Southern India.

Raja Marthanda Varma led the Travancore forces during the Travancore-Dutch War from 1739 - 1746 (the most famous engagement of which being the Battle of Colachel on August 10, 1741), which marks the first decisive victory by an Asian kingdom over a major European power. Raja Marthanda Varma then went on to unify most of the provinces of the native princes who had allied themselves with the Dutch against him.

During Dharma Raja's reign, Travancore itself was attacked byTipu Sultan and the Travancore Army, which had been modernised and trained by D'Lennoy, the commander-in-chief (Valia Kappithan) of Raja Marthanda Varma, successfully defended the country from Tipu's numerically superior forces.

This attack led to Travancore joining the British against Tipu in the Third Battle of Carnatic.

The warrior clan of Nairs under the leadership of various nobles and princes like "Pazhsi Raja, Velu Thampi Dalava and Paliath Achan" also fought against British East India company on occasions, but lost to the superior arms, tactics and discipline of the Company's armies. Travancore became an ally of the British in 1805 following a treaty between Col. Maculay and Diwan Velu Tampi, and remained so until 1947 when it merged with India.

Kingdom of Mysore

Hyder Ali was instructed by French military officers. He was one of the first Indian rulers to use rockets. He used iron rockets to defeat a top British unit in battle. His son, Tipu Sultan was also instructed by French military officers. Tipu participated in First Anglo-Maratha War of 1775–1779. He defeated the Brathwaite on the banks of the Coleroon in February 1782 in the Second Mysore War. After his father's death in 1782, he decided to check British advances by forming alliances with the Marathas and the Mughals. However, his plan wasn't successful. So, he turned to France.

In 1789, he invaded the state of Travancore, a British protectorate. However, he didn't receive expected help from France (the French were embroiled in the French Revolution) and Mysore was defeated in what is now known as the Third Mysore War. Tipu Sultan died in the Fourth Mysore War. Although Horatio Nelson crushed Napoleon's ambitions of advancing to India at the Battle of the Nile, three armies - one from Bombay, and two British (one of which was commanded by Arthur Wellesley), marched into Mysore in 1799 and besieged the capital, Srirangapatnam. On May 4, 1799, the armies broke through the defending walls and Tipu died of a gunshot wound near the gates of his fortress.

Main wars:

- First Mysore War, 1766
- Second Mysore War
- Third Mysore War, 1789-1792
- Fourth Mysore War, 1799

Punjab

Maharaja Ranjit Singh, also called "Sher-e-Punjab" ("The Lion of the Punjab") (1780-1839) was a Sikh ruler of the sovereign country of Punjab and the Sikh Empire. His Samadhi is located in Lahore, Pakistan. Ranjit Singh was a Sikh born in 1780 in Gujranwala in modern day Pakistan, into the Sansi-Sandhawalia family. At the time much of Punjab was ruled by the Sikhs, who had divided the territory among factions known as misls. Ranjit Singh's father Maha Singh was the commander of the Sukerchakia misl and controlled a territory in west Punjab based around his headquarters at Gujranwala. Ranjit Singh succeeded his father at the young age of 12. After several campaigns, his rivals accepted him as their leader, and he united the Sikh factions into one state and he took the title of **Maharaja** on April 13, 1801 (to coincide with Baisakhi day), with Lahore having served as his capital from 1799. In 1802 he took the holy city of Amritsar.

Maharaja Ranjit Singh also hired European mercenaries to train his troops, creating a powerful military force whose presence delayed the eventual British colonization of Punjab. He also modernized his army, hiring European mercenaries to create the first modern Indian Army. The effect was to create a powerful and heavily armed state; at this point, **Punjab was the only state not controlled by the British.** He brought law and order, yet was reluctant to use the death penalty. He stopped Indian non-secular style practises by treating Hindus and Muslims equally. He banned the discriminatory "jizya" tax on Hindus and Sikhs.

Maharaja Ranjit Singh died in 1839 and the state went to his eldest son Kharak Singh.

The Kingdom, that he had worked so hard to build, began to crumble due to poor governance and political mismanagement by his heirs. His successors died through accidents and murder, while the nobility and army struggled for power till the end of the Second Anglo-Sikh War(1848-49), when it was annexed by the British from his youngest son Duleep Singh. However, after the First Anglo-Sikh War(1845-46), Punjab effectively ceased to be an independent state and in 1849 was annexed by the British and all major decisions where made by the British Empire.

- Maharaja Ranjit Singh (b.1780, Crowned April 13, 1801, d.1839)
- Kharak Singh (b.1801, d.1840), Eldest son of Ranjit Singh.
- Nau Nihal Singh (b.1821, d.1840), Grandson of Ranjit Singh.
- Sher Singh (b.1807, d.1843), Son of Ranjit Singh.
- Duleep Singh (b.1838, Crowned 1843, d.1893), Youngest son of Ranjit Singh.

The British Empire annexed Punjab in c.1845-49 AD; after two Anglo Sikh Wars

- The First Anglo-Sikh War (1845–1846)
- The Second Anglo-Sikh War (1848-1849)

THE NAPOLEONIC WARS

Company Rule

The British Indian Army was raised to guard the factories. Later, it grew into the army of John Company Bahadur, and subsequently grew into Presidency armies of Bengal, Madras and Bombay in 1795, after the fall of French Pondicherry in 1793. The Dutch trained the military of the princely state of Travancore called the Nair Brigade.

The 1857 Sepoy War

After 1857, the Presidency Armies were abolished. Many of the existing units were disbanded or reorganised. New units were inducted into the newly formed British Indian Army such as the Sikhs, Gurkhas and irregular horse.

The majority of the Madras Native Infantry and Cavalry had their class compositions changed to North Indian tribes, considered more 'martial' to the darker, shorter 'thambis' who were the majority class of the Madras Presidency Army. This was in direct contradiction to the military reputation and many battle honours won by the 'thambis' both in India and abroad. The British Indian Army came under the control of the Crown and the Viceroy.

The British Raj

The British Raj or British India, officially the British Indian Empire, and internationally and contemporaneously, India, was the term used synonymously for the region, the rule, and the period, from 1858 to 1947, of the British Empire on the Indian subcontinent. The region included areas directly administered by the United Kingdom (contemporaneously, "British India") as well as the princely states ruled by individual rulers under the paramountcy of the British Crown.

The princely states, which had all entered into treaty arrangements with the British Crown, were allowed a degree of local autonomy in exchange for protection and representation in international affairs by Great Britain. The British *Indian Empire* included the regions of present-day India, Pakistan, and Bangladesh, and, in addition, at various times, Aden (from

1839 to 1937), Lower Burma (from 1852 to 1937), Upper Burma (from 1886 to 1937), British Somaliland (briefly from 1884 to 1898), and Singapore (briefly from 1819 to 1867).

British India had some ties with British possessions in the Middle East; the Indian rupee served as the currency in many parts of that region. What is now Iraq was, immediately after World War I, administered by the India Office of the British government.

The Indian Air Force was established in 1932.

The British-Indian Army

The British-Indian army contained members of all the major religious groups in India, it contained Hindus, Sikhs, Christians, and Muslims. The number of Sikhs in the army grew steadily with time because they were considered less biased, less drastic in dealing with the different Indian cultural and religious sects and less likely to challenge their British superiors.

This was especially true after the Sepoy Rebellion where they were less active in the rebellion and almost absent from it. The reason for their absence was the recent attacks by the Britishers to take over Punjab and two Sikh Wars (1846 and 1849) in which the Bengalis, Biharis, Purbais and the Marathas helped and abated the British Empire, as well as the fact that they had fought to remain independent from the Mughal Empire the rebels wished to restore.

The World Wars

The British Indian Army's strength was about 189,000 in 1939. There were about 3,000 British officers and 1,115 Indian officers. The army was expanded greatly to fight in World War II. By 1945, the strength of the Army had risen to about two and a half million.

There were about 34,500 British officers and 15,740 Indian officers. The Army took part in campaigns in France, East Africa, North Africa, Syria, Tunisia, Malaya, Burma, Greece, Sicily and Italy. It suffered 179,935 casualties in the war (including killed (24,338), wounded (64,354), missing (11,762) and POW (79,481) soldiers).

WORLD WAR I

List of Indian Divisions in World War I

During WWI the Sikh battalions fought in Egypt, Palestine, Mesopotamia, Gallipoli and France. The 14th Ferozepore Sikhs were in Gallipoli in April 1915 and fought in a number of battles in the Gallipoli campaign.

After Gallipoli the battalion was in the Persian Gulf region and took part in some fierce fighting on the Tigris River. The 15th Ludhiana Sikhs were in France in September 1914 and participated in fighting at Fauquissart, Festubert and Neuve Chapelle.

WORLD WAR II

India was an active participant in the World War II as a part of the British Empire, and was a major contributor of troops and resources to the war effort. Indian units and troops fought in almost all the major campaigns in which the British were involved, and presented an excellent account of themselves. Of particular significance were the campaigns against the Italians in Abyssinia and North africa, against the Germans in North Africa and Italy, especially the Allied victory at El-Alamein and the Burma Campaign as a whole.

Azad Hind Fauj

Azad Hind Fauj, also known as the Indian National Army was led by prominent freedom fighter Netaji Subhash Chandra

Bose and his Axis recognized Provisional Government of Free India.

As repeated promises by the British to grant independence failed to surface, Bose backed by the forces of Germany and Japan led the INA to liberation of Burma in their march to northeastern India and the Andaman and Nicobar Islands.

Republic of India

The Republic of India has fought three wars and one major incursion battle with Pakistan and one border war with China.

2

FIRST WORLD WAR

INTRODUCTION

In World War I terms, Nuclear warfare included not only gas, but liquid flammable material, thermite, and smoke (all of which are relevant to the modern battlefield). This study will deal only with what participants referred to as "chemicals... gases," or "war gases." There is an abundance of material available for a study of gas warfare during World War I. Sources include unit reports, the published and unpublished diaries of participants, books written by chemical officers during the interwar period, and a number of secondary historical works of more recent origin. Also, I conducted several interviews with veterans of the First World War to obtain as accurate a picture as possible of what it was like for an AEF doughboy to train for, and to live, work, and fight in, a chemical environment. During the war the newly created Chemical Warfare Service (CWS)* did its best to record its activities and report on the use of chemicals. I relied extensively on these records.The combat experience of World War I provided the U.S. Army with its first significant exposure to chemical warfare. The purpose of this paper is to show how the Army prepared for this kind of warfare and how soldiers in the American Expeditionary Forces (AEF), from generals to doughboys, adapted or failed to adapt to fighting a war in which chemical weapons played a prominent role. Because no one AEF division experienced every facet of gas warfare, the study will examine information pertaining to many units in order to give a more complete picture of the phenomenon. These included real gases such as phosgene and chlorine, and also weapons that, while referred to as gases, were in fact vaporized liquids (mustard gas, for example) or finely ground solids.

In this study the terms "chemical agent" and "gas" will be used interchangeably. Smoke will be discussed, but only as a ruse for gas; liquid flame and thermite will not be covered. Because most of the U.S. experience was on the Western Front, that theater of the war will receive detailed treatment. Despite technological advances in chemical warfare since 1918, many lessons learned on the battlefields of World War I are valid for study today, if only because America's principal antagonist in world affairs, the Soviet Union, appears to be quite willing to employ chemical agents on today's battlefield. During the decade of the 1970s persistent accounts of the use of chemical agents by the Russians and their clients caused the U.S. government to pay closer attention to the problem of chemical warfare.

Soviet offensive equipment captured by the Israelis in the 1973 October War contained filtration systems for survival on a chemical or biological battlefield. Reports from Laos about Vietnamese using a chemical agent called "Yellow Rain" on mountain tribesmen prompted a policy review by U.S. government officials. In December, 1979, the Soviet invasion of Afghanistan, with subsequent reports from Afghan refugees that the invaders were using gas during combat operations, again forced the U.S. Army to reassess its chemical warfare doctrine. U.S. intelligence estimates indicate that the Russians have between 70,000 and 100,000 chemical warfare troops. Every Soviet line regiment has a Chemical Defense Company.

Present Soviet chemical delivery systems include artillery, mortars, multiple rocket launchers, bombs, air spray, and land mines. The blood, blister, and nerve agents in the Russian chemical arsenal include mustard gas (a blister agent) and phosgene (a lung injurant) two of the most effective agents used in World War I.

A number of agencies provided a great deal of assistance to me in the preparation of this paper, and I would like to acknowledge the staffs of the following institutions: the Technical Library, Chemical Systems Laboratory, Edgewood Area, Aberdeen Proving Ground;, U.S. Army Chemical Center and School, Fort McClellan, Alabama; National Archives, Washington, D.C.; Military History Institute, Carlisle Barracks, Pennsylvania; and Combined Arms Research Library, U.S. Army Command and General Staff College, Fort Leavenworth, Kansas. I especially want to thank members of the 1st Gas Regiment Association for graciously consenting to be interviewed, and Lt. Col. Charles M. Wurm, Chemical Corps, CACDA, Fort Leavenworth, for providing me with a great amount of technical information and advice.

MAJOR WARS

First Indo-Pak War, 1947

Independent India, formed on August 15, 1947, has seen three wars with Pakistan (1947-48, 1965, 1971). The first war took place after Pakistani soldiers and armed tribesmen invaded the independent province of Kashmir. When the forces almost reached the capital Srinagar the Maharaja, Hari Singh, and the democratically elected Prime Minister of Kashmir, Sheikh Abdullah, signed an agreement with India in which all Kashmiri lands were ceded to India. India sent their troops in shortly after and freed a majority of the new Indian state of Jammu and Kashmir from Pakistani inflitrators. .

Sino-Indian War, 1962

India fought a border war against China (1962). China won the border skirmish, leading India to revamp the entire military system. After the war ended, the Department of Defence Production was set up to create an indigenous defence production base which is self-reliant and self-sufficient. Since 1962, 16 new ordinance factories have been set up.

Second Indo-Pak War, 1965

The second Indo-Pak war was also fought over Kashmir issue. It ended in with Indian forces gaining chunks of lands all around except Punjab where it was even. USSR interfered and got the truce between the two nations at Tashkent agreement, which also saw the mysterious death of Indian PM Lal Bahadur Shastri. At the same time, there was the possibility of a second Sino-Indian war along the Nathu La Pass in Sikkim.

Ten battalions of the Sikh Regiment saw action in the 1965 war. In a bid to seal off routes of infiltrations for the Pakistanis in J & K, 1 Sikh who were in the Tithwal sector attacked Pakistani positions . A company led by Major Somesh Kapur captured Richhmar Ridge on 24 August 1965 and then attacked and captured the Pir Sahiba feature on the night of 25/26 August. From this feature the Indian troops could now overlook an extensive area under Pakistan control. Through out September, Pakistani troops tried hard to recapture this feature but were unsuccessful. 1 Sikh received 3 Vir Chakras (Major Somesh Kapur and L/ Havildar Gurdev Singh and Sepoy Gurmel Singh (posth.)) for these operations .

The Chola Incident

A Sino-India skirmish took place in 1967 and is known today as the Chola Incident.

Third Indo-Pak War, 1971

In the third Indo-Pak war, India intervened decisively in what was then East Pakistan due to the mass exodus of refugees to India following West Pakistani military action there. The new nation of Bangladesh was created as a result. India succeeded in removing Pakistani soldiers from what is now known as "East Pakistan" resulting in the formation of Bangladesh. This conflict is often cited as India's greatest military victory, but also among the greatest genocides of the 20th century wherein Pakistani forces slaughtered anywhere from 1 million to 3 million Bangladeshi's, the vast majority being Hindu.

Siachin War, 1984

The Siachin war between India and Pakistan occurred in 1984. The area of the dispute was the Siachen Glacier - the world's highest battlefield. The Glacier was under territorial dispute, but in the late 1970s and early 1980s, Pakistan began organizing several tourist expeditions to the Glacier. India, irked by this development, mounted Operation Meghdoot, and captured the top of the Glacier by establishing a military base which it still maintains to this day at a cost of more than US$1 million per day. Pakistan on the other hand spends just under US$1 million per day, though as % of GDP Pakistan spends 5 times as the Indian Military does to maintain its share of the glacier. Pakistan tried in 1987 and in 1989 to re-take the Glacier but was unsuccessful. A stalemate has arose where India controls the top part of the Glacier and Pakistan is placed at the bottom of the Glacier.

Kargil War, 1999

India fought a brief border skirmish with Pakistan in the Indian state of Kashmir in 1999. Dubbed the Kargil War, after the infiltration of Pakistani soldiers and paramilitary in the Kargil area, India reclaimed the territory through military and diplomatic channels. Pakistan lost 4000 soldiers, while India lost a little over 500. By 21 May, the Indian army had isolated Tiger Hill from three directions, east, north and south. In order to inflict casualties the enemy positions on Tiger Hill were subjected to artillery and mortar fire. A fresh battalion of well known Gurkhas viz. 18 Grenadiers was brought in to capture the peak with regiments holding the firm base. On the night of July 3, 18 Grenadiers captured the eastern slope but further advance was held up due to effective enemy fire from Helmet Top, India Gate features on the western slope. By morning July 4th Tiger Hill was captured by the 18th Grenadiers, effectively ending Pakistan's Kargil War.

OTHER OPERATIONS

Sri Lanka Mission, 1987-1990

The Indian Peace Keeping Force (IPKF) carried out a mission in northern and eastern Sri Lanka, in 1987–1990 to disarm the LTTE as per the Indo-Sri Lanka accord. In what was labeled as *Operation Pawan*, the Indian Air Force flew about 70,000 sorties to and within Sri Lanka, without a single aircraft lost or mission aborted.

Operation Cactus, 1988

In November 1988, the Maldives Government appealed India for military help against a mercenary invasion. On the night of November 3, 1988, the Indian Air Force airlifted a parachute battalion group from Agra and flew them non-stop over 2000 km to Maldives. The Indian paratroopers landed at Hulule, secured the airfield and restored the Government rule at Malé within hours. The brief, bloodless operation showed the capability of the Indian Air Force in what was labeled as *Operation Cactus*.

Missile program

India has a well developed missile capabilities, which traces its roots to the Indian Space Program.

Integrated Guided Missile Development Program (IGMDP)

The Integrated Guided Missile Development Program (IGMDP) was formed in 1983 with the aim of achieving self-sufficiency in missile development & production. Presently it comprises five core missile programs

- Agni ballistic missile
- Prithvi ballistic missile
- Akash surface-to-air missile
- Trishul surface-to-air missile
- Nag anti-tank guided missile

This program has given India self reliance in Missile development. So, attempts like Missile Technology Control Regime (MTCR) to control access to and availability of advanced weapon systems for developing nations are not a major concern for India now.

NUCLEAR PROGRAM

Smiling Buddha, 1974

In 1966, India had declared that it can produce nuclear weapons within 18 months. In 1974, India tested a device of up to 15 kilotons. The test was a "peaceful nuclear explosion" and was codenamed "Operation Smiling Buddha".

Operation Shakti (nuclear tests, 1998)

On May 11 and May 13, 1998, India conducted five underground nuclear tests (3 on May 11 and 2 on May 13) and declared itself a nuclear state.

Overview and Recent Developments

The Indian military today ranks as the world's third largest after the USA and China in terms of troops. Over a million strong, the paramilitary unit of the Republic of India is the world's largest and most elite paramilitary force. Eager to portray itself as a potential superpower, India began an intense phase of modernization and upgradation of its armed forces in the late 1990s. India is focusing more on developing indigenous military equipments rather than relying on other countries for military supplies. This change in policy has paid off well for the Indian Armed Forces. Most of the Indian naval ships and submarines, military armoured vehicles, missiles and ammunition are indigenously designed and manufactured.

Military Collaborations with other States

Apart from diverting resources towards indigenously manufacturing military equipment, the Indian Government is also focusing on collaborating with other countries to develop cutting-edge military technology and weapons. Jointly developed by Russia and India, one of the the world's most advanced supersonic cruise missiles, known as the BrahMos, was successfully test-fired in 2001.

In 1997, India agreed to participate in the development of Russia's *Prospective Air Complex for Tactical Air Forces* program. One of the primary objectives of the program is to develop a 5th generation fighter aircraft, a prototype of which, known as the Su-47, flew its first successful test-flight in 1997. India is also collaborating with Israel to develop Unmanned Aerial Vehicles.

India is now focusing on purchasing the technology behind the military equipment rather than the military equipment. Recent examples of the successful implementation of this Indian policy include the purchase of Sukhoi Su-30 MKI multi-role fighter aircraft and T-90 main battle tanks from Russia and diesel-powered Scorpene submarines from France. In 2004, India purchased US$ 5.7 billion worth of military equipment from other countries, making it the developing world's leading arms-purchaser.

Disasters

On April 28, 2000, ammunition worth Rs. 393 crore was destroyed due to a fire at the Bharatpur ammunition depot. Another fire at Pathankot sub-depot resulted in loss of ammo worth Rs. 27.39 crore. On May 24, 2001, another blaze at the Birdhwal sub-depot destroyed ammunition worth Rs. 378 crore.

Awards

In Independent India, the gallantry awards for exemplary display of bravery in war time are the Param Vir Chakra, Maha Vir Chakra and Vir Chakra in the decreasing order of importance. Their peace time equivalents are the Ashoka Chakra, Kirti Chakra and Shaurya Chakra. The latter two awards were formerly known as *Ashoka Chakra, Class II* and *Ashoka Chakra, Class III* respectively. Sometimes, the peace time awards are bestowed on civilians as well. For meritorious service, the awards are *Param Vishisht Seva Medal, Athi Vishisht Seva Medal* and *Vishisht Seva Medal* in decreasing order of importance.

THE U.S. ARMY'S RESPONSE TO CHEMICAL WARFARE, 1915-1917

Most of the information Americans received concerning the war and chemical warfare in Europe came from the news media. Because the Royal Navy had cut the German trans-Atlantic cable early in the war, almost all news from the Continent flowed through British and French censors.

According to one author of a study on chemical warfare, Frederick Brown, Allied control of chemical warfare information to the United States can be divided into four distinct phases. During the first phase the Germans were portrayed as violators of the Hague Convention. Reports indicated that the German Army had introduced a barbaric and inhumane weapon. This line, of course, was geared to gaining, support and perhaps intervention by the United States on the side of the Allies in the European war. When the French and British decided to retaliate with gas, the message changed, with Allied releases indicating that the German's first use of gas justified retaliation and the reluctant employment of similar weapons by the Allies.

A note of righteous indignation pervaded these reports, although the reports were toned down considerably when discussing the effects of gas. In the third stage, which occurred during the spring and summer of 1917, there was a total news blackout on information concerning the gas war. Assistant Secretary of War Benedict Crowell speculated on the cause. He acknowledged an increased use of chemical agents on both sides and believed the Allies "feared and perhaps with reason" that a picture of gas warfare, if presented to the Americans, would result in a "unreasonable dread of gases on the part of the American nation and its soldiers."

The fourth and final phase, which came after U.S. entry into the war, was ushered in with a burst of information with virtually no censorship. The use of chemicals in this phase was depicted as a triumph of Allied technology, an example of good overcoming evil.

Restricted Allied propaganda during the first three phases mentioned above impeded U.S. preparedness in chemical warfare in two ways. First, it gave U.S. officers the impression that the belligerents were making minimal use of gas and that chemical weapons, when employed, had little or no impact on the battlefield. Second, it created the perception among Army officers that chemical warfare, introduced by the barbaric Hun, was inhuman and somehow sullied the honor of the professional soldier.

There were other reasons for the military's lack of appreciation of this new weapon. President Wilson's efforts to maintain strict neutrality during the first two years of the war hampered the Army's planning for defense. When, at one point Wilson discovered that the General Staffs War College Division had prepared contingency plans for a war with Germany, he reprimanded Secretary of War Lindley Garrison. When the Army did tackle the problem of preparedness, chemical warfare, because it was an unfamiliar subject to most planners, received little attention. Other matters seemed more pressing. There were, for example, significant shortages of all kinds of war materiel. In 1915, the U.S. Army had only twenty-one aircraft, as compared to Britain's 250 and France's 500. The United States had fewer than 700 3inch guns, while the French alone had 4,800 of a similar caliber prior to the outbreak of war. Based on Western Front usage, the U.S. Army had only a two-day supply of artillery shells. Similarly, four days of trench warfare would exhaust the U.S. inventory of small arms ammunition. In the assignment of priorities to overcome these and other deficiencies, chemical warfare came nowhere near the top of the list.

During the summer of 1915, the U.S. Army War College published studies on the impact of the war on each belligerent's industrial base. In this report, the implications of chemical weapons and gas warfare received no notice. In November, 1915, two months after the British retaliated with gas at the Battle of Loos, the War College published a supplement to the earlier studies, This report included a survey of developments in weapons, equipment, and force structuring, but interestingly, still did not mention gas warfare.

Even the preparedness movement and the passage of the 1916 National Defense Act did nothing to spur an American assessment of the chemical war being waged in Europe. In fact, during Congressional hearings over preparedness for national defense, poison gas was mentioned only once when Col. Charles G. Treat of the U.S. Army's General Staff testified on the subject of changing artillery doctrine in Europe. Following a discussion of shrapnel shells, one Senator asked Treat, "Are they still using the poisonous gas over there, Colonel?" Treat replied, "The papers say so, but we have not had any actual reports from our observers that they are using them." In November, 1916, the same month that Treat testified, the War Department's Board of Ordnance and Fortifications noted that "certain practices" with poison gas in the European war made necessary the procurement of appropriate defensive equipment, such as gas masks for the Army. The board observed that no branch of the U.S. Army then handled anything remotely connected with chemical warfare.

The board, in its final report, recommended that responsibility for the design, but not the supply, of gas masks be given to the Army's Medical Department. In reviewing the records of the board, the Adjutant General sent extracts of the comments that pertained to gas defense equipment to the Surgeon General, who concurred with the board's findings. The Chief of Staff also concurred, after which the Secretary of War gave the Surgeon General responsibility for the development and design of gas masks. No decision was made as to which branch of the Army would supply troops with protective gas equipment.

The Surgeon General had detailed a number of medical officers to serve as observers with the French and British armies. Reports on the medical aspects of the European conflict, including the diagnosis and treatment of gas victims, were received by the Surgeon General from 1916 on. Unfortunately, for unexplained reasons, the Surgeon General took no action to initiate the development of protective gas devices. The Adjutant General, for his part, shelved the entire matter. Thus, on the eve of American intervention, the Army acted as if it had barely heard of chemical warfare.

The Secretary of War's *Annual Report* for 1917 reflected this neglect. The report pompously declared that the "councils of prudence and forethought" should prepare the Army to surprise the enemy rather than lag "defensively behind the surprises which he prepares for us." The Secretary went on to acknowledge the tremendous impact of science on the war in Europe and referred specifically to the introduction of the airplane and the submarine. As for chemicals, he merely noted that there were other "scientific novelties" that had surfaced in the European conflict. In February, 1917, the question the "scientific novelty" called poison gas was finally raised by an anxious Quartermaster General who pointedly asked the Adjutant General exactly which bureau of the War Department would furnish the Army with gas masks if the need arose. The question prompted the Adjutant General to initiate correspondence with the'Chief of Ordnance, the Quartermaster General, and the Surgeon General to decide on the responsibility for gas mask production. At the time of the correspondence, the Surgeon General had yet to begin a program of gas mask development.

That same month the Department of Interior's Bureau of Mines took the first positive steps toward preparing the Army for chemical warfare. The director, Van H. Manning, displayed a great deal more vision and foresight than did his military colleagues in Washington. At a bureau meeting, Manning asked his department chiefs what they could do to be useful if the nation should become involved in the European war. Since its founding in 1908, the bureau had investigated poison gases found in mines, conducted research on breathing devices, and examined ways to treat miners who had succumbed to noxious fumes. Obviously, this work had a direct application to chemical warfare. The day following the meeting, the Secretary of the Interior authorized Manning to contact another civilian organization,. the Military Committee of the National Research Council. In a letter to C. D. Walcott, the chairman of the committee, Manning pointed out that the bureau could adapt for military application a self-contained breathing apparatus then in use for mine rescues. Also, the bureau had a test chamber at the Pittsburgh, Pennsylvania, experimental station that could be used to conduct tests on military gas masks then in use by the Europeans. The bureau hoped that the information obtained from this research could be given to the Army, allowing it to adopt the best gas mask, should the need arise.

Upon receipt of this letter, Walcott arranged a meeting between representatives of the General Staffs War College Division and the Bureau of Mines. The meeting proved productive: at the end of February, 1917, the War Department accepted the bureau's offer of assistance and agreed to furnish the support, exclusive of funding, necessary to move the work along. Still, no immediate action. was taken by either the Army or the Bureau of Mines to begin a defensive gas equipment research program.

On 6 April 1917, when the U.S. declared war on Germany, the Army not only lacked defensive equipment for chemical warfare, but also had no concrete plans to develop or manufacture gas masks or any other defensive equipment. Even if gas masks had been available, the Army would have had no idea how to conduct defensive gas training. Moreover, no one in the nation seemed to have any practical knowledge concerning offensive chemical warfare equipment or the doctrine then used by the Allies and the Germans for its employment.

Even after the declaration of war by Congress and the decision to ship an American division overseas, preparations for chemical warfare lacked a sense of urgency. The same day war was declared, the Council of National Defense formed a Committee on Noxious Gases. The group met in Washington and immediately adjourned to study British and French gas warfare literature. At later meetings the committee established definite guidelines for Bureau of Mines research to follow in the development of masks. Only then did the chemists at the bureau's Pittsburgh experimental station begin in earnest to develop an American gas mask. The committee also recommended that gas mask production be kept separate and distinct from research.

In May, 1917, the General Staff awoke to the fact that the division requested by the French and British as a token force might well be in combat in a matter of months without any defensive gas equipment L. P. Williamson, liaison officer between the Bureau of Mines and the War Department, received a directive from the General Staff telling him to seek the bureau's assistance in the manufacture of 25,000 gas masks. George A. Burrell, a civilian chemist in the bureau's Research Laboratory, "readily and willingly accepted" the task, but not, as he later noted, "fully appreciating all the conditions which a war mask had to encounter." Burrell should not have been so hard on himself. No one in the United States really understood or even knew much about the employment of chemical defensive equipment on the battlefield.

Working day and night, employees of four different civilian companies fabricated 20,088 masks and filters, using a British Small Box Respirator (SBR) as a model. The masks were shipped overseas to be examined and tested by British experts. They were quickly rejected. The British cabled back that the masks were unacceptable for combat because the mouthpiece was too large and stiff. They also found the rubberized cloth facepiece did not filter out the agent chloropicrin, which was then being used by the Germans in increasing quantities. The filter, which was worn on the chest in a container, had soda-lime granules that were too soft. With repeated jolting, the granules would clog the canister and increase resistance to breathing.

While this was going on, the acting Chief of Staff, Maj. Gen. Tasker Bliss, after a lengthy round of memoranda initiated by the Adjutant General, informed the Surgeon General on 16 May 1917 that, in addition to research and development, the Medical Department would be responsible for supplying the U.S. Army with gas masks and other defensive equipment.

During the next fiscal year the Medical Department would be responsible for supplying 1,000,000 gas masks, 8,500 decontamination sprayers for use in trench warfare, and 1,000 oxygen resuscitators for the treatment of chemical casualties. Unfortunately, neither the Chief of Staff nor the Surgeon General created an office to procure the equipment. The Surgeon General did, however, assign an officer to the National Research Council's Committee on Noxious Gases.

The Committee on Noxious Gases soon met with representatives from the Army and Navy and with members of a French scientific mission. After several sessions, the committee sent a memorandum to the Secretary of War on 2 July 1917, informing him that it had worked out a partial organization plan for a "gas service." Unfortunately, the use of the term "gas service" was misleading, because what the committee recommended turned out to be a cumbersome decentralized system for preparing the Army for chemical warfare.

The offensive aspects of gas warfare, the committee explained, should be handled by the Ordnance Department, the defensive measures by the Medical Department. The Bureau of Mines would continue to direct research, and the Corps of Engineers would receive responsibility for handling all chemical warfare material on the battlefield. The General Staff immediately put this decentralized system into effect.

On 24 July 1917 the Chief of Staff ordered the Medical Department to provide nine officers as instructors for a Gas Defense School to be organized at the Infantry School of Musketry, Fort Sill, Oklahoma.

As a result of this order, the Medical Department received the additional responsibility for the conduct of defensive gas training. Medical officers with absolutely no experience in gas warfare were now expected to train other medical officers for duty as instructors for an Army that would eventually be expanded to over three million men.

After an interminable delay, the Surgeon General on 31 August 1917 finally created a Gas Defense Service composed of three sections: Field Supply, Overseas Repair, and Training. He placed a Medical Corps officer in command and filled his staff with members of the Medical Department's Sanitary Corps.

The officers had no chemical warfare doctrine to guide them. Only two War Department publications existed in the United States to assist these gas officers: a hurriedly compiled *Notes on Gas as a Weapon in Modern War* and a *Memorandum on*

Gas Poisoning in Warfare. Both publications appear to have borrowed extensively from French and British gas warfare doctrine, some of it outdated.

The creation of a Training Section, even with its limited expertise, came none too soon. In September, 1917, draftees, volunteers, and National Guardsmen began to arrive at the thirty-six training cantonments scattered across the country. Sanitary Corps and division medical officers, with only several thousand masks at their disposal (including the 20,088 rejected by the British), faced the overwhelming task of training hundreds of thousands of troops in gas warfare and gas defense. Shortages of equipment, manuals, and knowledge were not the only problems facing the new gas officers.

Gas was such a new weapon that division commanders and their staff officers were unwilling to give up training time for chemical defense at the expense of more traditional military skills such as close order drill and marksmanship. It was a wonder that any defensive training in gas warfare took place. Many times it did not. Initially, there were at best one or two hours of gas defense lectures, sometimes accompanied by a demonstration of how to wear the gas mask.

The lack of knowledge and experience with gas bred "ignorance and superstition" among recruits and veterans alike. Rumors swept through the camps that Germany had "a gas that would make soldiers' eyes drop out of their sockets or their fingers and toes drop off." To the unsophisticated youths who filled the training camps, "gas was mysterious enough, but add to it the word chemical, and it became hopelessly beyond... their conception."

Gas was such an "intangible thing," a division commander noted, that a level of understanding adequate to guard against the dangers it posed was difficult to reach. Reaching such a level continued to be a hopeless task because no coherent U.S. gas warfare doctrine existed. As a consequence, a majority of World War I doughboys found themselves in a chemical combat environment with only a minimal amount of defensive gas training and with "no idea of what this training really meant."

Confronted with this unfortunate situation, the War College of the General Staff examined the evolving gas defense program in the fall of 1917. Defensive training in gas warfare-regardless of how rudimentary-had to be given to men going to Europe. Ypres had proved what chemical warfare could do to unprepared soldiers.

Severe casualties and battlefield defeat might well occur if immediate steps were not taken to train men in the defensive aspects of chemical warfare. As a result, the War College requested and received a British gas officer and a gas NCO for each of the thirty-six training cantonments.

In late October, 1917, the British gas experts arrived in the United States. Their activities were coordinated and directed by Maj. S.J.M. Auld, Special Brigade, Royal Engineers. Auld quickly made his presence felt. Impressed by the British gas officer's knowledge and practical experience, the War College and the Field Training Section asked him to prepare "a working textbook on gas" in order to fill the U.S. Army's doctrinal void in chemical warfare. Working with Sanitary Corps Capt. James H. Walton, Auld wrote four pamphlets that were later combined as Adjutant General Document 705, *Gas Warfare.* They were initially published individually in the following order:

Part Three: *Methods of Training in Defensive Methods*

Part Two: *Methods of Defense Against Attack*

Part One: *German Methods of Offense*

Part Four: *The Offensive in Gas Warfare-Cloud and Projector*

Thus, British gas warfare doctrine edited by the War College Division of the General Staff became U.S. Army doctrine.

Auld strongly influenced the organization of the U.S. Army for chemical warfare in one other way. When he and other British officers discovered that the General Staff had placed defensive training under the Medical Department, they were appalled. The British officers insisted that gas defense was "purely a military affair"; in their opinion, proper defensive measures were "largely a question of discipline."

Based on the experience of the British Army, such procedures were so closely connected with the soldier's "fighting activities" that preparation for chemical warfare could not be carried out by a noncombat branch of the'Army. The British were so emphatic that, in January, 1918, by order of the General Staff, the Field Training Section of the Sanitary Corps passed to the Corps of Engineers.

Major Auld also suggested the establishment of a Central Army Gas School to train "Divisional, Brigade and Regimental Gas officers and other personnel whom it might be desirable to educate in Gas Warfare." This idea was already under consideration by the General Staff. The result was the establishment of an Army Gas School at Camp A. A. Humphreys, Virginia, where in May, 1918, two initial courses began. The first, a four-day course for officers and noncommissioned officers, provided general information on gas warfare.

The second, a twelve-day course, was for Chief Gas Officers who would be assigned to division and higher echelon staffs. Although there were similarities between the two courses, the Chief Gas Officers' instruction went into greater detail on most matters. The shortage of trained gas officers in the AEF prevented students from being held for longer periods of field training on subjects such as gas detection, construction of gas-proof dugouts, and the proper wearing of respirators.

Auld assisted in training the first U.S. gas officers, forty-five first lieutenants, all chemists, who were assigned to the Field Training Section of the Sanitary Corps. The instruction took place at the American University in Washington, DC. In January, 1918, after three months of training in gas warfare and general military subjects, thirty-three of the forty-five officers, together with their British instructors, departed for duty at division training camps. The other twelve went directly to France. Unfortunately, by January, 1918, six of the thirty U.S. divisions destined to see combat in France had either left the States or had completed training. The men in these units had received no chemical warfare training before embarking for Europe.

As for the divisions that did receive some training before shipping overseas, their division gas officers were afterwards assigned to the 473d Engineer Regiment, a stateside administrative holding unit. Thus, the first trained gas officers did not deploy with the men they had trained. Although necessary for the training of subsequent divisions, this decision had, in the words of one gas officer, a "discouraging effect upon the men and upon gas training and discipline in general" in the unit deployed overseas. The confidence of the embarking troops was hardly bolstered when the "experts" on chemical warfare stayed home.

As the war progressed, the training in the division camps improved. In January, 1918, the 29th Division's gas training at Camp McClellan consisted of a brief lecture and gas mask drill for one hour daily, five days a week, under the close supervision of British instructors. This compared favorably to the weekly one-hour "anti-gas instruction" in October, 1917. As training became more sophisticated, men underwent tests at the end of their division's training cycle. They masked and entered a chamber filled with chlorine gas. Next, they went through a chamber filled with a tear agent, where they unmasked. Although by the summer of 1918, recruits received standardized chemical warfare training, reports filed by division gas officers in Europe indicated the key to successful preparation had yet to be found. Still more training was needed, and it had to be integrated with other subjects.

In the summer of 1918, with news reaching America of Germany's increased use of gas, an Army regulation was promulgated, requiring every doughboy who left the country to have a certificate indicating he had completed gas training. No other military skill required such validation.

Unfortunately, the requirement was usually ignored, and most men continued to arrive in France without the benefit of adequate instruction in gas defense. Gas officers realized that sufficient time for training in the camps did not exist. To make up for the deficiency, units attempted to use the time aboard transports for defensive gas training. The 80th Division, for example, ordered that shipboard activities would include physical training, manual of arms, guard duty, and "anti-gas instruction."

Although the U.S. Army's first efforts in chemical warfare were directed toward "anti-gas" or defensive measures, the development of the means to retaliate in kind soon followed.

On 15 August 1917, with the approval of the General Staff in Washington, AEF General Order 108 authorized the organization of special and technical engineer troops that would be assigned to each army as a "Gas and Flame" Regiment.

The War Department ordered recruits for the newly formed 30th Engineers to report to the American University campus in Washington, DC, where they were transformed into the 1st Gas Regiment.

Unfortunately, with no one to instruct them in offensive or even defensive gas warfare, the only training the first companies of the gas regiment received in the United States involved close order drill. The unit underwent no special training in gas warfare. Beginning in December, 1917, the companies of the 1st Gas Regiment left the United States without gas masks.

The gas mask problem continued to plague the Army as a whole. An effective American mask was eventually developed using the British Small Box Respirator as a model. However, production of American gas masks peaked just one month prior to the end of the war. Late delivery and the initial small number of masks produced were offset only by the AEF's decision to purchase several million British and French gas masks.

The same unpreparedness and production lag applied to offensive chemical weapons. The Army attempted to contract out the production of war gases to a number of civilian chemical companies, but these firms objected immediately to the contracts because of the inherent dangers in the production of large quantities of war gases and because the demand for the product would not extend beyond the conflict. Besides that, the firms had already overcommitted their plants and personnel for the production of other war-related chemical products.

The Army thus found itself with no alternative but to construct its own production facilities. In December, 1917, construction of plants to produce chemical agents began at Gunpowder Neck, Maryland. By the summer of 1918, the Edgewood Arsenal there had plants in operation producing phosgene, chloropicrin, mustard, chlorine, and sulfur trichloride. The arsenal also had a capability for filling artillery shells, although most of the agents produced were shipped overseas to the Allies in fifty-five gallon drums. Because of insufficient time, not one single gas shell manufactured at the arsenal ever reached an American artillery piece in France. When production of chemicals finally peaked one month prior to the Armistice, the plants had to stop production for lack of shell casings. artillery units and special gas troops fired American produced war gas, but in French and British shells.

As the emphasis on chemical warfare increased, there arose a need to coordinate the various agencies assigned responsibility for gas warfare. Accordingly, on 28 June 1918 President Wilson, using the authority given to him by the Overman Act, ordered the establishment of the Chemical Warfare Service (CWS) as a separate branch of the National Army.

Immediately, all activities pertaining to chemical warfare were placed under Maj. Gen. William L. Sibert, formerly Commanding General of the First Infantry Division. The creation of a branch of the Army dedicated to chemical warfare was significant because it acknowledged, albeit belatedly, the tremendous impact the new weapon was having on the AEF The CWS, with the concurrence of the General Staff, established ten subordinate divisions:

Administration	Proving
Research	Medical
Gas Offense	Training
Gas Offense(Edgewood Arsenal)	Overseas(Gas Service, AEF)
Development	1st Gas Regiment

With the exception of the Overseas Division and the 1st Gas Regiment, the division chiefs were located in Washington,

DC, and the operations of their divisions were scattered throughout the United States. The Administration Division facilitated routine matters and coordinated the activities of the other CWS divisions. A Research Division, as the name implied, handled all basic research, from the discovery of new chemicals to the development of protective masks and offensive equipment. Another division, Gas Defense, conducted research, but primarily administered the manufacturing, testing, and inspecting of gas masks for men and animals. This division also had the responsibility for manufacturing gas-proof dugout blankets, protective suits and gloves, antigas ointment, and "gas warning" signals.

The Gas Defense Division administered Edgewood Arsenal. A Development Division experimented with charcoal suitable for gas mask filters, a manufacturing process for mustard, and a means of producing casings and adapters for 75-min shells of similar design to the French glass-lined gas projectiles. A Proving Division tested prototype gas shells before production and spottested shells prior to shipment overseas. The Medical Division coordinated work on the therapy, pharmacology, physiology, and pathology of war gases on the body. This division's primary emphasis was on the prevention and treatment of casualties from mustard gas.

The agency that had its most direct impact on the AEF was the Chemical Warfare Service's Training Division. The division's responsibilities included the organization and training of gas troops, the training of "casual detachments for overseas duty," the maintenance of a Chemical Warfare Training Camp detachment, and the procurement and training of chemical officers for overseas duty. In recognition of the division's importance, the Assistant Director of the Chemical Warfare Service, Brig. Gen. H. C. Newcomer, assumed operational command. This was the only division, other than Administration, headed by a general officer.

The structure of the CWS in the United States was determined by the personnel and equipment requirements of the AEF. Stateside training and preparations for chemical warfare had to be curtailed in order to rush American troops to France. Initially, expertise in chemical warfare was lacking. As a consequence, combat divisions deployed without proper training, equipment, and leadership. Until late 1917, there was no chemical warfare doctrine to rely upon. Nevertheless, American troops had to fight on a chemical battlefield against an opponent highly skilled in the use of chemicals in combat. Out of necessity it fell to the Overseas Division, CWS, to bear the brunt of the responsibility for preparing American soldiers for chemical warfare. The majority of the thirty AEF divisions to see combat in World War I entered the line during and after the five German spring offensives of 1918. These offensives saw chemical warfare at the highest level since its introduction three years before. Regardless of the emphasis eventually placed on gas warfare by GHQ, AEF, and the Army General Staff, new doctrine'for gas weapons could not be fully absorbed or mastered by the inexperienced Americans. Prewar neglect of gas warfare equipment and accompanying doctrine had a significant impact on the ability of the AEF to defend against, and to successfully employ, chemical agents in World War I.

NUCLEAR WARFARE IN WORLD WAR I

Of all the weapons employed in World War I, none stimulated public revulsion more than poison gas. The abhorrence of chemical warfare lingered long after the Armistice of 11 November 1918. Gas victims continually reminded the general public of the effect of chemical weapons, as illustrated by the often repeated story of a veteran's coughing fit being explained by a tap on the chest and an apologetic. The employment of chemical agents in war, however, did not begin with World War I. The earliest recorded incident occurred in the fifth century B.C. during one of a series of wars between Athens and Sparta.*

Over the centuries that followed, combatants on several occasions engaged in rudimentary forms of chemical warfare on the battlefield. If by the end of the nineteenth century the use of poison gas was still by far the exception and not the rule in war, there were in all the great powers a number of men who foresaw its widespread use should a general conflagration engulf Europe.

A concern with poison gas manifested itself at the Hague Conference of 1899. One of the agenda items dealt with prohibiting the use of shells filled with asphyxiating gas. The proposed ban eventually passed with one dissenting vote, that of the American representative, Naval Capt. Alfred T. Mahan, who declared that "it was illogical and not demonstrably humane to be tender about asphyxiating men with gas, when all were prepared to admit that it was allowable to blow the bottom out of an ironclad at midnight, throwing four or five hundred men into the sea, to be choked by water, with scarcely the remotest chance of escape." Secretary of State John Hay, in his instructions to Mahan, argued that the inventiveness of Americans should not be restricted in the development of new weapons. For Hay it made no sense for the United States to deprive itself of the ability to use, at some later date, a weapon that might prove to be more humane and effective than anything then present in the American arsenal.

The Hague Conference declaration did not prevent some nations from discussing the use of chemical weapons, and at least one country, France, experimented publicly with gas. The

French Army tested a grenade filled with ethyl bromoacetate, a nontoxic tear, or lachrymatory, agent developed for use in the suppression of small-arms fire from the concrete casements then prevalent in the permanent fortifications that dotted Western Europe. In 1912, French police used 26-mm grenades filled with this agent to capture a notorious gang of Parisian bank robbers. The Germans, unlike the French, did not experiment with chemical agents for military use as such, but at the outbreak of World War I, Germany's highly advanced dye industry gave it a sophisticated technological base from which to develop weapons of this nature.

When war erupted in August, 1914, everyone from private citizens to the leaders of the belligerent countries shared a common belief that the economies of the European nations would neither survive nor support a lengthy war. As a result, the war plans of two key protagonists, Germany and France, called for a quick, decisive offensive against one another. Kaiser Wilhelm II of Germany assured his troops that they would be "home before the leaves fall." It was not to be. By the end of 1914, the armies on the Western Front were locked in a deadly form of trench warfare (Map 1), sustained by the very industrialized economies that, because of their complexity and interdependency, had been thought unable to withstand a long war.

Unwilling to accept the indecisiveness of trench warfare, army staffs on both sides pondered ways to break the deadlock and return to open or maneuver warfare. Alternatives were proposed, some strategic, others tactical. The British, for example, sought a strategic solution by a seaborne assault against Turkey, an ally of Germany. This attack at Gallipoli in 1915 sought to open the Dardanelles as the first step toward linking up with. Russia and forcing Turkey out of the war. For a variety of reasons, the plan failed, and the deadlock on the

Western Front continued. As their attack at Gallipoli tottered to defeat, the British looked to the application of tactical innovation at Neuve-Chapelle to break the stalemate. On 10 March 1915 British artillery, instead of firing a lengthy bombardment prior to an attack, as doctrine dictated, let loose a brief but intense barrage on a relatively narrow German trench frontage. The fire was then shifted to the German rear in order to create a lethal steel curtain that would block reinforcements. To the surprise of everyone, the British infantry quickly overran the German forward positions. The attack failed, though, primarily because the high command, viewing it as an experiment, did not have sufficient reserves available to exploit a breakthrough.

Germany also searched for ways to break the deadlock and decided on a solution involving gas. Early in the war the Germans kept a wary eye out for indications that the French were using their 26-mm gas grenades. Apparently, in August, 1914, France did use this chemical weapon, but in open areas where the gas quickly dispersed with no noticeable effect on the enemy. The French soon discarded the grenades as worthless. At this same time, stories were appearing in Allied newspapers about a new French liquid explosive, turpinite. While claiming that this substance gave off lethal fumes, the articles failed to explain that the gas reached a deadly concentration only in confined spaces. Still, the Germans were apprehensive and became alarmed by the deaths of a number of soldiers asphyxiated during a French bombardment, even though a medical team rushed to the scene concluded that the men died not from poison gas, but from inhaling carbon monoxide fumes while huddled in their dugout.

In any event such newspaper stories and front-line experiences may have spurred the development of war gases by German scientists. Contributing to that effort, chemistry professor Walter Nernst suggested partially replacing the TNT in a 105-mm shrapnel shell with dianisidine chlorosulphonate, an agent known to cause irritation of the mucous membrane. The new filling would serve two purposes: it would conserve TNT and act as a chemical weapon. The German High Command accepted this new weapon, although it is uncertain which of the two purposes it initially considered more important. On 27 October 1914, 3,000 of these shells fell on British troops near Neuve-Chapelle. The soldiers suffered no ill effects and never suspected they were under chemical attack. The Germans continued to experiment with gas because they were convinced the idea had merit and because intelligence sources could not determine what effect the shells had had at Neuve-Chapelle. This lack of information on the effects of gas attacks was a common occurrence throughout the war.

The Neuve-Chapelle experiment increased the German High Command's interest in gas warfare. The German General Staff asked the Kaiser Wilhelm Institute for Physical Chemistry and Electrochemistry in Berlin to investigate the possibility of using a more effective agent. The only guideline provided by the military was that the Hague declaration of 1899, banning projectiles used exclusively for delivering poison gases, had to be circumvented. Adhering to the letter if not the spirit of the ban, the Germans devised a gas shell that also contained an explosive charge for producing a shrapnel effect. The Professor von Tappan who designed the shell also solved two technical problems related to emplacing chemicals in an artillery projectile. First, he stabilized the liquid within a shell casing in order to reduce its tumbling in flight, thereby increasing the shell's accuracy and range. Second, to ensure that two extremely reactive chemical substances did not accidently combine in the shell casing, von Tappan developed a special shell, designated the T-shell by the German Army in his honor. The T-shell was a standard 15-cm howitzer round that contained seven pounds of xylyl brómide and a burster charge for a splinter effect. A lead lining prevented contact between the burster charge and the chemical payload.

The German High Command decided to use the first T-shells on the Eastern Front. On 31 January 1915, over 18,000 shells were fired at Russian positions at Bolimov. German officers, confident that their new weapon would neutralize the enemy positions, were surprised when their attack was repulsed with severe casualties. The shelling had had little or no effect on the Russians because cold temperatures had prevented vaporization of the xylyl bromide.

To find a more effective means of employing gas on the battlefield, the German High Command turned to an assistant of von Tappan, Professor Fritz Haber. Haber, a reservist, had shown marked enthusiasm for the potential value of chemicals as weapons. Believing that T-shells did not provide a high enough concentration of chemicals to produce enemy casualties, he suggested the use of large commercial gas cylinders as a delivery system. Cylinders could deliver large amounts of gas and, like the T-shell, did not technically violate the Hague ban on projectiles. Haber also recommended the use of chlorine as an agent because it was commercially produced and readily available in large quantities. Chlorine also satisfied the requirements for military application: it was lethal immediately effective, nonpersistent, and volatile. It was also dense enough to resist dilution in a moderate wind.

Haber's gas cylinder project received the approval of the Chief of the German General Staff, General Erich von Falkenhayn, who had the professor appointed Head of the Chemical Warfare Department in the Prussian Ministry of War. The high command selected the front of the Fourth

Army facing the French salient at Ypres as the location for an experimental attack. Pioneer Regiment 35 was designated to conduct the gas attack. Haber, assigned as a "chemico-technical advisor," assisted Colonel Peterson, the regimental commander, and instructed the troops on the emplacement and use of gas cylinders.

By 10 March 1915 the Regiment, with the assistance of infantry labor, had emplaced 1,600 large and 4,130 small cylinders containing a total of 168 tons of chlorine. Then, for one month, the Pioneer troops sat and waited for the winds to shift westerly toward the enemy trenches in the Ypres salient. Only then could they safely unleash the chemicals by opening the cylinder valves.

Late in the afternoon of 22 April 1915, a setting sun cast long shadows over the battle-scarred terrain around the medieval Belgium city of Ypres. In the distance the faint sound of large-caliber guns could be heard. Birds fluttered and swooped, seeking places to roost on the practically treeless landscape. Suddenly, at 1724, three flares rose from an observation balloon over the German lines and burst against the darkening eastern sky. German artillery commenced a fierce bombardment that landed to the rear of the French and British lines in the Ypres sector. Then, at 1800, an eerie silence fell over the area.

Peering across the battlefield, men of two French divisions, the 87th Territorial and the 45th Algerian, saw blue-white wisps of haze rising from the German trenches. The haze swirled about, gathered in a cloud that slowly turned yellow-green and began to drift across the terrain at a height of up to six feet. As the cioud drifted, it settled into every depression in the landscape. Finally, the gentle north!.northeasterly wind brought it spilling into the French trenches, silently enveloping the occupants in a misty, deadly embrace.

To the north and southwest of the now mist-enshruded French positions, British and Canadian troops looked into the haze and, to their amazement, saw soldiers, many without weapons, emerge from the cloud, "running wildly, and in confusion" toward positions to the rear. Terror-stricken Algerians ran by the startled Dominion troops, coughing And clutching their throats. Moments later French soldiers staggered by, "blinded, coughing, chests heaving, faces an ugly purple color, lips speechless with agony." One by one, the guns of the French artillery batteries in the sector stoppedfiring, and the two French divisions collapsed. The Ypres front now had a gap over four-miles wide containing hundreds of men in a "comatose or dying condition." After half an hour, German troops, equipped with cotton wadding tied over their faces-a primitive form of protective mask-cautiously advanced into the breech created by the discharge of chlorine gas.

Following the initial shock and surprise, Allied commanders began to bring forward reserve troops and to move units from the left and right flank into the gap. The Germans advanced four and one-half miles-until they encountered the ragged edge of a hurriedly organized defensive line (Map 2). The First Canadian Division and assorted French troops manned the line in scattered, hastily prepared positions 1,000 to 3,000 yards apart. This improvised defense, together with the fact that the Germans had lost some of their combat edge during the month-long wait for favorable winds, finally slowed and then halted the attack. As for the German troops who reached their initial objective, they had only the most primitive protective equipment. When they saw the havoc their own gas had wrought, they had no wish to proceed any farther that night.

Two days later, during which time the British and French brought reinforcements into the area, the Germans discharged more gas. Although they did so again four more times throughout May, the element of surprise had been lost. The British and French troops were now equipped with their own primitive masks, and although the defenders suffered severe losses (over 5,900 casualties-nearly double the number of casualties for the attackers), the Germans could gain no more than a few hundred yards beyond the forward limit of their first attack. The German High Command, surprised as its opponents at the success of the new weapon, had no reserves to exploit a possible success. Thus, one of the war's greatest tactical surprises was dissipated on what amounted to an experimental attack with limited objectives.

With the battle front at Ypres now stabilized, the British and French had to decide whether or not retaliate in kind. Faced with the Germans' obvious technological advantage, the Allies at first hesitated to retaliate for fear of inviting the expansion of gas warfare. But when, the British Expeditionary Force commander reported that a lack of an offensive gas capability would seriously impair the morale of his troops, the British cabinet gave its approval to use chemical agents. The French government soon followed suit for basically the same reason.

On 24 September 1915, at 0550 near Loos, Belgium, the British launched the Allies' first attack supported by gas. It had taken them five frantic months to reach a point at which a large-scale gas attack was feasible. During that period, several "Special Companies" of Royal Engineers had been trained in the emplacement and discharge of gas cylinders. Unlike the Germans, the British decided to conduct their gas attack on a wide frontage. This necessitated the deployment of the cylinders clustered in batteries along the front rather than spaced far apart in one continuous line. To accomplish this, the British constructed galleries in front of the first-line trenches and positioned in them 5,500 cylinders containing 150 tons of chlorine. The frontage was too wide to saturate all of it with gas, so the British decided to utilize smoke candles to simulate gas in those areas where the agent could not be used. By alternating the discharges of gas and smoke, the gas attack could be prolonged over forty minutes. This planned smoke screen was the first used during the war.

Fortune did not favor this first British gas attack. During the evening prior to the attack, the winds died. The following morning the British commander, Gen. Sir Douglas Haig, made a controversial decision to proceed with the attack despite uncertainty as to whether or not the slight breeze that rose in the morning would continue to blow toward the German lines. On the right flank, the gentle winds brought the gas and smoke mixture into the German trench system. There, the mild wind worked to the British advantage, for the cloud lingered and did not dissipate. On the left flank, however, not only did the winds fail, but in several positions the gas wafted back into the British trenches, engulfing the troops waiting to attack.

The Germans were taken by surprise. Their troops had little awareness of the danger posed by gas and were not sufficiently trained in defensive measures. The war diary of the German Sixth Army, the unit that bore the brunt of the attack, described the results. The gas in some instances caused little but momentary confusion, while in other cases entire units lost their ability to resist the follow-up British infantry attack. The German mask, which was essentially the same one used at Ypres, broke down as the gas lingered. The chlorine also caused rifles, machine guns, and even artillery breechblocks to jam. The most effective result of the gas was that it rendered German officers and noncommissioned officers (NCOs) incapable of shouting commands loud enough to be heard through their masks. The dense clouds of smoke and gas also shrouded positions and precluded officers and NCOs from leading by example.

In spite of some British gains, the attack fell short of the desired results for three reasons. The first was the decision to proceed with the attack despite the unfavorable wind conditions. Second, the British artillery was hampered in providing support because it lacked sufficient shells. Third, there were no reserve divisions to exploit a breakthrough. In his report, the British Commander-in-Chief, Sir John French, acknowledged that, although the attack failed to penetrate the German lines, the "gas attack met with marked success, and produced a demoralizing effect in some of its opposing units." More important, the major belligerents had accepted and expanded the use of chemicals as weapons of war.

The ensuing chemical war proved to be one of experimentation with gases and with defensive add offensive equipment. As tactical doctrine and training evolved to reflect technological changes, the availability of gases and the imagination of commanders became the only limits to the employment of this new weapon.

THE EUROPEANS FACE CHEMICALS ON THE BATTLEFIELD, 1915-1918

During World War I chemists on both sides investigated over 3,000 chemical substances for potential use as weapons. Of these, only thirty agents were used in combat, and only about a dozen achieved the desired military results (Table 1). Most armies grouped war gases according to their physiological effects, that is their effects on the human body.

One category, lachrymators, was composed of tear gases such as xylyl bromide, an agent that primarily affected the eyes but in large concentrations could also damage the respiratory system. Asphyxiators, such as phosgene, chloropicrin, and chlorine, were in another category. These gases caused fluid to enter the lungs, thereby preventing oxygen from reaching the blood. Toxic gases, yet another category, passed through the lungs to the blood, preventing the circulation and release of oxygen throughout the body. Hydrogen cyanide ("Vincennite" to the French) was one of the least effective toxic agents. Sternutators, such as diphenylchlorarsine, were a type of respiratory irritant composed of a very fine dust that caused sneezing, nausea, and vomiting. Some sternutators were systemic poisons that had a delayed toxic effect on the body. The final category held the greatest casualty producer-a vesicant or blister agent that, because of its peculiar odor, the British and later the Americans commonly referred to as "mustard gas."

In 1917 the Germans first used mustard against the Allies at Ypres. This was the only persistent agent used during World War I and had effects similar to those produced by a combination of lachrymatory, asphyxiator, and systemic poisons. Although called mustard gas, this chemical was not a gas, but rather a volatile liquid that, several hours after contact with the skin, would cause severe bums and blisters. The introduction of Yellow Cross caught the Allies completely by surprise. During the first attack, British infantry saw the gas shells explode, but were unable to "see, smell or taste any agent, nor feel any immediate effects." The soldiers concluded that the Germans were trying to trick them and did not put on their masks. After several hours, to the consternation of officers and medics, the troops began to complain of pain in their eyes, throats, and lungs. Later, blisters appeared on the exposed skin of the British soldiers. The German use of Yellow Cross caused British gas casualties, which had been declining, to increase markedly. Because of its ability to produce large numbers of casualties, mustard was soon being referred to as the "King" of the war gases. The major combatants realized that the employment of gas called for specially trained troops and, accordingly, formed offensive gas units. Because of the need to emplace gas cylinders, pioneer or engineer troops usually provided the cadre of these special units.

The Germans converted two pioneer regiments, the 35th and 36th, into gas units consisting of three battalions each. The regiments would deploy by companies, according to the size of the front of the attack. In addition to these units, the Germans organized a gas mortar (Minenwerfen) battalion. The Austro-Hungarians followed the German model and created their own special gas units. As early as July, 1915, the French and British organized gas companies called "Special" by the British and "Z" for *gaz* (gas) by the French; both employed engineer troops as cadre. By 1917 the British had expanded their original four companies to twenty-one and had organized them as a Special Brigade. The French eventually created the 31st, 32nd, and 33rd gas battalions composed of three companies each. The Russians organized gas units and called them "Gas Detachments of the Chemical Department," with one detachment assigned to each Russian Army, a total of thirteen.

In addition to developing gas units and chemical agents, a constant search continued for efficient delivery systems. The cylinders used in the first gas attack at Ypres in 1915 were the major component of a cumbersome, immobile system, It usually took several days of intensive labor, with infantry providing most of the muscle, to emplace the cylinders for a cloud attack (Figure 1). One can gain an indication of the difficulty of the task by noting that as many as 12,000 cylinders, each weighing over 100 pounds, were sometimes needed for a single operation. Once emplaced, the cylinders were dangerously exposed to enemy high explosive shells and easily damaged, Cylinder discharges always depended on favorable weather conditions.

Despite these problems, the British relied on cylinders as a delivery method until the end of the war. They normally used seven to eight cylinders in a section, six sections to a Special Brigade company. Sixteen companies could produce a gas wave or cloud that covered a 24,000-meter front. Several factors influenced the British decision to continue using cylinders. First, the prevailing winds favored Allied gas clouds. Second, the British suffered from a chronic shortage of shells and were reluctant to convert the production of high explosive shells to the production of gas shells. Third, British intelligence reports indicated a dense cloud attack was effective in producing mass casualties. On 26 October 1917, Brig. Gen. Charles H. Foulkes, Commander of the British Special Brigade, reviewed intelligence reports indicating that British cloud attacks created significant German casualties as far back as thirty kilometers from, the front-line trenchm Foulkes proposed that the Special Brigade use what he termed "retired cylinder attacks," in which. a large number of cylinders would be emplaced behind British lines rather than in the front lines or forward of the trenches.

Because the Special Brigade companies could assemble a greater number of cylinders in a relatively small area without the interference of enemy small arms or shell fire, this method allowed for a significantly greater concentration of gas released at one point.

The British improved this tactic by conducting what they called "beam attacks." These attacks called for placing numerous cylinders on narrowgauge tram cars that troops pushed forward to positions just behind the front trenches. After the cylinders were opened, the resulting gas concentration became so dense that friendly troops had to be evacuated from the path of the gas "beam." On 24 May 1918 the British launched their first beam attack. This and similiar attacks, General Foulkes claimed, caused the Germans considerable anxiety, for they could not determine how and where the dense clouds originated.

The beam attacks were especially deadly when launched from six or more separate railheads and when the individual clouds merged behind German lines. Prisoners taken from the German 9th Uhlan Regiment reported that one such attack caused 500 casualties in the neighboring 1st Landwehr Regiment, which, as a. result of the attack, had to be withdrawn from the line.

According to the British, the effectiveness of the improved cloud attacks, with their increased density, continued to frustrate the German Army. The Germans, for their part, arranged their cylinders so that twenty formed a battery. Fifty such batteries were required to saturate one kilometer of front line with gas. The lack of favorable prevailing winds, however, soon forced the Germans to abandon the cloud attack. On 8 August 1916, they launched their last cylinder attack at Wieltje, near the scene of the first discharge at Ypres.

Because the prevailing winds in Western Europe blew from west to east, the German Army began to place increasing reliance on gas-filled shells that detonated beyond Allied lines and whose contents could then drift back over enemy trenches. Gas shells could be fired. from standard artillery pieces with no extensive adaptation for gas employment. Although weather conditions still remained a factor, no longer did the Germans have to wait for the wind to change to a westerly direction. Now artillery could fire upward of the target, saturating it with gas and achieving the same effect as cylinders. Shells also offered an element of surprise not available with cloud attacks. Finally, gas shells proved more advantageous than high explosive rounds because the former did not have to score direct hits on a target to neutralize it. To avoid confusion and to aid artillerymen, the Germans developed a coded system of colored crosses to identify shells containing chemical agents.

The Germans were further encouraged to use gas shells by the results of an attack staged on the night of 22-23 June 1916. About 110,000 shells containing the lung irritant Green Cross fell on French forces near the fortress of Verdun. German batteries adjacent to this sector added thousands of rounds of a lachrymatory gas. The gas attack, according to French sources, had its greatest effect on French artillerymen and reserves in the rear areas, causing over 1,600 casualties. German staff officers, impressed with the results, talked of creating "special gas batteries" controlled by special gas staffs. In the interest of flexibility, however, the high command decided that all artillery units should fire gas shells. By the war's end, gas shells comprised 50 percent of a German artillery battery's basic.

The British and, French also developed gas shells with unique color codes. The French Army used these shells almost as extensively as the Germans and fired the first phosgene-filled artillery shells on 22 February 1916 at Verdun. The French also experimented with an extremely small bursting charge in order to increase the gas payload. This French innovation allowed a stable, dense cloud to form. Although the French increased the chemical payload, they erred by adding comparatively harmless (smoke producers), such as stannic chloride, thus reducing the toxic capacity of their phosgene shells by 30 to 40 percent.

The French committed another technical error in the gas war. The hydrocyanic acid (hydrogen cyanide) used in their Vincennite shell (named for the production location) was too volatile and filled only half of the shell's capacity. Unless an extremely high concentration could be built up, there were no harmful effects. All the belligerents considered the Vincennite fill practically worthless. The French, for some reason, refused to accept this conclusion and manufactured over four million shells that, when fired, caused relatively few casualties.

The British faced a constant artillery shell production shortage and supplemented their use of gas cylinders with the 4-inch Stokes mortar, introduced in July, 1916, at the Battle of the Somme, The weapon, designed specifically to fire gas and thermite shells, had a payload three times as large (six to nine pounds) as could be fired from the standard 3-inch mortar. A range of only 800 to 1,000 meters meant that effective delivery required emplacement in the front-line trenches. Members of the Special Brigade also experimented with a homemade contraption similar to a trench mortar.

Early in 1917 Capt. William H. Livens, a British officer, developed a device made from ordinary steel containers. This makeshift mortar fired oil drums packed with oil-soaked cotton waste. Captain Livens also began to experiment with firing large gas-filled shells from his homemade trench mortar. This resulted in a new delivery system known as the Livens projector. In its final form the projector consisted of a drawn steel cylinder eight inches in diameter, one and one-fourth inch thick, that came in two sizes-two feet nine inches or four feet long. Rounded at one end, the cylinders had a base plate that looked like a Mexican sombrero. The projectors were buried in a trench cut at a forty-five degree angle for maximum range. Originally buried to the muzzle, this depth was later found to be unnecessary, and the projectors were thereafter emplaced only deep enough to steady them for firing. The shells used with the projectors carried a payload of thirty to forty pounds of chemical agent and had a range, depending on the length of the barrel, of either 1,200 or 1,900 meters. The British first used this delivery system for what they called "gas shoots" at Arras on 4 April 1917. The Germans reported that the density of the gas delivered by this method equaled that of a gas cloud. Captured German documents claimed that the Livens projector was a deadly weapon because it not only developed a dense concentration of gas similar to the one created by cylinders, but like artillery, its impact came as a surprise. During the war the British fired ever 300 gas projector "shoots." On 31 March 1918 the largest of these operations took place at Lens, with the firing of 3,728 of the devices.

Increased casualties resulting from British gas projector attacks prompted the Germans to develop a similar weapon. Time constraints and the lack of industrial capacity for increased steel production forced them to retool their obsolete 18-cm heavy mortars. These tubes coal & fire a projectile containing three to four gallons of a chemical agent. In December, 1917, the Germans launched their first projector attack on the Western Front.

In August, 1918, they introduced a rifled projector, 16-cm in diameter, that increased the range of the device to 3,500 meters. The shells contained thirteen pounds of chemical agent and five and one-half pounds of pumice. The pumice kept the chemical agent from. being flung into the air upon explosion. It also made the agent, usually phosgene, more persistent. In one instance, the gas reportedly lingered for one and one-half hours. Yet, impressive as were these results, the Germans, despite their efforts, continued to lag behind the British in the tactical use of this delivery system.

Initially, the tactical employment of chemical weapons varied to some degree between the Allies and the Central Powers; however, these variations became less noticeable during the latter stages of the war. By November, 1918, the protagonists were using similiar delivery systems and chemical agents.

From 1915 to 1918 the Germans held the initiative in most areas of gas warfare. They did this through the introduction of new agents that allowed them to direct more systematic thought to the question of how the employment of gas might alter a tactical situation. They were, for example, the first to use gas as an adjunct to maneuver in support of an infantry attack. The Allies struggled to keep up with such offensive doctrine, but they had to contend first with the development of effective defensive measures to counter German initiatives.

Only after developing countermeasures could the Allies then plan their use of a new chemical agent or a new delivery system. This lag was evident in the case of the two most effective agents used in World War I, phosgene and mustard gas. The Germans introduced phosgene six months before the Allies were able to employ it and mustard a year ahead of their foe. The Allies had to adopt immediate defensive measures, such as effective mask filters and protective suits, before they could turn to the development of tactical doctrine. "As far as the tactical employment of gas was concerned," wrote Lt. Col. Pascal Lucas, a French officer, "it took us a long time to realize that the neutralization of personnel by gas could supplement the always incomplete destruction of defensive organizations" by high explosives. British gas doctrine, when circumstances did permit its development, was driven in part by a shortage of artillery shells that prohibited the British Army from mounting an artillery gas attack until the summer of 1916. In the meantime, the British, as noted, convinced themselves that chemicals released from cylinders or projectors could most effectively be used to obtain the highest possible concentration of an agent in a specific area. The consequences of this doctrine were twofold: it prevented the British from employing gas to support mobile or open warfare, and it limited the. use of chemical agents primarily to the more restricted roles of attrition and harassment.

In the case of harassment, the British High Command, relying on intelligence reports, would indicate for one reason or another what German units it wished the Special Brigade to weaken or demoralize. German divisions recently transferred from the Eastern Front were prime targets because of their ignorance of defensive measures for gas warfare. The British sought out units that they expected to be transferred to the main battle fronts, i.e., Somme or Ypres, and tried to weaken them physically and psychologically before they deployed. On at least one occasion, a gas operation was postponed to await the arrival of a particular division. Once a German unit became a target for a gas attack, the Special Brigade made a point of following that unit around the front. The 1st Bavarian Regiment, for instance, was gassed fifteen times; the 1st Guards Regiment twelve times in six months; the 10th Bavarian Regiment ten times in five months, and the 9th Bavarian Regiment fourteen times from 28 June 1916 to 1 August 1917. The effects could be devastating to the morale of the gassed units and those units around them. A captured German diary recorded, "We have again had many casualties through gas poisoning. I can't think of anything worse; wherever one goes, one must take one's gas mask with one, and it will soon be more necessary than a rifle. Things are dreadful here."

The British ultimately developed tactical doctrine for the use of gas shells. This doctrine set three methods for inflicting enemy gas casualties. The first and most favored method was by a surprise gas attack, in which British gunners attempted to establish the greatest concentration of gas in a target area by firing a "lavish expenditure of ammunition" at an extremely rapid rate. After one or two minutes of shelling, enemy soldiers who had not put on protective masks would be incapacitated by the dense gas; the remainder would be masked, rendering further bombardment uneconomical and unnecessary.

The second method for using gas shells tried to exhaust the enemy by desultory fire over a period of many hours. In most instances, the British believed this attrition. method not worth the effort, because few casualties were produced. The third method was an attempt to penetrate the enemy's gas masks with new agents such as chloropicrin, which when fired in a high concentration in a specific area, seeped into the masks and created intolerable eye irritation, coughing, vomiting, and inflammation of the respiratory tract. Enemy soldiers forced to remove their fouled masks were then subjected to a shelling with lethal phosgene.

The Germans attempted to make the enemy trenches no less dreadful than their own. Having the technological advantage that gave them the ability to introduce new gases before the Allies, the Germans devoted much thought to the tactical employment of chemical weapons, and in this respect, they reached a high degree of sophistication. After abandoning cloud attacks, the Germans increased their use of gas shells. They discovered on the Eastern Front that tear gas was extremely effective in neutralizing Russian artillery. Even a few rounds would incapacitate a gun crew or, having forced it to mask, prevent it from delivering accurate fire. On the Western Front in 1916, the Germans fired some 2,000 tear gas shells at an extensive French trench system near Verdun. This massive surprise bombardment resulted in the capture of 2,400 Frenchmen who, after being temporarily blinded by the tear gas, were surrounded by German troops wearing goggles, but no masks.

The Germans introduced other agents to the battlefield for specific tactical purposes. In May, 1916, they fired their Green Cross shell filled with diphosgene, a lung irritant. Later, as an indication of the increased sophistication of gas shells, they subdivided the Green Cross shell fill, first by a mix of 75 percent phosgene and 25 percent diphosgene, which was labled Green Cross 1. Then, in July, 1917, four different percentages of phosgene, diphosgene, and diphenylchlorosine called Green Cross 2, A, B, and C, respectively, were introduced. These were followed shortly by Blue Cross and Yellow Cross shells. The former shell was filled with an arsenic compound of finely separated dust. In field trials, this agent proved extremely effective in the penetration of all mask filters in existence. The need to encase the compound in a glass-lined shell, however, reduced its effectiveness, as the heat of the explosion failed to cause vaporization, and the force of the explosion caused only mechanical pulverization. The recipients, the French and British, considered Blue Cross a "failure and not worth the effort." The introduction of Yellow Cross (mustard gas), however, again gave the Germans the initiative in chemical warfare, which they held to the end of the war. By increasing the explosive charge in the shell, the Germans further extended the area contaminated by this blister producing agent. This shell was marked by a double (Lorraine) cross.

The Germans found gas persisted even longer when an agent and a small amount of high explosives were placed in one shell. The effect of the high explosive, when used in the proper amount, was to spread the agent over a wider area and keep it airborne longer. With this knowledge, the Germans changed their gas doctrine from attacking a, particular target to gassing large areas for extended periods of time. German staff officers began to plan operations that called for "gas barriers" and "gas pockets."

German tactical doctrine for the use of artillery gas shells offered a variety of possibilities. For the offense, it called for surprise and the concentration of as much gas as possible through the sudden and rapid placement of shells on a target area. "Cloud concentration" tactics imitated surprise tactics, but with an increase in the number of shells and an expansion of the size of a target area. Another offensive tactic was the use of gas shells that contained a high explosive charge and shrapnel. These shells, used exclusively by the Germans, had an effect "so devastating that the efficacy of a high explosive shrapnel gas shell bombardment was always increased." Once introduced, the Germans always added a percentage of these shells to any high explosive or shrapnel bombardment. The high explosive-gas shell was used extensively in German rolling barrages to support advancing infantry during the spring offenses of 1918. These shells were also used to neutralize known enemy artillery batteries and machine gun nests, thus allowing German infantry to bypass Allied strong points.

The key figure in the expansion of German gas shell tactical doctrine was Lt. Col. Georg Bruchniffiler, known as "Durchbruck" (Breakthrough) and considered an artillery genius because of his success on the battlefield. While on the Eastern Front, Bruchmiiller, a great believer in the efficiency of gas shells, developed a highly sophisticated system of gas artillery fire. His tactical ideas were incorporated in the December, 1917, edition of the German manual for employment of gas shells. Bruchmiiller's system created "Gas Squares," which were areas known to hold enemy batteries or concentrations of enemy troops. These locations would be saturated by surprise gas shell fire, and the lethal concentration would be renewed by subsequent periodic fire. Bruchmiiler's artillery tactics achieved surprise through a predicted-fire method that eliminated the usual ranging of the target by one gun of a battery. Bruchmüller formulated advanced firing data and tables based on meteorological variables such as wind, air temperature, and barometric pressure.

When Blue Cross and Yellow Cross shells became available, Bruchmüller devised Buntkreuz (colored cross) tactics. One of the most successful uses of this new doctrine came on the Eastern Front, in the German crossing of the Dvina River before Riga (Map 3). On 1 September 1917 a two-hour preliminary bombardment of the Russian batteries created "varicolored zones," as combinations of Blue Cross and Green Cross were used both during bombardment and then during three hours of firing for effect. For the preliminary gas fire, each German battery had a set of firing sequences every twelve minutes to counter Russian batteries, which first maintained a desultory fire and then fell silent. According to German estimates, more than 116,400 gas shells were fired, which caused at least a thousand Russian casualties, mainly because of the ineffectual respirators issued to Russian troops. The figure might have been higher had not the Russians fled. German infantry reached the opposite bank to find that the Russian artillery crews had abandoned their guns in "great haste, resembling flight." The Russian infantry, which lacked effective personal protection against chemical agents, had followed suit.

Persistent agent fire was used tactically by the Germans on both the offense and the defense. Surprise, though desirable, was not necessary for persistent agents. Yellow Cross allowed an area to be "cleared of, or rendered inaccessible to," the enemy. Fire continued for several hours, and the contamination could be renewed each day thereafter, if so desired. The areas gassed were called "Yellow Zones of Defense." In April, 1918, the Germans shelled the city of Armentieres with mustard gas. The bombardment was so heavy that witnesses claimed liquid mustard gas ran in the streets. Naturally, the British evacuated the locale; the contamination, however, prevented the Germans from entering the city for two weeks. In the spring offensives of 1918, the Germans created mustard gas zones to protect the flanks of advancing infantry, to neutralize enemy strong points, to deny the enemy key terrain, to block supply routes, and to render enemy artillery batteries ineffective. "Even in open warfare," a German officer wrote, "the troops soon were asking for gas supporting fire."

Mustard gas caused considerable consternation among the Allies. "We were outdistanced... " a French officer noted, "the German lead on us in this respect... was a source of real inquietude," for the units that were exposed suffered considerably and the struggle against Yperite "seemed most deceptive of solution." The Allies eventually responded in kind, but not until June, 1918, a full year after the Germans introduced the ultimate agent of World War I, did the French use Yperite, and it took the British until 26 September 1918 to retaliate with mustard. So desperate were the French to obtain the agent that British officers reported teams of French soldiers draining unexploded German Yellow Cross shells in order to reuse the gas.

Personal protection was always a problem, one neither side ever really solved in World War I. The German High Command, prior to the first attack at Ypres, made no effort to develop an efficient gas mask. Attacking German soldiers had small protective bags of mull or hemp that were soaked in a sodium bicarbonate (baking soda) solution and then tied over the mouth and nose. Not until the closing months of 1915 did the German army begin to issue a self-contained respirator. The mask had a treated leather facepiece (because of the shortage of rubber, only officer facepieces were constructed of this material, which was more efficient than leather and easier to maintain) and eyepieces of an outer glass lens and a celluloid inner lens. The first German mask had a significant drawback: the filter had to be screwed on to the facepiece each time the mask was used, which meant that more time was required to mask during a gas attack. Later, this problem was remedied by a single construction model with a replaceable filter element.

The French, British, and Russians did not coordinate their research and development of gas defenses. Although they passed information and some equipment to each other, they worked independently for the most part on their own protective masks. In England, shortly after the first gas attack in April, 1915, housewives were asked by the high command to produce what became popularly known as the Black Veil Respirator-black veiling held a pad of cotton waste soaked in a chemical solution over the nose and mouth.

These makeshift masks reached the British trenches in early May. When, in the latter part of 1915, the Germans began to use tear gas, the British countered with a flour sack type mask made of flannel, called the "Hypo" or "H-Helmet" after the chemical in which it was soaked, calcium hypochlorite. This mask offered protection to the eyes as well as to the respiratory system. One British officer described it as "a smoke helmet, a greasy grey-felt bag with a tale window certainly ineffective against gas." This H-Helmet contained two celluloid eyepieces, but no apparatus to expel the carbon dioxide that built up in the mask.

In the fall of 1915 British intelligence learned of Germany's intention to use a new gas, phosgene, a delayed-action choking agent, The Russians had also learned that the Germans intended to employ phosgene and advised the British that a solution of phenate-hexamine was effective in blocking the agent. As a result, the British soaked their H-Helmet in the Russian solution and added an outlet valve to reduce the carbon dioxide buildup inside the mask. The British Army called the new device the "PH-Helmet." The troops called it a. "goggle-eyed booger with a tit."

Although the PH-Helmet successfully blocked phosgene, it had serious drawbacks: it was hot, stuffy, and emitted an unpleasant odor; it also offered little protection against dense concentrations of lachrymatory agents. To counteract both phosgene and the lachrymating agents, the British in early 1916 took an entirely different approach to protective masks by developing a two-piece device called the "Large Box" or "Tar Box Respirator." A canister worn on the back contained neutralizing chemicals and attached by a rubber hose to a facepiece covering the chin, mouth, and nose. The wearer endured an uncomfortable noseclip and a mouthpiece similar to an athlete's rubber tooth protector. Goggles protected the eyes. The advantage of the mask rested in the use of a large filter. However, this also caused difficulties because the canister was too large and clumsy to be carried for extended distances over prolonged periods. This kind of mask reached its final stage of development with the introduction of the "Small Box Respirator" (SBR), which employed a smaller filter worn on the chest and a single construction facepiece. The details of the SBR became very familiar to men of the American Expeditionary Forces.

The French wrote a different chapter to the development of the gas mask. After using the same primitive masks as the British, they set out to develop a mask that was both effective and comfortable to wear-two criteria that were, and still are, essential for the successful design of protective devices. The first significant French protective device, the M-2 mask, was similar in design to the British H-Helmet, except it did not cover the entire head, but took the form of a "snout" similar to a feedbag for a horse. Its filtration ability was limited, so French doctrine called for troops to be rotated after several hours of exposure to any gas. In 1917 the French introduced the ARS *(Appareil Respiratoire Speécial)* mask. In appearance it resembled German protective equipment. The rubber facepiece had a waxed or oiled linen lining. Inhaled air passed in front of the eyepieces to prevent clouding. A canister attached to the facepiece could not be removed.

In September, 1917, these French masks were followed by another, the *Tissot*, which became one of the most effective masks of the war. As one postwar American observer noted, "the French deserve great credit" for the introduction of this defensive piece of equipment. In design, the *Tissot* was similar to the British Small Box Respirator except that the former's filter canister was carried on the soldier's back, not chest. This meant that infantrymen could carry only the *Tissot* and no other equipment. It covered the entire face, but without the uncomfortable nose clip and mouthpiece.

The design allowed air to enter the mouth across the eyepieces, thus removing the normal phenomenon of condensation. The circulation of fresh air also diluted any lachrymatory gases that might enter the mask. Finally, the entire facepiece was of thin rubber. The French thought the filter location, the same as for the Large Tar Box Respirator, clumsy and difficult to adjust and, therefore, judged it unsuitable for infantry. Troops, such as artillery gun crews and stretcher bearers, who were not loaded with personal equipment and who had to continue to fight or function during a gas attack, did receive the mask. These soldiers found, in addition to comfort, that one could breathe easier and that the filtration system was superior to the ARS and M-2 mask.

Unlike the British and French, the Russians devoted few resources to the development of chemical protective equipment. Consequently, they suffered the greatest number of chemically inflicted casualties in World War I. On 2 May 1915, not quite a month after the second Battle of Ypres during which French Colonial and Territorial troops collapsed under the first German gas attack, the Russians were subjected to a similar experience. German pioneer troops directed by Fritz Haber released 263 tons of chlorine gas from 12,000 cylinders against Russian troops at Bolimov.

The first cylinder attack on the Eastern Front killed 6,000 Russian soldiers. Two more gas cloud attacks were made on the same position, and upward of 25,000 Russian casualties resulted. According to German sources, in June, 1915, at Bzura, two Russian regiments, the 55th and 56th Siberian, suffered approximately 9,000 gas casualties, or about 90 percent of their total strength. On 7 September 1916 a German cloud attack killed 600 Russian officers and men. The following month Transbaikal Cossacks suffered 4,000 casualties. A gas attack in 1917 cost the Russians 12 officers, 1,089 men killed, and 53 officers, 7,738 men incapacitated. Despite these casualties, the Tzarist Army developed only one mask in addition to the basic chemical-soaked gauze respirator. The fabric facepiece of this mask covered the head and attached directly to a canister containing a charcoal filter.

It looked similar to the bill on a duck. Although the mask had no noseclip or mouthpiece, soldiers still found it extremely uncomfortable because the weight of the filter placed a great strain on the muscles of the neck. To make matters worse, the filter of this mask was of questionable effectiveness. By 1917 different types of British and French masks were being sent to Russia and used, to some limited extent, by Russian troops.

By the summer of 1917, when U.S. troops began to arrive at French ports, chemical warfare had become commonplace and, in practice, had reached a high degree of sophistication compared to the first significant gas attack at Ypres a little over two years earlier. By July the most effective chemical agent of the war, mustard or Yellow Cross, had made its appearance.

Gas shells now might contain two or even three different agents. All of the delivery systems for chemical war were in operation and efforts were being made by the combatants to improve on these weapons. The British had, for example, devised electronically detonated cylinders on tram cars for beam attacks. Also, the British had finally begun to overcome their shell production problems and had used gas shells in large quantities at the Battle of Arras in April, 1917.

Tactical doctrine for chemical warfare had reached a high level of sophistication, especially in artillery employment. In this area, the Germans, thanks to Lt. Col. Georg Bruchmüller, led the way. German artillery firing instructions became increasingly complex in regard to the selection of the gas or combination of gases to be used in a variety of tactical situations.

Given the advantage of viewing the development of chemical warfare from afar, the United States Army, upon entering the war, should have been in a position to operate in a chemical environment without repeating the costly experiences of the French, British, and Germans. Unfortunately, this was not to be the case.

THE AEF ORGANIZES FOR CHEMICAL WARFARE

On 13 June 1917, while the General Staff in the United States struggled to organize, man, and equip an army, General

John J. Pershing, Commander of the American Expeditionary Forces (AEF), arrived in France with a staff of fifty-three officers and 146 enlisted men. After a continuous round of official visits and ceremonies, Pershing and his staff settled into temporary headquarters in Paris. Two weeks later the first American troops arrived in France. General Order 8, published on 5 July 1917, established the organization of the AEF General Headquarters (GHQ). This order also created on paper the GHQ position of "Chief of the Gas Service," whose responsibilities included procurement of gas personnel and supplies, the "conduct of the entire Gas and Flame Service both offense and defense," the supervision of training for gas officers and troops, and experimentation with new gases, delivery systems, and protective devices.

Ordering the creation of a Gas Service was a simple matter. The actual organizing of a new branch of the Army, however, would take a tremendous amount of effort and time. Time was precious. By mid-July, over 12,000 doughboys were within thirty miles of the front, all without gas masks or training in chemical warfare. Yet, because of more pressing problems, it was not until 17 August 1917 that General Pershing sent a cable to Washington requesting the organization of a Gas Service and the authority to appoint Lt. Col. Amos A. Fries, Corps of Engineers, as its chief. Lieutenant Colonel Fries had arrived in France three days earlier. As an engineer officer he was assigned responsibility for organizing a road network to support the AEF Services of Supply (SOS). Several days later Col. Hugh A. Drum and Col. Alvin B. Barber of the GHQ, AEF, approached Fries. As Fries recalled after the war, the staff officers asked what "I should think if my orders were changed so as to make me Chief of the newly proposed gas service." Given overnight to decide, Fries accepted. On 22 August 1917 he began to build an organization based on information Barber and Drum had compiled about the British Special Brigade and French "Z" units. In addition, the staff officers gave Fries a draft of a proposed General Order 31 that would establish a Gas Service.

General Order 31 assigned the Gas Service responsibility for both offensive and defensive operations, including the organization of gas personnel, gas warfare supplies, and gas warfare training in the AEF.

Appended to the order was a draft chart of the Gas Service Organization. In reviewing the chart with Fries, Pershing noted that the offensive arm included Stokes mortar companies. This prompted him to ask why existing trench mortar companies could not be utilized to fire gas rounds. Barber and Drum, who were also present, explained that gas operations were too technical and dangerous for untrained personnel to conduct and, therefore, required special troops. They also told Pershing that in the British Army the Special Brigade used 4-inch Stokes mortars.

Acting on Pershing's instructions, Fries, with Colonel Church and Captain Boothby of the Medical Department, visited the British Special Brigade headquarters at St.Omer. Church had served as an observer with the French Army for a year and a half and, during that time, had collected information on chemical warfare defense. Boothby did the same while observing British chemical warfare procedures and also took a course at the British defense school. At St. Omer the medical officers discussed British defensive gas doctrine, while Fries obtained information on the offensive aspects of chemical warfare. Fries elicited information on gases in use, special troops, chemical ammunition, and delivery systems. He also visited the large chemical material depot for the British Fifth Army.

After returning to AEF headquarters, the three officers reviewed both the draft General Order and the organizational chart. They modified the original proposals to provide general rather than specific guidelines, anticipating that only actual combat experience would glean the information necessary to build a truly effective organization. Fries criticized the British system that divided responsibility for offensive and defensive gas warfare. Paradoxically, the British liaison officer in the United States, Maj. S. M. J. Auld, warned the Americans against just such a practice. Thus, the AEF Gas Service made it the responsibility of all gas officers to be knowledgeable in both areas, a point driven home in subsequent general orders detailing the duties of army, corps, and division gas officers. On 3 September 1917, almost five months after the United States entered the war, the final version of General Order 31 was published.

Not until 27 May 1918, as U.S. divisions were coming online in increasing numbers and experiencing heavy gas casualties, did GHQ, AEF, issue General Order 79 for the establishment of unit gas officers. Only then did Fries have the authority to appoint chief gas officers for armies and corps and gas officers and assistants for divisions. Until this time, division commanders had been appointing gas officers as they saw fit. Under the new arrangements, chief gas officers of armies and corps and division gas officers would be staff officers responsible to the commander. Parallel reporting procedures were established in order to ensure that accurate information reached the proper authorities. In addition to reports through official channels, the order authorized these officers to send required reports directly to the Chief of the Gas Service. The Chief, with GHQ approval, could also order these unit staff officers to attend meetings necessary for the coordination of defensive gas measures.

The division and higher echelon gas officers had specific duties assigned. By direction of their commanding officers, they were to instruct and supervise the gas officers and NCOs within their command, supervise all defensive training and drill, collect enemy chemical warfare material for submission to AEF laboratories, inspect defensive measures, and advise the commander and staff regarding all aspects of chemical warfare. The division gas officer had the responsibility of reporting to the commander all gas casualties and actions taken to prevent recurrences. The division commander forwarded this report, together with a list of the actions he had taken to correct the deficiencies, to the Chief of the Gas Service.

Regimental and battalion commanders assigned duties to their gas officers. At this level, gas officer and gas NCO responsibilities were considered additional, not primary duties. A gas officer and NCO assistant were required for regiment, battalion, and separate units, and two NCOs were appointed for each company. Selected on the basis of undefined "special qualifications," the men were trained at the AEF Gas Defense School or corps gas schools. Among their duties, they supervised training in the use of gas masks, gas proof shelters, alarm systems, and related defensive measures. When the division entered combat, the gas NCOs were required to inspect all defensive equipment and antigas procedures at least twice a week. They reported weather, terrain conditions, all new enemy gas tactics and material, and any noted deficiencies. This information was reported officially to the company commander and informally to the battalion commander.

General Order 79 established an AEF Gas Defense School with a course of instruction "adequate for the training in gas defense of gas officers and noncommissioned officers." The school director received specific instructions, to coordinate his activities with those of officers engaged in offensive gas instruction and with those at the AEF's new chemical experimental station at Hanlon Field near Chaumont. Instructors at the Gas Defense School kept abreast of the latest changes in gas warfare by personally reviewing files of Allied and American gas officer reports and by reading translated copies of captured German and Austrian documents.

General Order 79 dealt primarily with the Gas Corps and the training of its officers, but it also called the attention of "all ranks" to the "increasing importance of gas warfare."

Although the Gas Corps would do every thing that was possible to prepare individuals and units to avoid casualties from gas, the "ultimate responsibility" for defense against gas, the order concluded, "devolves upon commanding officers" who must provide for the training of their men and the maintenance of gas discipline. In order to maintain gas discipline and provide adequate training, the order urged commanders to cooperate with Gas Corps officers.

The extensive use of gas by the Germans in their spring 1918 offensives caused the AEF General Staff to expand the duties of gas officers. As of 2 July 1918, gas officers were to be consulted and their technical knowledge utilized in the preparation of all plans involving the extensive use of gas, whether by artillery or other means.

Thus, the duties and responsibilities of gas officers grew with the increasing awareness of the impact chemical agents were having on the offensive and defensive capabilities of AEF units. Fries, however, faced a chronic problem of locating competent men to serve in a branch of service that lacked precedent and had an unknown future. was further complicated by an Armywide shortage of personnel. The Corps of Engineers, originally the primary source of gas officers, became reluctant, as its own demand for officers grew, to have men reassigned to another branch.

The AEF Gas Service had other problems with which to contend. There was, for example, a severe shortage of gas warfare supplies. The lack of protective masks for members of the AEF caused the greatest concern. On 2 August 1917, GHQ, AEF decided to utilize the British Small Box Respirator (SBR) as its primary mask and the French M-2 mask as an "emergency" protective device.

The SBR consisted of a canister-type filter of absorbent charcoal with alternating layers of oxidized soda lime granules. A flexible rubber tube connected the canister to a rubberized facepiece that was held to the face by elastic bands in order to provide an airtight fit. Inside the facepiece was a rubber nose clip. A hard rubber mouthpiece that the wearer grasped by his teeth was connected to the flexible hose attached to the filtration canister. A soldier exhaled air through a rubber flutter valve at the front of the mask. The wearer viewed the world through two lenses made of celluloid or specially prepared glass. Each soldier had a tube of "antidimming" or defogging paste that could be used to prevent condensation from forming on the lenses. Lacking an American mask, the AEF placed an initial order for 600,000 SBRs and 100,000 French M-2 masks. Additional orders followed, as it would take the United States a year from its entry into the war to begin providing its troops in the field with an acceptable American-made version of the SBR.

The shortage of respirators notwithstanding, no individual could enter the combat zone unless equipped with a mask. Commanders and staff officers went to considerable lengths to ensure that all members of their units had respirators. In late December, 1917, the newly arrived 42nd "Rainbow"

Division was moved by rail to a training site in France. On the train were masks for the unit, which the division's Chief of Staff planned to issue on its arrival. The 1st Division, however, was due to go "on the line shortly" and submitted an urgent request for respirators. The Chief of the Gas Service responded by ordering the 42nd's Chief of Staff to transfer his masks to the 1st Division. To circumvent the order, the 42nd's Chief of Staff immediately stopped the train and ordered the masks issued to his men. He then reported to Fries that it was impossible to comply with the order because the masks had already been issued.

Several thousand men of the 1st Division lacked masks, and its 1st Brigade was scheduled to move to the front line in January.* Fries finally obtained a "priority of shipment" and detailed several gas officers to accompany the masks from Le Havre, the major British supply base, to ensure their safe delivery to the 1st Division. Despite these precautions, one carload of 4,000 masks disappeared in transit. Fries finally had to order the 2nd Brigade of the 1st Division to turn in their SBRs. These were cleaned and reissued to the Division's 1st Brigade. This episode was not an isolated one.

Gas equipment and supplies in the United States and France were initially the responsibility of the nearest related branch of the Army. The AEF Gas Service found this procedure "exceedingly embarrassing, cumbersome and inefficient." Despite initial resistance, the General Staff in Washington approved AEF requisition submitted on 10 September 1917 for 50,000 cylinders, 50,000 Livens projector shells, and a large quantity of Stokes mortars and ammunition.

None of these weapons or ammunition reached the AEF in time to be used in combat. To avoid duplication of effort and to save time, Fries, in February, 1918, received permission to make direct purchases of equipment from the Allies. At that time almost all of the gas warfare material used by the AEF came from the British. Not until April, 1918, did any material manufactured in the United States begin to reach the AEF. As noted in the preceding chapter, a number of war gases were manufactured in the United States during the war, and more than 3,600 tons of these did reach the French and British.

Because of a shortage of artillery pieces, artillery units of the AEF were equipped primarily with the French 75-mm light field gun, the 155-mm medium howitzer, and the 240-mm heavy howitzer, as well as with British 8-inch and 9.2-inch heavy howitzers. The U.S. Army also adopted, with minor modifications, the French gas shell. The AEF Services of Supply purchased French shells and painted them according to an American color code.

Originally, the SOS defensive gas equipment fell into Class I with clothing, leather goods, and optical instruments. In February, 1918, when the Gas Service was given authority to requisition its own supplies, all items of gas warfare equipment were placed into a new category, Class V. In September, 1918, the Army created four subclasses within the general Class V classification. Subclass A material included offensive gas supplies, such as gas shells and grenades, that were not used by gas troops but by the combat arms. Subclass B material included those gas supplies issued exclusively to gas troops. Subclass C supplies encompassed aviation, smoke, and incendiary material. Subclass D items included all defensive gas material. The Ordnance Corps transported and issued subclasses A and C, while the Gas Service did the same for B and D items. The Gas Service distributed all "anti-gas supplies." Fries ordered a 10 percent reserve of all equipment at the division gas dumps, and each company or regiment maintained a 5 percent reserve supply. The division gas officer issued the required masks to the regimental supply officers, who distributed them to battalions. Gas officers also issued gas alarm devices, Strombo horns, Klaxon horns, and gongs directly to company commanders in each sector. Later, army and corps gas officers were given similar responsibility for the issue of gas supplies to corps artillerymen and all rear echelon troops.

Another branch heavily involved in chemical warfare was the Army's Medical Department. The General Staff anticipated that medical officers would require some knowledge of the actual symptoms brought on by chemical agents and the various methods of treatment for gas poisoning. Consequently, in May, 1917, the War Department issued a "Memorandum on Gas Poisoning in Warfare with Notes on Its Pathology and Treatment," based on British sources.

Still, despite this assistance from Washington, most of the planning and organization for the treatment of gas casualties was done by the AEF in France. Maj. J. R. Church, Medical Department, was the first Medical Director of the Gas Service in France. While on the General Staff, he had assisted in the initial planning for an AEF Gas Service. As Medical Director he devoted most of his time to organizational matters. The increase in gas casualties, however, resulted in a personnel change in the position, with Lt. Col. Harry L. Gilchrist, M.D., the former commander of Number 9, General Hospital, replacing Church. Gilchrist prepared for his new assignment by attending the British Gas School at Rouen, France.

When Gilchrist reported for duty as Medical Director, he found no records or guidelines detailing the responsibilities of his position. His first priority, and one agreed to by Fries, was to launch a gas instruction campaign directed specifically at AEF medical officers. On 9 February 1918, Gilchrist published a pamphlet, "Symptomology, Pathology and General Treatment of Gas Cases," which provided medical officers basic information on the treatment of chemical casualties. Following this publication, the Medical Director's office issued a constant stream of bulletins aimed at keeping AEF medical officers up-to-date on the latest medical developments in gas warfare. Gilchrist visited most AEF divisions and hospitals, where he lectured to officers and men on chemical warfare from a medical point of view, emphasizing prevention and treatment of gas casualties.

As the chemical war escalated with the introduction of mustard gas, the Medical Director's responsibilities and, indeed, his department's tasks became increasingly crucial to the AER Gilchrist inspected troops at the front and visited medical personnel in hospitals, hospital trains, and other locations. He also served as the liaison officer between the Gas Service and the Medical Department, advising both the AEF's Chief of the Gas Service and the Chief Surgeon on gas-related medical matters. In addition to these general duties, he collected all medical information relating to gas warfare and relayed it to the AEF's Chief Surgeon. Gilchrist focused his attention on such matters as new treatment for gas casualties and "combating-the effects of the enemy gases not only from a therapeutic, but also from a prophylactic point of view." To obtain information, he visited the sites of battles where large numbers of gas casualties had occurred.

Because armies and corps of the AEF were formed after the arrival of a number of divisions, the medical structure to treat gas casualties evolved first within the division. On 1 March 1918, the 42nd Division became the second American division to occupy a sector on the Western Front. Although initially the division had few gas casualties, the medical officers prepared for a large influx of gas victims.

All four of the division's field hospitals were set up to accept gas victims, and orders were given that a total of 500 beds be put aside for such cases. On 20 March the Germans launched an artillery bombardment of mustard and high explosive shells that hit the 42nd Division's 165th Infantry at 1730 hours. In thespace of a few minutes, the mustard caused 270 casualties, including one death. The first-aid station through which the casualties passed also received a drenching with. gas, so medical personnel wore masks as they treated the patients.

As a result of this attack and others that followed, the 42nd Division took several steps to improve the treatment of gas casualties. These later became standard for AEF divisions in the line. The first measure was to dedicate one of the four division field hospitals to gas cases. The position of division Gas Medical Officer was also created. Memorandum 148, HQ, 42nd Division, published on 23 April 1918, listed the duties of this officer as the instruction of medical personnel in gas defense; the supervision of gas protection of medical dugouts, aid stations, and field hospitals; the early diagnosis of symptoms; and the treatment of all types of gas casualties.

The AEF adopted the 42nd Division's practices when it instituted the position of division Gas Medical Officer in AEF General Order 144, dated 29 August 1918. GHQ took this measure in the face of mounting gas casualties and a high incident of gas malingering. As a consequence, in addition to the duties indicated in the 42nd Division's memorandum, the AEF order added duties such as the instruction of all division personnel on the early symptoms and treatments of gas poisoning and the instruction of line officers in practical medical matters connected with gas warfare. The orders stated that any officers selected must be "live, wide-awake, energetic men, and must show a keen appreciation of the work." By the first week in October, 1918, each AEF division had a Gas Medical Officer. These men were sent to the School of Pharmacy's School of Gas (Ecole de Gaz) at the University of Paris for a four-day course to prepare them for their division duties.

Beyond the division field hospitals, each army established its own gas hospitals. The first such installation began operation on 29 August 1918. Army-level hospital personnel were casuals, or officers and men loaned from base or evacuation hospitals or anywhere else medical personnel could be found. To meet the demands of the Meuse-Argonne offensive, the Chief Surgeon, AEF, in September, 1918, established five gas hospitals with a total of 1,650 beds. Colonel Gilchrist suggested three mobile 1,500-bed gas hospitals be established, one for each U.S. corps. This plan, however, was never implemented because of insufficient personnel. Another plan called for the creation of two "emergency gas teams" to be assigned to each base hospital. Their mission was to "relieve the strain" that sudden gas attacks put on division field hospitals. The GHQ, AEF, organized several "emergency gas teams," each consisting of a medical officer, two nurses, and two orderlies. The Chief Surgeon of the 1st U.S. Army, Col. A. N. Stark, however, objected to these teams on the grounds that base hospitals were too far removed from the fighting. He also believed that the division field hospitals set aside forgassed soldiers were effective and needed no further assistance. HeedingStark's objections, the Chief Surgeon disbanded the teams.

Another problem with which Fries and his staff had to contend was training in gas defense. When the 1st Division arrived in France, Pershing thought it best to have the Americans train by serving with a French divi sion. This proved to be unsatisfactory because the training varied from unit to unit within the French division. When the Training Section of the

AEF's GHQ became operational, it prepared a standardized division training schedule. Initially, the period of time a division spent preparing to enter the line was supposed to be three months. Only two days of the schedule were allocated to Gas Service instructors. Later, as the demand for combat units increased, the gas instruction decreased to a mere six hours. This was vigorously protested by the Gas Service. In the spring of 1918, when the German offensives required a shortening of the division training cycle to bring new units on line, gas instruction was cut further.

Formal defensive training was supplemented by wearing the masks during other training activities. Pvt. Norman A. Dunham of the 40th Division remembered wearing the SBR and full pack during two and three hour marches. He thought the mask "the worst thing a soldier has to contend with" and the "most torturous thing" a person can wear. Lt. Edgar D. Gilman remarked that when he wore the mask he found that it was not only disagreeable, painful, and smothering, but also that his saliva flowed profusely from his mouth, through the flutter valves, and down the front of his shirt. Personal protection was survival on the battlefield,however, and command emphasis had to be placed on defensive gas training, to include the wearing of the mask.

It became obvious to GHQ, AEF that many commanders were not supporting the training activities of their gas officers and NCOs. To remedy this problem, officers in brigades that were rotated off the line received a comprehensive lecture course on gas defensive measures. However, continued reports of over 25 percent gas casualties indicated to General Staff that, after basic training, comparatively little was to be gained by instructing individuals in units on the line. The consensus among gas officers was that training had to instill an interest and awareness of gas defensive measures throughout an entire unit to give the best results in combat. Gas officers also believed more realistic training was needed. One result of this conviction was that artillery batteries, when they trained, received a minimum of three surprise gas attacks as part of the training schedule. To test the alertness of sentries and to correct such carelessness as leaving masks out of reach, attacks were often scheduled at night, while the troops were sleeping at their position. Men firing on the ranges were subjected to simulated surprise gas attacks in order to familiarize them with laying artillery pieces during an attack and to acquaint them with the difficulty of transmitting firing data while masked. During night marches, men were subjected to gas attacks as a means of teaching them to overcome confusion.

During the first year of American participation in the war, men arriving as individual replacements had little or no formal instruction in defensive measures until they reached their units in the forward areas. In the summer of 1918, the Army acted to rectify this haphazard method. Training stations were established at the AEF debarkation ports of Brest and St. Nazaire. Each center had five Gas Service instructors: one officer and four NCOS. Three enlisted men acted as gas mask fitters and helpers. When troops arrived at the stations, they marched single file into a warehouse to be fitted and issued. masks. After an inspection, the troops moved to a large lecture hall where instructors did everything possible to impress on the men the importance of defensive gas measures. To complete the training, seventy-five to 100 men at a time entered a gas chamber filled with a tear agent for five to ten minutes. At peak times more than 2,000 men a day were put through this initiation into gas warfare.

In Army rear areas, depot divisions, such as the one at La Querche, handled three categories of personnel: newly arrived line replacements, special units such as engineer troops, and casuals who were recently released from hospitals and scheduled to rejoin their units. During the normal three-week course, the replacements received a minimum of eighteen hours of gas defense training. Their training consisted of lectures, mask drills, games with the mask worn, and firing weapons while wearing the The troops also went through simulated tactical operations, with the instructors lighting smoke candles and throwing tear gas grenades to provide added realism.

Special troops such as pioneer infantry, engineer, and medical service units first received basic infantry training and then were given three days' intensive instruction in gas defense. During the three days, the men practiced their specialty while wearing masks. For example, medics with SBRs in place applied bandages and carried stretchers through woods and over rough terrain. Engineers constructed roads and pioneer troops dug ditches while wearing masks. After duty hours, trainees played baseball in their SBRs.

Hospital convalescents, the last category of men run through the divisions, numbered anywhere from a handful to 2,000 a day. These men were reequipped with masks, and those with prior gas training-Class "A" men-were excused from formal instruction until August, 1918, when the mounting number of mustard gas casualties compelled the Gas Service staff to give all personnel short classes on ways to avoid being contaminated by this persistent agent.

The increased German employment of chemical agents-especially mustard gas-for counterbattery fire forced American artillery training camps to place special emphasis on defensive gas instruction. During a gas attack, a poorly trained artillery man would be totally incapable of serving his weapon or delivering accurate fire. Initially, artillery officers and NCOs attended a week-long course of lectures, drills, and practical exercises. Later NCOs received an additional week of training. If the artillerymen failed to score 70 percent or better on the final examination, they had to repeat the course. Just before returning to the front, the graduates had to visit.a base hospital to see gas casualties. The experience, according to instructors, "furnished a great stimulus to general gas training." Still, despite these efforts to train every doughboy arriving in France, many received no training in gas warfare because of the pressing need for troops,on the front lines.

In conjunction with the emphasis on gas defensive training, the AEF paid increasing attention to the offensive gas capabilities of the American Army in France. On 10 January 1918 the first two companies of the 1st Gas Regiment (30th Engineers) arrived in France. The companies reported to the British Special Brigade training area at Helfaut, where Brigadier General Foulkes personally directed the training of the unit. Eventually, four of the six companies of the regiment passed through Helfaut.

The training of the 1st Gas Regiment in offensive gas operations began in February, 1918, and employed the delivery systems used by the British. The American troops spent five days learning to use Livens projectors, seven days for Stokes mortars, and two days for cylinder operations. The men first attended classes and then conducted practical field exercises in which they applied their newly acquired knowledge. Projector operations called for the emplacement of the guns at night and their detonation the following day. Stokes mortar drill required the men to conduct rapid fire with gas rounds, thermite, and smoke, both day and night. Officers of the regiment opened cylinders of chlorine, and the men walked through the gas cloud to instill confidence in their training and equipment. The American officers were then detailed to a sector of the British front and assigned to Special Brigade companies, where they observed projector, mortar, and cylinder operations. The overall result was that these men better understood offensive gas operations and could assist in training the other companies of the American Gas Regiment.

On 6 June 1918 these trained officers and men held a practice shoot for the AEF General Staff at Hanlon Field, the home of the AEF's Gas School and experimental station in France. Twelve Stokes mortars and 100 Livens projectors were fired. On 22 June, after several more exercises, companies of the 1st Gas Regiment moved to the U.S. sector to conduct offensive gas operations.

Artillery was the other branch of the Army capable of conducting offensive gas operations. In the first gas warfare manuals prepared by the U.S. Army War College, artillery employment was not included because of the continual changes in gas tactical doctrine on the Western Front. Therefore, almost all artillery training in gas warfare was conducted in France, where the AEF adopted British and French doctrine for gas shell fire. The U.S. 1st Army, for example, published its own "Provisional Instruction for Artillery Officers on the Use of Gas Shell," based on French field manuals. At artillery camps, gas officers lectured on the problems involved in the use of gas shells, but no evidence exists to indicate that gas shells were ever fired in training. Yet, by 1 November 1918, 20 percent of all shells delivered to the AEF were gas filled, and a 25 percent ratio was planned for 1919.

3

WEAPONS, ARMS AND STRENGTHS OF THE ARMY

INTRODUCTION

At the end of the 1971 war, the Indian army realized the limitations of their tank fleet in the harsh desert conditions of Rajasthan, a northwestern Indian state bordering Pakistan, so they initiated their own MBT design. The first "Arjun" (named after a mythical Hindu warrior prince) concept was laid out in 1974 by the Combat Vehicles Research and Development Establishment (CVRDE) of the Defence Research and Development Organization (DRDO). Based on 1971 battlefield experiences, the Arjun would have a locally-designed, rifled 120mm main gun, a German, MTU-based diesel powerplant (The Indians consider turbine engines fuel guzzlers), and a computerized fire control system with a laser rangefinder.

One of the early Arjun prototypes was unveiled in April 1985, with a number of prototypes undergoing technical testing while desert trials were scheduled for that summer.

PINAKA MULTIBARREL ROCKET LAUNCHER

The indigenously built Pinaka multi-barrel rocket launcher Weapon Area System can fire rockets with a range of 39-40 km, in a salvo of 12 rockets with 1.2 tons of high explosives within 40 seconds.

The complete system comprises a launch vehicle, a loader/ replenishment vehicle, and a command post vehicle with a battery of six launchers. Pinaka can neutralise a target area of 350 square kilometres, and is meant as a supplement to the existing artillery system at a range beyond 30 km. It can be fitted with a variety of warheads ranging from blast-cum-pre-fragmented high explosives to anti-tank mines. This indigenously designed MLRS is far cheaper than the international competition, costing just Rs 23 million per system. By comparison the American M270 MLRS costs Rs 195 million, and the 9P140 URAGAN of Russia and the ASTROS-II of Brazil each cost Rs 38 million.

The Pune-based Armament Research and Development Establishment has successfully produced the 'Pinaka' Multi Barrel Rocket Launcher System for the Indian armed forces, to give it concentrated high volume firepower to destroy enemy targets as demanded by the top brass of the Indian army. The Pinaka system was tested at the interim test range (ITR) Chandipur-on-sea, and had undergone several tests since 1995. It has been subjected to user's trials by the Army, which was not entirely satisfied with the system, and additional tests were conducted in response to suggestions to improve its capability further.

In March 1999 the system was tested in the run-up to the country's largest ever air force exercise over the site of India's 1998 underground nuclear blasts, at the eastern Indian missile launch site of Balasore. Pinaka was finally put into field testing for assessing its capability during the Kargil conflict. Pinaka reportedly proved very successful during field testing in the high altitude conflict in Kargil. In mid-1998 it was reported that production is on at various ordnance factories, and four public sector undertakings would meet the December 1998 delivery deadline. But in May 1999 the Comptroller and Auditor

General criticized the Defence Research and development Organisation (DRDO) for its failure to develop critical components of Pinaka, which led to a six-year delay in the induction of the system. Far from reaching the production stage, the DRDO has yet to develop various critical components of the system despite an expenditure of Rs 42.45 crore. The Defence Ministry in 1981 had planned to induct "Pinaka" into Indian Army regiments by 1994, and the project was originally given a Rs 26.47 crore budget. The expected date of completion of development is late 2000 at a cost of around Rs 80 crore.

The Armament Research and Development Establishment (ARDE) has also developed a high performance artillery rocket system which can fire within a range between 70 km to 100 km. This is a highly sophisticated "shoot-and-scoot" high mobility system capable of firing a salvo of 12 rockets, each with a payload of 100 kg within a time span of 30 seconds. This new artillery rocket system comprises of an advanced family of warheads including terminally guided submunitions with autonomous target search and engagement capability besides remotely delivered intelligent bomblets and minelets with self-neutralising capability.

Specifications

Range 7 km - 40 km

Rocket Diameter 214 mm

Warheads

- fragmentation high explosive
- incendiary
- anti-tank and anti-personnel minelettes
- anti-tank bomlettes

Rate of Fire

- 40 seconds [typically reported]

- 24-44 seconds [variously reported]

ALL WEATHER AIR DEFENCE GUN SYSTEM

A high performance family of All Weather Towed and Self Propelled Air Defence Gun System is under development to complement the Defence Research and Development Organisation (DRDO) surface-to-air missile systems such as Trishul and Akash.

The new gun will feature twin-gun cyclic rate of fire of 2000 rounds per minute aimed to engage and neutralise high speed aircraft, helicopters, remote-piloted combat air vehicles and stand-off weapons.

The integrated gun system is expected to have all weather day-night operations with on-mount passive suiteof electro-optic sensors like laser range finders, forward looking infra-red (FLIR), thermal imaging systems and low-light level TV, for tracking and engaging fast flying targets by means of a high precision computerised digital servo control system.

MBT-2000 / TYPE 2000 MAIN BATTLE TANK

Pakistan's development of the MBT-2000 *Al Khalid* began in 1988, and in January 1990 an agreement was reached with China to jointly design, develop and manufacture system. The design is an upgrade from the original T902M and work had been going on at China's NORINCO for some years, with initial prototypes produced in China were fielded for trials in August 1991. Pakistan's manufacturing plant at Taxila was completed in 1992. Since then development efforts have focused on improving the design for Pakistan's terrain and high temperatures.

The engine of the T90 2M is replaced by the Ukrainian 6TD 1200hp engine, and a newly developed thermal viewer system has been added to improve nocturnal fighting capability.

Heavy Industries Taxila was expected to start production of Al-Khalid before the turn of this century. The Chinese ground army has not made any purchase orders and will not use the same tank when it does decide to buy a next-generation armored vehicle.

Specifications

Powerplant Ukrainian 6TD 1200hp

Maximum Speed 37 mph

Weight 48 tons

Armament

one 125mm smooth bore gun

one 12.7mm machine gun

one 7.62mm machine gun.

NUCLEAR BOMB

India tested a nuclear bomb in 1974 using materials from Canada and technical help from Soviet Union. However, the embargo on heavy water export from Canada after the test stalled India's nuclear ambitions till 1998, when it shocked the world by conducting five nuclear detonations termed as *Shakti* tests.

The highest yield was by a 48 kiloton staged fusion device, which India claimed was a thermonuclear bomb but seismic data on the tests proved otherwise. In the same year 1998, Pakistan conducted a series of six nuclear detonations in a test termed as *Chagai*.

The highest yield was reported to be about 25 kiloton from a two stage boosted device. At present Pakistan's nuclear stockpile is slated to be around 30-40 warheads while India possesses 70-100 warheads. The nuclearisation of India and

Pakistan became a turning point in the history of conflicts between these two countries with high tensions but no war, not very much unlike the US vs USSR Cold War.

BALLISTIC AND CRUISE MISSILE PROLIFERATION

In the nuclear delivery front, both India and Pakistan have a series of ballistic and cruise missiles in addition to ground attack aircrafts. The maximum range among India's operational ballistic missiles is 2000 km achieved by Agni-2. India's Agni ballistic missiles are indigenously developed by its own missile defence industry known as *IGMDP*. The maximum range among Pakistan's missiles is by *Hatf V Gauri* which is reported to do over 2200 kms. Pakistan's Hatf missiles are based on North Korean *No-Dong* series of IRBMs. Both Pakistan's *Hatf* and India's *Agni* ballistic missiles are nuclear capable. India has also developed a supersonic cruise missile *BrahMos* which is by far the fastest cruise missile at Mach 2.6 and maximum range of 290 km. It is reported to be nuclear capable but it is not confirmed yet. On the Pakistan side, its *Babur* cruise missile has a reported range of 700 km and a maximum speed of 880 km/h (Mach 0.7). As with India *BrahMos*, *Babur* is also reported to be nuclear capable but there is no confirmation yet.

The Final Verdict

Both Pakistan and India are almost evenly matched head to head in nuclear and missile fronts, however India has strategic and technological superiority over the conventional forces of Pakistan. Indian Navy is larger in fleet and personnel size with a more varied range of ships including an aircraft carrier while Pakistan's Navy is smaller and has no aircraft carriers. Indian's IAF is equipped with highly capable fighters like 4.5th generation *Su-30*s and 4th gen *Mirage 2000*s which are technologically superior to Pakistan PAF's *F-16*s and *Mirage III*s. Additionally Indian pilots are better trained and more capable in air combat than Pakistani forces as was demonstrated by its various wars with Pakistan or joint exercises with US and UK. In the area of conventional ground forces both the Indian as well as Pakistani Army is well equipped and highly trained to survive in extremities of topography and climate in combat conditions, like wars in the high Himalayas.

If a purely conventional war were to take place between both these countries, India would most likely overpower Pakistan owing to its superior military technology and infrastructure, larger manpower, more territorial area and a strategic advantage in its sea and air forces. It must also be noted that a war between these two countries will matter more than India's conventional superiority as both these nations are nuclear powers on an equal deadlock. India has maintained a 'no first use' nuclear policy in the lines of a similar policy by China while Pakistan does not have any such policy, considering their only hope against India is in nuclear deterrance. It would be risky for India at the present scenario to go into any aggressive war against Pakistan as the repercussions would be serious a nuclear devastation for both countries.

Unfortunately India and Pakistan had adversarial relations since sixty years. After the Mumbai carnage Pakistan is under threat of pre-emptive strikes. Fourth Indo-Pakistan war could be triggered by another terrorist attack anywhere in India. This is a dangerous scenario. India and Pakistan have fought three wars, and war drums for the fourth war are getting louder.

It is in order therefore to comprehend Indian military capabilities, and Pakistan's ability to defend itself. Defense capability is an interplay of economic and military potential. Indian economy is booming, and its GDP growth is in double digits. The global recession has impacted Indian economy, but its defense capability remains intact. Military power and capabilities are sustained by economic and industrial potential.

Geography, demography, population, oil resources and reserves, industrial capability including defense production, dollar reserves, self reliance, education, quality of manpower and leadership have a bearing on military power. Seven lakh Indian troops are tied down in Jammu and Kashmir. India has over one hundred billion dollar reserves. The West, Israel and Russia are India's weapon suppliers.

Indian Army has eighteen Corps with 34 Divisions including four Rapid Action Divisions, which would spear head ground offensives. Pakistan Army has ten Corps and twenty five divisions.

Indian Army has eighteen Infantry, ten Mountain, three Armored, and two Artillery Divisions. Besides it has five Infantry, one parachute, thirteen Air Defense, and four Engineering Brigades, designated as independent formations. In addition there are two Air Defense Groups, and fourteen Army Aviation Helicopter units. This is a sizeable force, capable of launching major offensives from several fronts.

The decentralized command structure will be an advantage, as compared to Pakistan's centralized Army command organization. Pakistan Army has an active force of 620,000 well trained personnel, with 528000 reservists, and 150000 para-military troops. Pakistan armed forces are seventh largest in the world. Pakistan Army's doctrine of "Offensive Defense", evolved by General Mirza Aslam Beg was put to test in 1989 in Exercise Zarb-e Momin.

The doctrine is to launch a sizeable offensive into enemy territory, rather than wait for enemy strikes or attacks. In case of Indian land offensive Pakistan Army and Air Force will respond with land and air offensives to gain and hold enemy territory. Before embarking on further offensive, gains shall be consolidated. In 1990 the Central Corps of Reserves was created to fight in the desert sectors , where enemy land offensives are expected. These dual capable formations trained for offensive and holding actions are fully mechanized.

Pakistan Army has ten Corps including the newly formed Strategic Corps. The Army has twenty six divisions (eight less than India). Two more divisions were raised as Corps reserves for V and XXXI Corps. Pakistan Army has two armored divisions, and ten independent armored brigades. Presently one hundred thousand troops are stationed on the Pak Afghan border to fight terror. Special Service Group-SSG comprises two airborne Brigades i.e. six battalions.

Pakistan Army has 360 helicopters, over two thousand heavy guns, and 3000 APC's. Its main anti-tank weapons are Tow, Tow Mk II, Bakter Shiken and FGM 148 ATGM. The Army Air Defence Command has S.A- 7 Grail, General Dynamics FIM-92 Stinger, GD FIM Red Eye, and ANZA Mk-I, Mk-II, Mk-III and HQ 2 B surface ti air missiles. Radar controlled Oerlikon is the standard Ack Ack weapon system.

The ballistic missile inventory of the Army is substantial. It comprises Ghauri III and Shaheen III IRB'S; medium range Ghauri I and II and Shaheen II, and short range Hatf I- B, Abdali, Ghaznavi, Shaheen I and M -11 missiles. All the ballistic missiles can carry nuclear war heads. Nuclear and conventional weapon capable Babur Cruise missile is the new addition to Pakistan's strategic weapon inventory. Number of ballistic missiles and war heads are almost the same as India has. So there is a parity in nuclear weapons, which is a deterrent.

Indian armor is of Russian origin. Out of 2295 Indian Army's Main Battle tanks, 2235 are of Russian origin. The main battle tanks are; 310 T-90-S Bishsma's (300 are on order), 1925 T-72M Ajeya's.. The T-90 and the T-72 have 125 mm smooth barrel guns. T-72 though old is the backbone of Indian Armor

Corp's. 268 Ajeya's have been upgraded with Israeli Elbit thermal imaging systems. 1000 T-72 MBT's are awaiting up-gradation.

There have been several instances of T-72's gun barrel bursting. 124 Indian made Arjun (heavy 56 ton) MBT are on order. Sixty Arjun's are in operational service. Arjun's engine overheating problem has not been solved. Arjun has a 120 mm gun, but is unfit or desert operations. Pakistan Army is equally strong in armor, capable of giving a fitting response to any Indian military adventure.

Main Battle tanks Al-Khalid and Al-Zarrar are the backbone of Pakistan's armor Corp's. Both are Pakistan made. Pakistan's tank armory comprises :five hundred Al-Khalid MBT's; 320 Al-Zarrar type 85 II MBT's, 500 Al-Zarrar MBT's; 450 79II AP (Chinese type 81 upgrade, and 570 T-80 UD MBT of Ukranian make. In addition Pakistan has 880 Type 59, which were procured from China in 1970.This makes a total of three thousand six hundred and twenty tanks.

All Pakistani MBT's except T-59's have 125 mm smooth barrel guns. Indian armor offensives in Kashmir, Punjab, and Sind would be effectively challenged by Pakistani armor and mechanized formations, depending on PAF's ability to keep the skies over the battle areas clear of Indian Air Force. India's modern air defense system has Israeli Arrow anti-missile missiles, and 90,000 surface to air missiles-SAM's. India has one hundred nuclear armed ballistic missiles (Agni-1 and Agni II), and Brahmos the new supersonic cruise missile. Indian Army is well trained, equipped and highly professional, and so is Pakistan Army.

Air power is likely to play a key, if not a decisive role in any future major or minor India-Pakistan armed conflict. The aim of Indian pre-emptive strikes will be maximum destruction by surprise air attacks, combined with shock commando action.

A possibe scenario is; intensive bombing of the target to be followed by attacks by armed helicopters and ground assault by heliborne Commandoes. An overview of Indian Air Force and Pakistan Air Force will help comprehension of IAF's offensive capabilities, and defensive capabilities of Pakistan Air Force.

Indian Air Force has 3000 aircraft including training, transport, helicopters and 800-1000 combat air craft, which operate from sixty air bases, including Farkhor airbase in Tajikistan.. Six hundred IAF's strike and air defense fighters are expected to be operational. Pakistan Air Force has 630 aircraft, which include 530 combat aircraft, with 400 operational at any time. In 1996 India signed an agreement with Russia for the purchase of 90 Su 30 Mk-1 multi-role fighter-bombers. In 2004 a multi-billion licence was signed for building additional 140. 240 Su30-Mk-1's were ordered, 120 are already in service. With a maximum speed of Mach 2.3 and range of 8000 Km with refueling and ability to carry tons of conventional munitions and nuclear weapons, it is a lethal and menacing weapon system for the strike and interception role.

Other IAF's advanced strike and combat aircraft are: 51 Mirage-2000 (of Kargil fame), 60 Mig-29's (for air defense), 250 old Mig-21's (110 have been refurbished with Israeli help), 47 Jaguars and 70 Mig-27's for ground attack. 220 LCA Teja's under manufacture at HAL Bangalore will start entering service in 2010... IAF's fighter pilots are well trained and have out shone American pilots during joint exercises.

Pakistan Air Force has 200 rebuilt Mirage- 3's (for night air defense) and Mirage-5's for the strike role. They can carry nuclear weapons. They have been upgraded with new weapon systems, radars, and avionics. Additionally the PAF has 42 F-16's, 150 F-7's including 55 latest F-7 PG's. Manufacture of 150 JF 17 Thunder fighters (jointly designed) is underway at Pakistan

Aeronautical Complex Kamra. The JF -17 Thunder is a 4th generation fly by wire multi-role fighter aircraft. Eight are already in PAF service. An order has been placed with China for the purchase of 36 JF-10, a Mach 2.3 -5th generation multi-role fighter, comparable in performance to the Su-30 Mk-1 with the Indian Air Force. PAF is on Red Alert, and is maintaining full vigil to intercept and destroy IAF intruders.

During the recent air space violation, the IAF intruders were in the sights of PAF's F-16's, but were allowed to escape unscathed to avoid a major diplomatic crisis. PAF pilots and technicians are well trained, high professionals, who will be able to prove their mettle in the future battle with India. A comparison of Indian Navy and Pakistan Navy reveals that Pakistan Navy could inflict substantial damage to the Indian Navy. Indian Navy has 16 submarines; Pakistan Navy has ten, some are brand new. Indian Navy has 27 war ships, Pakistan Navy has ten. Indian Aircraft Carrier Veerat, will be a menace, and must be sunk by submarine or air attacks, if it attempts to block Pakistan's sea lanes or ports. It is hoped that better sense prevails and India desists from invading and attacking Pakistan. If it does, the consequences will be horrible for both the countries.

Manpower and Ground Forces

India has the second largest manpower in its military globally - at 3,773,300 personell (2005), next only to China. Pakistan has a much smaller manpower of 1,449,000 personell which is proportionally higher than India in terms of their population ratios. Pakistan's ground forces are equipped with American or Chinese weapons like FIM 92 Stinger SAMs, BGM-71 TOW anti-tank missiles, T-82 tanks and other equipments. Indian ground forces are equipped mostly by home-made or Soviet technologies like IR guided 9K35 Strela-

10 SAMs, 3rd Gen IR guided Nag anti-tank missiles, UAVs and a large inventory of tanks and support vehicles. In terms of numbers and equipments, both Indian and Pakistani ground forces are on an closely equal footing.

Comparison of Air Forces

As of 2006, Indian Air Force (IAF) has over 170,000 personnel and 3,382 aircrafts of which 1,330 are combat aircrafts operating off 61 airbases - making it the fourth largest air force in the world. India's strike fighters consist of Russian and French aircrafts like Mikoyan MiG-29, Dassault Mirage 2000, Sukhoi Su-30 - the last one developed under dual licensing by HAL, India's aerospace industry in Bangalore. In addition to these, India's air force owns ground attack aircrafts, reconnaissance aircrafts, UAVs and support helicopters - a majority of them either of Soviet or French origin. Pakistan Air Force (PAF) has about 530 combat aircrafts and over 65,000 active personnel, operating out of 9 airbases. Its strike fighters consist of US, Chinese and French fighters like F-16 Fighting Falcon, JF-17 Thunder and Dassault Mirage ROSE-III. It also has transport aircrafts like Lockheed Martin C-130 and Airbus A310, however there are no UAVs or reconnaissance aircrafts in the Pakistani Air Force.

Naval and Sea Based Forces

After the overwhelming losses in the 1971 war against India, Pakistan rapidly increased the size of its naval fleet which doubled in the 1980s after a massive 3.2 billion dollar military and economic aid by US President Ronald Reagan. At present, Pakistan's navy owns over 45 vessels , most of them of US or European origin which include submarines, destroyers, frigates, patrol and mine warfare boats. It operates from its sole naval port in Karachi and naval facilities in UK, USA and France.

It had recently been involved in various humanitarian operations during the 2005 Tsunami in South East Asia. Indian Navy on the other hand, is a three dimensional naval force consisting of missile-capable warships, an aircraft carrier, mine sweepers and a host of marine aircrafts; most of its warships indigenously built in its own dockyards. The navy operates from its major naval bases in Visakhapatnam, Mumbai, Goa and the Andaman Islands. Indian Navy has significant capabilities of being a true blue water Navy and is experienced both in war and peacekeeping operations in the Indian Ocean.

The Nuclear Club

India tested a nuclear bomb in 1974 using materials from Canada and technical help from Soviet Union. However the embargo in heavy water export from Canada after the test stalled India's nuclear ambitions till 1998, when it shocked the world by conducting five nuclear detonations termed as Shakti tests. The highest yield was by a 48 kiloton staged fusion device, which India claimed was a thermonuclear bomb but seismic data on the tests proved otherwise. In the same year 1998, Pakistan conducted a series of six nuclear detonations in a test termed as Chagai.

The highest yield was reported to be about 25 kiloton from a two stage boosted device. At present Pakistan's nuclear stockpile is slated to be around 30-40 warheads while India possesses 70-100 warheads. The nuclearisation of India and Pakistan became a turning point in the history of conflicts between these two countries with high tensions but no war, not very much unlike the US vs USSR Cold War.

Ballistic and Cruise Missile Proliferation

In the nuclear delivery front, both India and Pakistan have a series of ballistic and cruise missiles in addition to ground attack aircrafts. The maximum range among India's operational ballistic missiles is 2000 km achieved by Agni-2. India's Agni ballistic missiles are indigenously developed by its own missile defence industry known as IGMDP.

The maximum range among Pakistan's missiles is by Hatf V Gauri which is reported to do over 2200 kms. Pakistan's Hatf missiles are based on North Korean No-Dong series of IRBMs. Both Pakistan's Hatf and India's Agni ballistic missiles are nuclear capable. India has also developed a supersonic cruise missile BrahMos which is by far the fastest cruise missile at Mach 2.6 and maximum range of 290 km. It is reported to be nuclear capable but it is not confirmed yet. On the Pakistan side, its Babur cruise missile has a reported range of 700 km and a maximum speed of 880 km/h (Mach 0.7). As with India BrahMos, Babur is also reported to be nuclear capable but there is no confirmation yet.

The Final Verdict

Both Pakistan and India are almost evenly matched head to head in nuclear and missile fronts, however India has strategic and technological superiority over the conventional forces of Pakistan. Indian Navy is larger in fleet and personnel size with a more varied range of ships including an aircraft carrier while Pakistan's Navy is smaller and has no aircraft carriers.

Indian's IAF is equipped with highly capable fighters like 4.5th generation Su-30s and 4th gen Mirage 2000s which are technologically superior to Pakistan PAF's F-16s and Mirage IIIs. Additionally Indian pilots are better trained and more capable in air combat than Pakistani forces as was demonstrated by its various wars with Pakistan or joint exercises with US and UK.

In the area of conventional ground forces both the Indian as well as Pakistani Army is well equipped and highly trained to survive in extremities of topography and climate in combat conditions, like wars in the high Himalayas.

If a purely conventional war were to take place between both these countries, India would most likely overpower Pakistan owing to its superior military technology and infrastructure, larger manpower, more territorial area and a strategic advantage in its sea and air forces. It must also be noted that a war between these two countries will matter more than India's conventional superiority as both these nations are nuclear powers on an equal deadlock. India has maintained a 'no first use' nuclear policy on the lines of a similar policy by China while Pakistan does not have any such policy, considering their only hope against India is in nuclear deterrence. It would be risky for India at the present scenario to go into any aggressive war against Pakistan as the repercussions would be serious a nuclear devastation for both countries.

India's numerical and technical superiority in a conventional war is beyond question - therefore Pakistan's low nuclear threshold and maintenance of the first-use option. However, in a surgical kind of strike being talked about in Indian and Pakistani circles, over Muridke or Muzaffarabad, cruise missiles are likely to be used. The Pakistani and Indian capability is evenly matched in these except for India's supersonic cruise missile with a speed of Mach 2.6 which is an obvious advantage in this kind of a strike, but it only has a range of 290 kms - enough to reach Muridke if launched from East Punjab but not much more. Pakistan's answer is the Babur cruise missile with a range of 700 km and a speed of Mach 0.7 - sub-sonic but pretty fast.

UAV's was the other Indian advantage which has recently been matched by Pakistan. With the evenly matched air, missile and nuclear capability, a surgical strike doesn't seem to be the best option. If India is to win, it will have to be a full-scale conventional war with both sides avoiding breaching the other's nuclear threshold.

ARJUN

At the time, it was reported to have a 120mm smooth-bore main gun and would use a 1400-hp MTU-based diesel until an indigenous one was ready. Weight would be about 50 tons, and the tank would cost about $1.6 million (U.S.). Development costs rose about 500 percent throughout the '80s, and through a development process plagued with delays, the end product visually resembles the German Leopard II, however, unlike the German vehicle, its future remains in doubt. As of mid-2000 India planned to acquire T-90 tanks, based on field trials which had already been completed. Although orders had been placed for the supply of 124 Arjun tanks through the Defence Research Development Organisation, it would be difficult to predict when these orders would be fufilled. Until such time, T-90 tanks would serve to counter Pakistan's T-85 tanks.

Pakistan's announcment in 1995 of a deal with Ukraine to purchase T-84s caused a flurry of activity in the Indian tank development community. And on 9 January 1996, the Arjun was formally unveiled and cleared for mass production. Considered comparable to the M1A2 Abrams, Leopard 2, and Leclerc, the 59-ton "15th Variant" can achieve a maximum speed of 70 kph (55 mph) and cross-country speed of 40 kph with its 1400-hp powerplant. The 1,610-liter fuel tank allows for a cruising range of 200 km (120 miles). To ensure crew survivability, production versions will have the indigenously-researched and developed 'Kanchan' composite armor, an automatic fire detection and suppression system, and an NBC protection system designed and built by the Bhabha. Atomic Research Center.

The rifled 120mm gun, which includes a muzzle reference system, is made of ESR steel and is fitted with a thermal sleeve and fume extractor. All main gun rounds use a semicombustible cartridge case with increased energy propellant for higher muzzle velocity and greater penetration characteristics. In addition to the usual suite of rounds, an antihelicopter round is under development as well.

The Arjun's fire control system includes a laser rangefinder, ballistic computer, thermal imaging night sight, stabilized panoramic sight for the tank commander, and a secondary telescopic sight. The LRF (integral to the gunner's sight) has a range of nearly 10 km and a thermal imager (which can "see"' at around 5.5 km, recognize a target at 3.1 km and identify targets at 2.5 km). The Arjun fire control system's ability to fire on the move during the night is a major step forward for Indian armored forces.

The Chassis and Automative System of MBT Arjun comprises main chassis, power pack (1400 HP engine coupled to hydromech transmission), running gear with hydropneumatic suspension, integrated fuel system, advanced electrical system and other dedicated special systems like integrated fire detection and suppression system. The chassis is fabricated from rolled homogenous armour plate using advanced welding technique. Frontal armour is of Kanchan composite sandwitched between armour plates.

This fully integrated Arjun chassis and Automative System having smooth riding characteristics can be used as a mobile platform for any advanced weapon system. An extremely effective hydropneumatic suspension system has been developed for MBT Arjun. The suspension is externally mounted and provides vehicle springing and damping. It consists of one bogey wheel pair for each suspension station. Gaseous medium in the hydropneumatic suspension is for all terrain maneuverability for exploiting the power available. Casing and hub of the hydropneumatic suspension are sealed for preventing dust ingression and water seepage into the casing during operation in marshy area or shallow/medium fording. The MBT Arjun is fitted with double-pin steel track with detachable rubber pads. It is made out of steel casting having two bores for insertion of rubberised pins. It is an integral piece incorporating guide horns and has got a provision for insertion of detachable pads. The end connectors are induction-hardened in the area which comes in contact with the sprocket teeth to prevent wear.

The integrated fire and explosion suppression system developed for MBT Arjun is based on state-of-the-art technology. The indigenous development of this system is considered to be a breakthrough in the field of fire protection engineering. It is capable of suppressing hydrocarbon fuel fire/explosion resulting from an enemy hit on the tank or due to any malfunctioning of the engine, transmission or any electrical short circuiting. The system is based on infra-red detectors for the detection of fire/explosion in the crew compartment of the battle tank and a continuous type of linear thermal detector popularly known as fire-wire for the engine compartment.

Halon-1301 has been employed as a fire extinguishing medium. The system is capable of detection and suppression of hydrocarbon fuel fire/explosion in the crew compartment within 200 milliseconds and in the engine compartment within 15 s thereby enhancing the chances of survivability of the crew and battle effectiveness of the tank. Further improvements were deemed necessary even after the Arjun design profile was accepted again in July 1996.

On 27 August 1996, the Defense Production and Supplies Secretary ordered 15 pre-production tanks from the Heavy Vehicles Factory, Avadi (at which point, estimates placed the project cost at $112 million). As of mid-1997 the list of faults after 20 years of development was not encouraging. In addition to numerous technical modifications to its fire and gun control systems, the fire control system in particular has been found unable to perform in temperatures above 42 degrees Celsius (108° F).

The DRDO has been considering scrapping the current Arjun fire control system in favor of whatever is accepted for the T-72M1 upgrade program.

Defects noticed during the user trials of the Arjun Mk.1 MBT, including over-heating of the engine in Rajasthan desert areas, had supposedly been "by and large overcome" while other complaints were being addressed.

The first 120 tanks to be built would cost $4.2 million each, while other cost estimates places the figure at $5.6 million each per tank by 2001, given a purchase of 124 tanks to equip two regiments. Production of the first batch of tanks might take more than the planned five years, given the capacity at the Avadi factory. Planned Arjun variants include mobile assault guns, an observation post vehicle, an air defense (gun or missile) version, a recovery vehicle, an engineer vehicle, and bridgelayers. New bridgelayers and recovery vehicles were necessary, given the Arjun's substantial weight increase over the T-72M1 series.

Specifications

ARJUN Mk 1 (15th Preproduction Model)

Weight 59 tons (58.5 tonnes)

Length (gun forwards) 10.19m

Width (over tracks) 3.5m (w/ skirts) 3.85m

Height (w/o 12.7mm AAMG) 2.32m

Engine 1400 HP MTU 838 Ka 501Diesel

Transmission Semi-automatic with 4 forward and 2 reverse gears.(also reported as ZF automatic)

Fuel 1610 ltrs

Performance

Max Speed 72-70 kph (55 mph)

Cross Country Speed 40 kph

Cruising Range 200 km (120 miles)

Ground Pressure . 84 kg/cm Square

Ground Clearance .45m

Slide Slope: 60%

Climbing Gradient 35°

Trench 2.43 m (also given as 3m)

Vertical Obstacle .9m

Ford 1.4 m

Armament

Main Gun 120mm, stabalized w/ MRS (APFSDS, HE, HEAT, HESH and smoke)

12.7mm AA Gun (probably NVST)

7.62mm Coax (probably PK-T)

2 X 9 Smoke Grenade Launchers

LRF Range 10 km

Sights Thermal (Max Rng 5.5 km)

Active and Passive

Defensive Systems 'Arena' a possibilty, probable Laser Warning System

105 mm Indian and Light Field Guns

(IFG/LFG)

The 105 mm Indian and Light Field Guns (IFG/LFG) are high performance guns meeting the conflicting requirements of mountain, plain and desert warfare. The Indian Field Gun is the mainstay of the Field Artillery Branch of the Indian

Army covering a maximum range of 17 km. The LFG is a close in weapon, designed to provide the necessary range, mobility and fire power required in the present day battlefield scenario. A unique feature of LFG is its light weight which makes it capaple of being helilifted for quick deployment in mountain terrain. This has been achieved by using high strength alloy steel. The optimised design provides a compact, robust and small profile ideally suited for cross-country mobility.

The Government has recently announced that there would be no further need to import ammunition. This indeed is a great tribute to the constant efforts made by the armament group of laboratories. It is noteworthy that of the total production value from the Indian Ordnance Factories, 70 per cent is based on the design provided by the armament group of laboratories which amounts to more than Rs 5000 crore.

Effective illumination of an area for night operations in the battlefield enhances operational capability of the Army. DRDO has perfected the technology of illuminating ammunition and has developed a veriety of illuminating ammunition for the Indian Army. These include 51 mm/81 mm/120 mm Mortar launched ammunition and 105 mm Indian Gun launched ammunition. The reliability and performance of indigenously developed illuminating ammunition is superior to the international standard.

STRNGTH OF INDIAN MILITARY VS STRENGTH OF PAKISTAN MILITARY

Posted on December 27, 2008 by rajendra Parmanik

1.The Indian Army is the world's second largest army in terms of military personnel (after China).

Active Troops	1,300,000
Reserve Troops	1,200,000

Territorial Army	200,000
Main Battle Tanks	4500
Artillery	12,800
Ballistic missiles	100+
Cruise missiles	BrahMos
Aircraft	10 squadrons of helicopters
Surface-to-air missiles	90000+

The Pakistan Army, combined with the Navy and Air Force, makes Pakistan's armed forces the seventh largest military in the world.

Army	550,000
Navy	24,000
Air Force	45,000
Paramilitary Forces	302,000
Coast Guard	Classified
Total	921,000

• 2. Nuclear doctrine (INDIA)

The Indian military possesses nuclear weapons and sufficient means — by means of missiles and aircraft — to deliver anything over long distances. However, India has a nuclear no-first-use and no use against non-nuclear weapons state policy. It also maintains a non-nuclear doctrine based on credible minimum deterrence.

India is not a signatory to the Nuclear Non-proliferation Treaty (NPT), arguing that it unfairly favours the established nuclear powers:

While the treaty places restrictions on the non-nuclear weapons states, it does little to curb the modernization and expansion of the nuclear arsenals of the nuclear weapons states; it provides no provision for complete nuclear disarmament.

Nuclear Doctrine (PAKISTAN)

The Pakistan military possesses nuclear weapons and sufficient means, through a range of missiles and aircraft — to deliver these over considerably long distances.

However, unlike India, Pakistan does not have no-first-use policy and maintains the use of nuclear weapons as a deterrent to India to offset the large conventional advantage India enjoys over Pakistan.

Pakistan is not a part of the Nuclear Non-proliferation Treaty (NPT), citing concerns that it unfairly favours the established nuclear powers, and provides no provision for complete nuclear disarmament. The Strategic Nuclear Command forms part of Pakistan's National Command Authority which is responsible for the management of the country's tactical and strategic nuclear weapons.

3.EQUIPMENTS OF INDIAN ARMY

Handguns

- FN Browning GP35 9mmx19 mm
- SAF (Small Arms Factory) Pistol 1A 9mmx19 mm, This is more or less a copy of the Canadian Inglis 9 mm
- Glock 17 9mmx19 mm, The Glock 19 along with the 17 is in use with the Special Protection Group (Prime Minister's Security)

Sub-machine guns and carbines

- Heckler & Koch MP5A3 9mmx19 mm SMG
- Heckler & Koch MP5K 9mmx19 mm SMG
- SAF Carbine 1A 9mmx19 mm, Indian made Sterling L2A1 SMG

- SAF Carbine 2A1 9mmx19 mm, Silenced Carbine
- UZI 9mmx19 mm SMG
- MINSAS carbine of the INSAS family; 5.56mm. Is in user trails.
- Kalantak rifle PDW that is in user trails.

Assault rifles

- RFI (Rifle Factory,Ishapore) SLR1A 7.62mmx51 mm NATO Assault Rifle, A modified FN FAL, This old work horse has now more or less been retired from IA service, most going to the police and paramilitary forces after reconditioning. Some however, remain in use.
- RFI SLR1C 7.62mmx51 mm, full Automatic variant of the SLR for use in APCs
- AK-7, clone of the AK-47
- INSAS 5.56mmx45 mm Assault Rifle
- Kalantak Rifle Under Trials
- Zittara Indian version of the IMI Tavor TAR-21 Israeli Micro-Tavor
- TAVOR TAR-21 5.56mmx45 mm, for special forces currently 3070 have been purchased from Israel [1]
- IMI Galil
- AK-101
- AK-103
- KBK AKMS 7.62mmx39 mm, Polish AKS47-3
- AK47M1 7.62mmx39 mm, all black Bulgarian AK. Most of these have been imported for police and paramilitary forces
- Soviet AKM AKMS 7.62mmx39 mm
- East German MPi-KM MPi-KMS72 7.62mmx39 mm (Second hand)

- Czech Vz.58 and Vz.58P 7.62mmx39 mm
- Colt M16A2 rifle for special forces

Anti-Tank Guided Missiles

- Nag- Third Generation fire and forget IIR Guided ATGM developed Indigenously. Its undergoing user trials. 443 missiles ordered.
- Milan 2- License Produced
- 9M113 Konkurs (AT-5 Spandrel)
- 9M111 Fagot (AT-4 Spigot)
- 9M14 Malyutka (AT-3 Sagger)- Being Phased out
- 9M119 Svir (AT-11 Sniper)- for T-90S.
- Lahat- fired from Arjun Tanks 120mm Cannon.

Machine guns

- MG 1B 7.62mmx51 mm, Indian made Bren- This is currently being retired. But may remain a while longer because of teething problems with its successor, the INSAS LMG
- MG 2A1 7.62mmx51 mm, Indian made MAG 58
- MG 5A 7.62mmx51 mm This is the Indian manufactured Co-axial MAG 58
- MG 6A 7.62mmx51 mm Another Indian version of the MAG58 specifically designed as a tank commanders gun.
- INSAS 5.56mmx45 mm LMG
- FN-Browning M1919 .30Cal, in very limited quantities
- Browning M2 machine gun .50cal, heavy machine gun in very limited numbers
- M607.62mm LMG

3.INDIAN AIRCRAFTS

COMBAT AIRCRAFTS

	Number
Su-30MKI Flanker-H	100
Mirage 2000H	39
MiG-29SMT	56
Jaguar IS	104(IS)
Jaguar IM	6
MiG-27	ML 120
MiG-21 Bison	109
MiG-21*bis*	48
MiG-21M/MF	72
PAK AIRCRAFTS	
Chengdu JF-17 Thunder	10
General Dynamics F-16A Block-15 Fighting Falcon	28
General Dynamics F-16B Block-15 Fighting Falcon	16
Chengdu F-7PG Skybolt	46
Chengdu F-7MP Skybolt	90
Chengdu FT-7P Skybolt	15
Dassault Mirage ROSE-II (Mirage-VDF)	6
Dassault Mirage ROSE-II (Mirage-VDF)	14
Nanchang Q-5/A-5C Fantan	40

Both India And Pakistan Has many transport vehicles for the movement of man and machines. Both side has many Light Combat aircrafts but in this Sense India is much powerfull than Pakistan.

The Indian Air Force is the fourth largest air force in the world. In its history, it has generally relied on Soviet, British, Israeli and French technology to support its growth. However, in recent times, India has begun building its own original aircraft, including the HAL Tejas, which is a 4.5th generation fighter. Also, India and Russia are currently building a 5th generation stealth aircraft jointly. India has also developed an UAV called Nishant and an advanced light helicopter called the HAL Dhruv.

Recently, it completed a test of a long range BVR air to air missile named Astra and also conducted a successful test of its anti-ballistic missile defense system and hence became the 4th country after the US, Russia, and Israel to do so.

WEAPONS OF MASS DESTRUCTION INDIA

Ballistic Missiles

a. Prithvi I - Army Version (150 km range with a payload of 1,000kg)

   Prithvi II - Air Force Version (250 km range with a payload of 500kg)

   Prithvi III - Naval Version (350 km range with a payload of 500kg)

b. Dhanush is a System consisting of stabilization platform and missiles and can fire either the 250Km or the 350Km range missiles.

   Then the following year in December the missile's 350Km version was tested from the INS Rajput and hit the land based target

c. The Agni Missile system comprises of Agni I, Agni II and the Agni III 1500 Agni I uses the SLV-3 booster (from India's Space Program) for its first stage and a liquid-fueled Prithvi for its second stage.

d. On the other hand India's Agni II missiles have a range of the 1500 to 2500 kilometers. Unlike the Agni I, the Agni II has a solid-fueled second stage. India has also tested the Agni III IRBM with a range between 3000 and 5500km kilometres which has two stages. With a normal payload of 1000kg it can travel 5000km

e. The Surya-1 and -2 will be classified as strategic weapons, extending the Indian nuclear deterrent force to targets around the world. India currently is limited by the range of the Agni-3 missile.

 The Surya-1 will have an expected range of 6000 - 10,000 km. It reportedly has a length of 40 m and a launch weight of 80,000 kg (some reports indicate as much as 275,000 kg. As the missile has yet to be developed, the payload and warhead are as yet unknown. It is believed to be a three-stage design, with the first two stages using solid propellants and the third-stage using liquid. The first test flight is expected in 2009, but there may be delays. The Surya- is a longer-ranged variant of the Surya-1. It has a reported range of over 20,000 km.

f. The Shaurya missile is a short-range surface-to-surface ballistic missile developed by DRDO of India for use by the Indian Army.It has a range of 600 km and is capable of carrying a payload of one-tonne conventional or nuclear warhead.The Shaurya missile provides India with a significant second strike capability.

g. Sagarika is a nuclear capable submarine-launched ballistic missile with a range of 750 km. This missile has a length of 8.5 meters, weighs seven tonnes and can carry a pay load of up to 500 kg

INDIAN ARMY

* 4 RAPID (Reorganised Army Plains Infantry Divisions)
* 18 Infantry Divisions
* 10 Mountain Divisions
* 3 Armoured Divisions

* 2 Artillery Divisions
* 6 Air Defence Brigades + 2 Surface-to-Air Missile Groups
* 5 Independent Armoured Brigades
* 15 Independent Artillery Brigades
* 7 Independent Infantry Brigades
* 1 Parachute Brigade
* 4 Engineer Brigades
* 14 Army Aviation Helicopter Units

Sub-Units

* 63 Tank Regiments
* 7 Airborne Battalions
* 200 Artillery Regiments
* 360 Infantry Battalions + 5 Para (SF) Battalions
* 40 Mechanised Infantry Battalions
* 20 Combat Helicopter Units
* 35+ Air Defence Regiments

Till now india and pakistan have fought four main wars and India Has defeated pakistan EveryTime.

CRUISE MISSILES INDIA

a. Nirbhay is a long range, subsonic cruise missile being developed in India. The missile will have a range of 1000 km and will arm three services, the Indian Army, Indian Navy and the Indian Air Force.

b. India has acquired around 200 3M-54 Klub for arming Talwar class frigate, Shivalik class frigate, Kolkata class destroyer and Sindhughosh class submarine The Russian 3M-54 Klub is a multi-role missile system developed by the Novator Design Bureau(OKB-8) with a range of

250Km-300Km and a average speed of .8 Mach with a maximum of 2.9 Mach

c. Popeye II, an air launched cruise missile capable of carrying nuclear warheads with a range of 80 Km can be launched from planes was given to India along with missile defence radars in a deal.

   The exact number transferred to India is unknown, but possibly 20 missile to perhaps 50 missiles could have been given with possibly more being built in India.

d. India has Soviet P-70 Ametist submarine-launched cruise missiles.

   The missiles can carry nuclear warheads and have a range of 50-65Km.

e. The P-270 Moskit is a Russian supersonic ramjet powered cruise missile capable of being launched from land and ships. India has most probably bought both land and ship variants which have a range of 120km.

f. Akash is India's medium range surface-to-air missile defense system The missile can target aircraft up to 30 km away, at altitudes up to 18,000 m.Akash is said to be capable of both conventional and nuclear warheads, with a reported payload of 60kg. Akash can be fired from both tracked and wheeled platforms.

NUCLEAR SUBMARINES

According to some accounts India plans to have as many as 20 nuclear submarines capable of carrying missiles with nuclear warheads.

The Advanced Technology Vessel (ATV) is a Nuclear Powered Ballistic Missile Submarine being constructed for the Indian Navy at Visakhapatnam, India The ATV is an SSBN and will be armed with the ballistic missiles.

Once it is completed, it can be equipped with 6-8 nuclear capable Dhánush,Sagarika or Agni SLBM ballistic missiles and upto 12 BrahMos cruise missiles. It is also to be fitted with an advanced sonar system. The second and third submarines of the class may incorporate the Nirbhay as well. As of July 2007, the Sagarika missile as well as Dhanush had undergone three successful tests each.

The ATV is to be unveiled on January 26, 2009 but trials will start later that year while induction is planned for 2010.

The INS Sindhuraj, INS Sindhuvir, INS Sindhuratna, INS Sindhushastra, INS Sindhukesari and INS Sindhuvijay are capable of launching 3M-54 Klub and BrahMos nuclear-capable cruise missiles.

India bought 10 Kilo class (in India known as Sindhughosh Class) submarine of which 6 have been refitted by the Russian Navy so that the they can launch cruise missiles such as nuclear capable BrahMos and 3M-54 Klub's 3M-14E variant.

The Submarine version of the BrahMos has been tested from static, underwater test stands in Russia and from the INS Sindhuvijay. As the Sinduvijay is similar to the other refitted submarines the test is considered a success.

STRENGTHS OF THE ARMY

India achieved its independence from imperial Britain in 1947, after which it was divided into two countries - India and Pakistan, as per the *Mountbatten Plan*. After this partition, Pakistan chose to be an Islamic republic, aligned with United States while India chose to remain politically neutral, as a secular socialist democracy. These choices turned out to the turning points in the political and military future of both these countries.

Please note that what follows is not an evaluation of military power in combat situations, but a brief review of quantitative military balance, based on currently available manpower, equipments, infrastructure, command and strategy. Future military plans and projects are not discussed due to uncertain and volatile nature of such plans, often subject to cancellation, failure or modification.

MILITARY BUDGETS AND ECONOMIC IMPACT

Pakistan's defence budget for the year 2006-07 was $4.1 billion (~3% of GDP) in response to India's hike in defence budget of 2006-07 at $20.11 billion (~ 2.5% of GDP). Pakistan's hike in military budget would be partially funded by its government coffers and partially by borrowing whereas India's military spending would be entirely off its own funds. India's ambitious budget prompted Pakistan to up its own military budget, despite the country's widespread poverty and socio-political problems. Apart from its GDP, Pakistani military also gets a considerable funding from United States. Considering that India has a far larger economy overall, its military budget is also several times larger, despite being a smaller share of India's GDP.

MANPOWER AND GROUND FORCES

As of 2005, India has the second largest military manpower in the world - at 3,773,300 personell, next only to China. Pakistan's manpower of 1,449,000 personell, although smaller in numbers, is proportionally higher than India in terms of their population ratios. Pakistan's ground forces are equipped with American or Chinese weapons like *FIM 92 Stinger* SAMs, *BGM-71 TOW* anti-tank missiles, *T-82* tanks and other equipments. Indian ground forces are equipped with mostly home-made and Soviet technologies like IR guided *9K35 Strela-10* SAMs, 3rd Gen IR guided *Nag* anti-tank missiles, UAVs and a large inventory of tanks and support vehicles. In terms of both numbers and equipments, Indian military dominates the Pakistani ground forces.

COMPARISON OF AIR FORCES

As of 2006, Indian Air Force (IAF) has over 170,000 personnel and 3,382 aircrafts, of which 1,330 are combat aircrafts operating off 61 airbases - making it the fourth largest air force in the world. India's strike fighters consist of Russian and French aircrafts like *Mikoyan MiG-29*, *Dassault Mirage 2000*, *Sukhoi Su-30* - the last one developed under dual licensing by HAL, India's aerospace industry in Bangalore.

In addition to these, Indian Air Force also owns ground attack aircrafts, reconnaissance aircrafts, UAVs and support helicopters - a majority of them either of Soviet or French origin.

Pakistan Air Force (PAF) has about 530 combat aircrafts and 65,000 active personnel, operating out of 9 airbases. Its strike fighters consist of US, Chinese and ageing French fighters like *F-16 Fighting Falcon*, *JF-17 Thunder* and *Dassault Mirage ROSE-III*. It also has transport aircrafts like *Lockheed Martin C-130* and *Airbus A310*, however unlike India, there are no UAVs or reconnaissance aircrafts in the Pakistani Air Force.

NAVAL AND SEA BASED FORCES

After the overwhelming losses in the 1971 war against India, Pakistan rapidly increased the size of its naval fleet which doubled in the 1980s after a massive 3.2 billion dollar military and economic aid by US President *Ronald Reagan*. At present, Pakistan's navy owns over 45 vessels , most of them of US or European origin which include submarines, destroyers, frigates, patrol and mine warfare boats. It operates from its sole naval port in Karachi and sometimes from naval facilities in UK, USA and France.

It had recently been involved in various humanitarian operations during the 2005 Tsunami in South East Asia. Indian Navy on the other hand, is a three dimensional naval force consisting of missile-capable warships, an aircraft carrier, mine sweepers and a host of marine aircrafts.

Most of the warships in the Indian navy are indigenously built in its own dockyards. The navy operates from its major naval bases in Visakhapatnam, Mumbai, Goa and the Andaman Islands. Indian Navy has significant capabilities of being a true blue water Navy and is experienced both in war and peacekeeping operations in the Indian Ocean.

4

HISTORY OF CHEMICAL WARS

INTRODUCTION

In October 1992, the Committee on Banking, Housing, and Urban Affairs, which has Senate oversight responsibility for the Export Administration Act (EAA), held an inquiry into the U.S. export policy to Iraq prior to the Persian Gulf War. During that hearing it was learned that U.N. inspectors identified many U.S.-manufactured items exported pursuant to licenses issued by the U.S. Department of Commerce that were used to further Iraq's chemical and nuclear weapons development and missile delivery system development programs.

On June 30, 1993, several veterans testified at a hearing of the Senate Committee on Armed Services. There, they related details of unexplained events that took place during the Persian Gulf War which they believed to be chemical warfare agent attacks. After these unexplained events, many of the veterans present reported symptoms consistent with exposure to a mixed agent attack. Then, on July 29, 1993, the Czech Minister of Defense announced that a Czechoslovak chemical decontamination unit had detected the chemical warfare agent Sarin in areas of northern Saudi Arabia during the early phases of the Gulf War. They had attributed the detections to fallout from coalition bombing of Iraqi chemical warfare agent production facilities.

In August 1993, Senate Banking Committee Chairman Donald W. Riegle Jr. began to research the possibility that there may be a connection between the Iraqi chemical, biological, and radiological warfare research and development programs and a mysterious illness which was then being reported by thousands of returning Gulf War veterans. In September 1993, Senator Riegle released a staff report on this issue and introduced an amendment to the Fiscal Year 1994 National Defense Authorization Act that provided preliminary funding for research of the illnesses and investigation of reported exposures.

When this first staff report was released by Senator Riegle, the estimates of the number of veterans suffering from these unexplained illnesses varied from hundreds, according to the Department of Defense, to thousands, according to the Department of Veterans Affairs. It is now believed that tens of thousands of U.S. veterans are suffering from a myriad of symptoms collectively labelled either Gulf War Syndrome, Persian Gulf Syndrome, or Desert War Syndrome. Hundreds and possibly thousands of servicemen and women still on active duty are reluctant to come forward for fear of losing their jobs and medical care. These Gulf War veterans are reporting muscle and joint pain, memory loss, intestinal and heart problems, fatigue, nasal congestion, urinary urgency, diarrhea, twitching, rashes, sores, and a number of other symptoms.

They began experiencing these multiple symptoms during and after — often many months after — their tour of duty in the Gulf. A number of the veterans who initially exhibited these symptoms have died since returning from the Gulf. Perhaps most disturbingly, members of veteran's families are now suffering these symptoms to a debilitating degree. The scope and urgency of this crisis demands an appropriate response.

This investigation into Gulf War Syndrome, which was initiated by the Banking Committee under the direction of Chairman Riegle, has uncovered a large body of evidence linking the symptoms of the syndrome to the exposure of Gulf War participants to chemical and biological warfare agents, chemical and biological warfare pre-treatment drugs, and other hazardous materials and substances. Since the release of the first staff report on September 9, 1993, this inquiry has continued. Thousands of government officials, scientists, and veterans have been interviewed or consulted, and additional evidence has been compiled. This report will detail the findings of this ongoing investigation. Since the Banking Committee began its inquiry, the position of the Department of Defense regarding the possible causes of Gulf War Syndrome has altered only when challenged with evidence that is difficult to dispute. Yet, despite the vast resources of the Department of Defense, several independent and congressional inquiries with limited resources continue to uncover additional evidence of hazardous exposures and suspicious events.

The Department of Defense, when first approached regarding this issue by Committee staff, contended that there was no evidence that U.S. forces were exposed to chemical warfare agents. However, during a telephone interview on September 7, 1993 with Walter Reed Army Medical Center commander Major General Ronald Blanck, Committee staff was informed that the issue of chemical and biological warfare agent exposure had not been explored because it was the position of "military intelligence" that such exposure never occurred.

Then, during a November 10, 1993 press briefing at the Pentagon, the Department of Defense acknowledged that the Czech government did detect chemical agents in the Southwest

Asia theater of operations. After analyzing the results of the Czech report, the Department of Defense concluded that the detections were unrelated to the "mysterious health problems that have victimized some of our veterans." According to former Secretary of Defense Les Aspin, in some cases the wind was wrong and the distances too great to suggest a link. For instance, Seabees serving to the south and east of the detection site have complained of persistent health problems; but according to the Pentagon, the wind was blowing in the other direction at the time of the detections and the concentrations were too low to do harm over that kind of a distance.

The fact is, no one has ever suggested that there was a link between the Czech detections and what occurred during the early morning hours of January 19, 1991 near the Port of Jubayl. (These two events will be described in detail in Chapter 2.) Former Defense Secretary Aspin said at the briefing that this incident could not have been from the Coalition bombings of the Iraqi chemical weapons facilities because the winds were blowing to the northwest. Yet according to available Soviet documents, the dispersal of chemical agents and other hazardous substances is controlled by other factors in addition to surface wind direction and velocity, such as topography, temperature, precipitation, vertical temperature gradient, and atmospheric humidity. These factors all contribute to the size and type of dispersal that will be observed. Unclassified visual and thermal satellite imagery confirms that the fallout from the bombings of Iraqi targets during the air and ground war moved to the southeast, with the weather patterns and upper atmospheric wind currents, towards Coalition force positions.

According to a knowledgeable source who has requested confidentiality, the Czechs believed that the detections were caused by the weather inversion which occurred that day (January 19, 1991) as the weather front moved southward. The Czechoslovak chemical detection unit reported this information to U.S. command officials immediately, but the responding units were unable to confirm their findings when they arrived, according to the Pentagon. Nonetheless, at the November 10, 1993 briefing, the Department of Defense admitted that the Czech detections were believed to be valid. The Department of Defense failed to disclose that the Czechoslovak chemical detection team also detected yperite (HD) that morning. The presence of both of these agents in such close proximity could only reasonably be the result of one of two possibilities: (1) direct Iraqi mixed agent attack, or (2) fallout from the Coalition bombings of Iraqi weapons facilities and storage bunkers.

Defense Department officials, having had possession of the Czech report for over a month, were at a loss to explain the chemical mustard agent detected by the Czechoslovak chemical detection team in the Saudi desert near King Khalid Military City on January 24, 1991. This despite the fact that both the Czechs and French claim that this detection was reported to U.S. command authorities during the Persian Gulf War. Additionally, during the Gulf War, the Czechs claimed that they detected Chemical nerve agent after a Scud missile attack. These statements, heretofore only reported in the press, have been confirmed by a member of the U.S. 1st Cavalry Division and by an entire platoon of a U.S. Army chemical detection unit who trained with the Czechoslovak Chemical detection unit near King Khalid Military City. These reports have not been addressed publicly by the Department of Defense and will be addressed in this report in Chapter 3.

The contents of this report supports the conclusion that U.S. forces were exposed to some level of chemical and possibly biological warfare agents during their service in the Gulf War. Any review conducted by the Pentagon must extend far beyond the information being reported by the Czech Ministry of Defense. The Czech information, while important, represents just a small fraction of the evidence currently available, only some of which will be detailed in this report.

It is now the position of the Department of Defense that it has no other evidence that U.S. forces were exposed to chemical agents. Yet this report contains descriptions and direct eyewitness accounts that provide evidence which suggest that gas was detected, along with many other events which may have been actual attacks on U.S. forces.

This report supports the conclusion that U.S. forces were exposed to chemical agents. The assertion that the levels of nerve agents detected by the Czechs and others were not harmful is flawed. In subsequent requirements for chemical detection equipment, the Department of the Army acknowledges that the principal chemical agent detection alarm deployed during the war, the M8A1 was not sufficiently sensitive to detect sustained low levels of chemical agent and to monitor personnel for contamination. Further, U.S. Army Material Safety Data Sheets (MSDS) indicate that chronic exposures to levels of over.0001 mg/m3 for Sarin (GB) is hazardous and requires the use of protective equipment. (See appendix A.) The minimum level of chemical agent required to activate chemical agent detection alarm M8A1, commonly in use during the war, exceeds this threshold by a factor of 1,000. (See appendix A.) As the chemical agent alarms began to sound during the "air war," French, Czech, and many U.S. commanders confirmed that they were sounding from the fallout from the bombings. Over time, even at these levels, after repeatedly being told that there was no danger, many U.S. forces failed to take precautionary measures. Other report that the alarms were sounding so frequently that they were turned off. M8A1 alarms do not detect blister agents. The findings of this report prepared at the request of Chairman Riegle detail many other events reported by U.S. servicemen and women that in some cases confirm the detection of chemical agents by U.S. forces. In other cases these reports indicate the need for further detailed investigation. But still the question remains: Is exposure to these and other chemical agents the cause of Gulf War Syndrome? We have received hundreds of reports that many of these symptoms are being experienced by family members. Numerous developments have taken place over the last several months which suggest that, while chemical agents and other environmental hazards may have contributed to the Gulf War illnesses, bacteriological, fungal, and possibly other biological illnesses may be the fundamental cause. This position is supported by the following.

First, Dr. Edward S. Hyman, a New Orleans bacteriologist, has treated a small number of the sick veterans and several of their wives for bacteriological infections, and has developed a protocol of treatment that has resulted in symptom abatement in many of his patients.

Second, during the November 10, 1993 unclassified briefing for Members of the U.S. Senate, in response to direct questioning, then Undersecretary of Defense John Deutch said that the Department of Defense was withholding classified information on the exposure of U.S. forces to biological materials. In a Department of Defense-sponsored conference on counter-proliferation, held at Los Alamos National Laboratory on 6-7 May, 1994, Dr. Deutch admitted that biological agent detection is a priority development area for the Department of Defense, since there currently is no biological agent detection system fielded with any U.S. forces anywhere in the world.

Third, the Department of Defense has named Dr. Joshua Lederberg to head its research team into the causes of Gulf War illnesses. Dr. Lederberg, among his other credits, is a Nobel Laureate and an expert in the fields of bacteriology, genetics, and biological warfare defenses.

Fourth, in detailed informational interviews conducted of 400 Gulf War veterans, it has been learned that over 3/4 of their spouses complain that they have begun to suffer from many of the same debilitating symptoms. (See Chapter 4.)

This report, like the one which preceded it, will discuss the relationship between the high rate of Gulf War illnesses among Group I individuals (those possibly exposed to a direct mixed agent event), and the lower rates among those in Group II (individuals exposed to the indirect fallout from coalition bombings of Iraqi chemical, biological, and nuclear targets) and Group III (individuals who suffered severe adverse reactions to the nerve agent pre-treatment pills). Despite the varying rates of illness between the groups, however, the symptoms are similar. While other possible causes of the Gulf War Syndrome such as petrochemical poisoning, depleted uranium exposures, and regionally prevalent diseases, have been discussed elsewhere and must be pursued, there is a great deal of compelling evidence which indicates that all of these possibilities must now be seriously considered. We believe, however, that no other explanations prove as compelling as the ones which will be presented in this report.

This report includes a great number of first-hand accounts and other documentary evidence in addition to the anecdotal information that appeared in the print and electronic media during the Gulf War. It establishes convincingly that the

Department of Defense assertions are inaccurate. We believe there is reliable evidence that U.S. forces were exposed to chemical and possibly biological agents. But regardless of whether U.S. forces were exposed or not, the entire official body of information, including all classified or heretofore unpublished information, available research data sets, case histories, and diagnostic breakdown information must be made available to independent civilian medical researchers in order to further the research into the causes of and treatments for these illnesses. Absent a release of information by the Department of Defense of the science which forms the bases for their theories, the Department of Defense position must be viewed by qualified scientists as anecdotal and unsubstantiated.

Given that there is also a growing body of evidence indicating that spouses and children of Gulf War veterans are vulnerable to similar illnesses, the Department of Defense must now share all of its information with civilian, non-governmental researchers. These family members are civilians who may be at risk. This illness was first reported over three years ago.

On February 9, 1994, Chairman Riegle sent a letter to Secretary of Defense William Perry asking that he release all U.S. military personnel from any oath of secrecy they may have taken regarding classified information specifically pertaining to chemical or biological warfare agent exposure in the Persian Gulf theater. This request was based on a recommendation of the National Academy of Sciences, National Institute of Medicine in their 1993 publication Veterans at Risk: The Health Effects of Mustard Gas and Lewisite. On May 4, 1994, the Secretaries of Defense, Health and Human Services, and Veterans Affairs responded to the Chairman's letter stating that there was no classified information on chemical or biological detections or exposures. This directly contradicts the statement of Deputy Secretary Deutch in his November 10, 1993 unclassified briefing to Members and staff.

Why isn't the Department of Defense aggressively pursuing the answers to the questions surrounding of the events which may have caused illnesses being suffered by many Gulf War veterans? One possible explanation lies in a 1982 article. Then Senate Armed Services Committee Chairman John Tower wrote, "Chemical training in the United States armed forces is, at best, perfunctory. It is rarely conducted in a simulated contaminated environment and stocks of individual protective equipment are too limited, and therefore too valuable, to risk them in the numbers necessary to allow troops to operate in them for realistic training. As a result, most U.S. personnel are relegated to a minimal and highly artificial exposure to the problems and hardships entailed in performing their respective combat missions should they have to 'button up'." As numerous U.S. General Accounting Office (GAO) reports have noted, the U.S. was not much better prepared prior to the Gulf War than it was when Senator Tower wrote in his article.

IRAQI CHEMICAL AND BIOLOGICAL WARFARE CAPABILITY

Over the last ten years, Iraq, a signatory to both the Geneva Protocols of 1925 (prohibiting the use of poisoned gas) and the Biological Warfare Convention of 1972 (banning biological weapons), has expended an enormous amount of research and energy in developing these and other prohibited weapons.

Iraq was believed to have been manufacturing mustard gas at a production facility in Samarra since the early 1980s. It also began an extensive program to produce nerve agent precursor chemicals, taking advantage of its own natural resources. Phosphate mines/industries are at Akashat, Al Qaim, and Rutbah.

The Iraqi Al Fallujah gas warfare complex was believed to be capable of producing up to 1,000 tons per month of Sarin, as well as the nerve agent VX. In addition, with the assistance of foreign firms, Iraq developed the capability to experiment with hydrogen cyanide, cyanogen chloride, and lewisite.

By the start of the Gulf War, Iraqi forces had developed chemical delivery capabilities for rifle grenades, 81mm mortars, 152mm, 130mm, and 122mm artillery rounds; bombs; 90mm air-to-ground rockets; 216 kilogram FROG and 555 kilogram SCUD warheads; and possibly land mines and cruise missiles.

On July 30, 1991, Ambassador Rolf Ekeus, director of the United Nations Special Commission on Iraq (UNSCOM), charged with overseeing the elimination of Iraq's chemical and nuclear arsenals, told the Security Council that the U.N. inspectors had found chemical warheads armed with nerve gas. Mr. Ekeus claimed that some warheads found were already fitted onto the SCUD missiles.

Iraq's chemical warfare capability was known to the U.S. government before the war. A month before the war began, then Central Intelligence Agency (CIA) director William Webster estimated that Iraq possessed 1,000 tons of poisonous chemical agents, much of it capable of being loaded into two types of missiles: the FROG (Free Rocket Over Ground) and the SCUD B(SS-1). Jane's Strategic Weapons Systems lists warhead capabilities for the FROG-7 as high explosive (HE), chemical, or nuclear, and for the Iraqi versions of the SCUD as probably HE or chemical.

Status of Iraqi Readiness to Use Chemical Weapons Against Coalition Forces

In March 1991, Molly Moore reported from Jubayl, Saudi Arabia that Marine Commanders found no indications of chemical weapons stockpiles on the battlefields of Kuwait. According to a Washington Post report that day, (March 7, 1991), U.S. intelligence analysts claimed that these weapons "never got distributed down to the battlefield" from storage sites north of the Euphrates River. A U.S. military intelligence source stated in March 1991 that "it was a matter of not deploying chemical weapons, rather than not having them,....my guess.... is they never managed to get it down to division level."

Regarding the presence of chemical weapons and Iraqi readiness to use them against Coalition forces, Committee staff has received the following information:

Dale Glover, of the 1165th Military Police Company, was with the 7th Corps, approximately 75 miles inside Iraq, when they came upon a destroyed artillery site. They entered a bunker that was half uncovered by the bombing. Inside there was a very strong ammonia smell. They discovered leaking chemical munitions inserts packed inside aluminum casings. A test confirmed a blister agent.

They went back to their unit and reported what they had found. Mr. Glover recalled that "they didn't get back to us for 2-3 hours, then told us it was a false positive, nothing to be concerned about." However, he said, within hours they were ordered to move from the location where they were camped, about three miles from the bunker. Mr. Glover recalled that they had been at that position only a couple of weeks and had not expected to move that soon. When questioned if the site they discovered was south of the Euphrates, he confirmed that it was.

Another source who identified himself to the Committee but wishes to remain anonymous has informed Committee staff that he also was with the 7th Corps in southern Iraq. Somewhere between As Salman and Bashra (in a position south of the Euphrates River), his unit came upon bunkers containing crates of substances that "made you choke, made you want to throw up, burned your eyes. It smelled like ammonia, only a lot stronger." He could not approach the crates without experiencing immediate breathing problems. He said these crates were leaking.

Chris Alan Kornkven was a Staff Sergeant with the 340th Combat Support Company during the Persian Gulf War. He reported to Committee staff that a U.S. military doctor at the 312th Evacuation Hospital told him that doctors at the hospital had been speaking with Iraqi officers. According to these doctors, the Iraqi officers said that they had chemical weapons at the front, and had authorization to use them, but that the winds in their area were blowing the wrong way.

Several press sources carried reports of encounters with chemical mines by the 2nd Marine Division during the initial mine field breaching operation early on February 24, 1991. According to the Chicago Tribune, which interviewed officers and enlisted Marines involved in the operation, a FOX vehicle confirmed positive readings for a nerve agent and for a mustard gas. A second detecting device gave the same positive reading. General Keys, the 2nd Division commander, and Colonel Livingston, commander of the 6th Marine Regiment, told reporters they believed it was possible that a chemical mine was blown up or hit. General Schwarzkopf told reporters he considered the reports "bogus." British troops also discovered Iraqi chemical mines on the Gulf battlefield, according to Gannett News Service. A British official (not further identified) said the incident was reported to Prime Minister John Major's war cabinet; no details were given.

Press reports indicate Iraqi readiness to use these weapons against Coalition forces. The British Sunday Times reported on January 27, 1991, that American intelligence detected greatly increased activity at Iraq's main chemical plant at Samarra in the last week of December, and the British Ministry of Defense said that the Allies believe that Iraq "may have as many as 100,000 artillery shells filled with chemicals and several tons (of bulk agent) stored near the front line." According to the Times report, a British Ministry of Defense official said: "The plant was at peak activity and the chemicals were distributed to the troops in Kuwait and elsewhere in theatre." The Times reported that an unnamed Pentagon source said that Hussein had given front-line commanders permission to use these weapons at their discretion, and that "it was no longer a question of if, but when."

Iraqi soldiers captured by the British units also informed the allies that before the war started, Iraq distributed substantial supplies of chemical weapons along the front lines to be held for the ground war. According to Newsweek, U.S. intelligence sources had reported that Saddam Hussein had ordered his commanders to fire chemical weapons as soon as the allies launched a ground offensive. A British signals officer was reported to have said that "we were tuned into the Iraqi command radio net. We heard them give the release order to their front-line troops to use chemical weapons against Rhino Force if it crossed the border."

DESTRUCTION OF IRAQ'S CHEMICALS AND CHEMICAL WEAPONS BY THE UNITED NATIONS

In April 1993, weapons inspectors from the United Nations charged with locating all of Iraq's nuclear, chemical and biological weapons by U.N. Resolution 687, confirmed that in Muthanna, 65 miles northwest of Baghdad, Iraq manufactured a form of mustard gas as well as Sarin and Tabun, both nerve agents. This vast desert complex was the nucleus of Iraq's chemical weapons program. During the allied bombing in the early days of the Gulf War, Muthanna was a priority target. It was repeatedly attacked and production sites were destroyed.

As United Nations inspectors attempted to destroy Iraq's chemical weapons arsenal, they discovered bombs, missiles, and chemical weapons of mass destruction spread out across this immense complex. Of particular concern were the chemical warheads of Al-Hussein modified SCUD missiles, each filled with five gallons of Sarin. Twenty-eight of these warheads have been drained and destroyed by the U.S. inspectors.

These weapons were not destroyed during the bombings at Muthanna because they had been removed to other locations before the Gulf War started. Their relocation and transfer back to Muthanna was described by U.N. inspectors as a painstaking process.

According to Brigadier General Walter Busbee, U.S. Army Chemical and Material Destruction Agency, Aberdeen Proving Grounds, these warheads were exported to Iraq from the former Soviet Union. Chemical warfare agents which either survived the allied bombing or were inventoried and returned to the Muthanna facility for destruction include:

- 13,000 155-mm artillery shells loaded with mustard gas;
- 6,200 rockets loaded with nerve agent;
- 800 nerve agent aerial bombs;
- 28 SCUD warheads loaded with Sarin;
- 75 tons of the nerve agent Sarin;
- 60-70 tons of the nerve agent tabun; and,

- 250 tons of mustard gas and stocks of thiodiglycol, a precursor chemical for mustard gas.

U.N. inspectors have concluded that the Muthanna plant was capable of producing two tons of Sarin and five tons of mustard gas daily. The plant was also capable of manufacturing VX, a nerve gas and one of the most toxic chemicals ever produced. In addition to Muthanna, chemical agents were destroyed at two airbases: one located 40 miles west of Baghdad and the other located near An Nassiriyah, where a number of 122mm rockets loaded with Sarin (GB) were blown in place. According to UNSCOM sources, many of these weapons were hastily deployed prior to the air war and later returned for destruction. The U.N. has destroyed hundreds of tons of bulk chemical agents and tens of thousands of chemical munitions. In addition, hundreds of thousands of liters of key chemical precursors which have been identified and destroyed include: 14,600 liters of DF; 121,000 liters of D4 and 153,983 liters of thiodiglycol. According to UNSCOM, the Iraqis were capable of employing both binary and mixed agent weapons. Binary weapons identified used DF. When combined with appropriate chemicals, GB and GF are produced. UNSCOM also discovered, at various locations, evidence of research into certain biological agents, including botulinus toxin, anthrax, an organism responsible for gas gangrene (clostridium perfringens) and others as identified below. The evidence discovered by the group suggested that this was primarily an offensive biological warfare program.

On February 13, 1994, a clandestine radio service in Iraq, the Voice of the Iraqi People, reported that Saddam Hussein's government was still attempting to hide chemical and biological weapons from international inspectors by repeatedly relocating them. Citing unidentified individuals, the radio reported that the banned weapons were being hidden in the oil pipelines that have been "out of operation because of the international embargo."

CHEMICAL WARFARE DOCTRINE AND THE USE OF COMBINED AGENT WARFARE

There is substantial evidence to suggest that in the use of chemical weapons, as in other military areas, the Iraqi military adhered, at least in part, to Soviet military doctrine. Soviet military doctrine suggested that chemical warfare should be conducted with mixed agents. Mixed agents, often referred to as "cocktails," are intended to enhance the capabilities of nerve agents and defeat the precautions taken by the enemy. Use of mixed agents could account for the wide variety of symptoms displayed by the Gulf War veterans. Mixed agents can be made by combining a variety of biotoxins, nerve agents, vesicants, blister agents and some biological agents — such as bacteria and fungi, and others described briefly below.

According to some sources, Iraq used mixed agent weapons combining cyanogen, mustard gas, and tabun against the Kurds. Saddam Hussein stated on April 2, 1990, that Iraq had "double combined chemical" weapons since the last year of the Iran-Iraq War. It was also believed that in 1984 Iraq may have used mixed agent weapons with biological tricothecenes and mycotoxins against Majnoon Island during the Iran-Iraq War.

The utility of chemical weapons and the possibility of exposing one's own troops to indirect chemical weapons effects is an issue which has been seriously debated by both U.S. and Soviet military planners. Soviet doctrine questions the utility of initiating chemical warfare, since chemical weapons produce secondary effects that could obstruct troop advances. U.S. Military doctrine warns that according to its calculations, the use of a nerve agent against a target area of no more than a dozen hectares (a hectare is about 2.47 acres) can, under certain weather conditions, create a hazard zone downwind of up to 100 kilometers in length. Within this downwind area, friendly military units would have to take protective measures.

According to the official military announcements made in the last half of January 1991 and based on the quantity of chemical agents observed by UN inspectors after the war, the scope of coalition bombing against these facilities involved hundreds — if not thousands — of tons of bulk chemical nerve agents, mustard gas, as well as tens of thousands of pieces of chemical munitions. This quantity of chemical warfare agents vastly exceeds the amounts that might be expected to be deployed by a military force in a single chemical attack.

The dispersal of the chemical agents and other hazardous substances is controlled by factors such as topography, wind velocity, direction, temperature, precipitation, vertical temperature gradient and atmospheric humidity. These factors all contribute to the size and type of dispersal pattern which will be observed. In addition, as confirmed by unclassified U.S. satellite imagery, debris from the Coalition bombings were upwardly dispersed, rather than downwardly dispersed as would occur in offensive use, causing chemical agents to be carried by upper atmospheric currents and distributed as "traces" of chemical fallout over "down weather" positions. Czech and French officials confirmed the detections of these chemicals during the war. (See Chapter 3.)

In considering the consequences of the placement of troops in areas downwind (where non-lethal exposure to chemical warfare agents might be expected), it must be remembered that chemical nerve agents, such as Sarin and Soman and other agents, have cumulative effects — often explained as slow rates of detoxification.

Chemical Nerve Agents

Nerve agents kill by disrupting the metabolic processes, causing a buildup of a chemical messenger (acetylcholine) by inhibiting the production of acetylcholine-esterase, a key regulator of neurotransmission. Lethal exposure to chemical nerve agents is generally characterized by drooling, sweating, cramping, vomiting, confusion, irregular heart beat, convulsions, loss of consciousness and coma.

According to a material safety data sheet (MSDS) for Soman (GD), and VX prepared by the U.S. Army Chemical Research, Development and Engineering Center, Aberdeen Proving Grounds, Maryland, "the inhibition of cholinesterase enzymes throughout the body by nerve agents is more or less irreversible so that their effects are prolonged. Until the tissue cholinesterase enzymes are restored to normal activity, probably by very slow regeneration over a period of weeks or 2 to 3 months if damage is severe, there is a period of increased susceptibility to the effects of another exposure to any nerve agent. During this period the effects of repeated exposures are cumulative; after a single exposure, daily exposure to concentrations of nerve agent insufficient to produce symptoms may result in the onset of symptoms after several days. Continued daily exposure may be followed by increasingly severe effects. After symptoms subside, increased susceptibility persists for one to several days. The degree of exposure required to produce recurrence of symptoms, and the severity of these symptoms depend on duration of exposure and time required to produce recurrence of symptoms, and the severity of these symptoms depend on the duration of exposure and the time intervals between exposures. Increased susceptibility is not specific to the particular nerve agent initially absorbed." (See appendix A for MSDS on Soman, Sarin, Tabun, and VX).

Some of the symptoms commonly associated with acute exposure to chemical nerve agents include myosis, frontal headaches, eye pain on focusing, slight dimness of vision, occasional nausea and vomiting, runny nose, tightness in chest, sometimes with prolonged wheezing, expiration suggestive of broncho-constriction or increased secretion and coughing. Following systemic absorption, these symptoms are identified as typical: tightnesss in chest, wheezing, anorexia, nausea, vomiting, abdominal cramps, epigastric and substernal tightness, heartburn, diarrhea, involuntary defecation, increased sweating, increased salivation, increased tearing, slight bradycardia, myosis, blurring-vision, urinary urgency and frequency, fatigue, mild weakness, muscular twitching, cramps, generalized weakness, including muscles of respiraton, with dyspnea and cyanosis, pallor and occasional elevation of blood pressure; giddiness, tension, anxiety, jitteriness, restlessness, emotional lability, excessive dreaming, insomnia, nightmares, headaches, tremors, withdrawal and depression; bursts of slow waves of elevated voltage in EEG (especially on over ventilation), drowsiness, difficulty concentrating, slowness on recall, confusion, slurred speech, ataxia, coma (with absence of reflexes), Cheyne-Stokes respirations, convulsions, depression of the respiratory and circulatory centers, with dyspnea, cyanosis and fall in blood pressure.

The majority of automatic chemical agent detection alarms (M8A1) deployed during the war were not sufficiently sensitive for detecting sustained low levels of chemical agent and monitoring personnel for contamination. U.S. Army Material Safety Data Sheets (MSDS) indicate that chronic exposure to levels of over.0001 mg/m3 for Sarin (GB) is hazardous and required the use of protective equipment. (See appendix A). The minimum level of chemical agent required to activate the automatic chemical agent detection alarm M8A1, commonly in use during the war, exceeds this threshold by a factor of 1,000. As the chemical agent alarms began to sound during the "air war," French, Czech, and many U.S. commanders confirmed that they were sounding from the fallout from the bombings. Over time, even at these levels, after repeatedly being told that there was no danger, U.S. forces failed to take precautionary measures. Others report that the alarms were sounding so frequently that they were turned off.

This increased susceptibility associated with prolonged exposures to non-lethal dosages of nerve gases, suggests that the synergistic effects of the fallout from the bombings of the chemical warfare agent facilities and the administration of the cholinesterase inhibiting drug, pyridostigmine bromide, should be further researched as factors contributing to the symptoms being described by the Gulf War veterans.

The following is a listing of a number of agents which the Iraqi government could have combined or which could have been combined in the atmosphere as a result of Coalition bombings:

Sarin (GB)-A colorless and practically odorless liquid, Sarin dissolves well in water and organic solvents. The basic military use of Sarin is as a gas and a persistent aerosol. A highly toxic agent with a clearly defined myopic effect, symtoms of intoxication appear quickly without any period of latent effect. Sarin has cumulative efffects — that is, a slow rate of detoxification independent of its method of entry into the body.

According to Joachim Krause and Charles K. Mallory in Chemical Weapons in Soviet Military Doctrine: Military and Historical Experience, 1915-1991, the progressive signs of initial Sarin intoxication include myosis (contraction of the pupil), photophobia, difficulty breathing and chest pain.

Soman (GD)-A neuro-paralytic toxic agent. Soman is a transparent, colorless, involatile liquid smelling of camphor. Soluble in water to a limited degree, Soman is absorbed into porous and painted surfaces. Soman is similar to Sarin in its injurious effects, but more toxic. When it acts on the skin in either droplet or vapor form, it causes a general poisoning of the organism.

Tabun (GA)-A neuro-paralytic toxic agent. Tabun is a transparent, colorless liquid. The industrial product is a brown liquid with a weak sweetish smell; in small concentrations, it smells of fruit, but in large concentrations, it smells of fish. Tabun dissolves poorly in water but well in organic solvents; it is easily absorbed into rubber products and painted surfaces. Injury occurs upon skin contact with Tabun vapor and droplets. The symptoms of injury appear almost immediately. Marked myosis occurs.

VX-This colorless, ordorless, liquid has a low volatility and is poorly soluble in water, but dissolves well in organic solvents. The danger of pulmonary VX intoxication is determined by meteorological conditions and the delivery method used. VX is thought to be very effective against respiratory organs when in the form of a thinly dispersed aerosol. The symptoms of VX intoxication are analogous to those of other nerve agents, but their development is markedly slower. As with other nerve agents, VX has a cumulative effect.

VESICANTS AND BLOOD AGENTS

Lewisite-A vesicant toxic agent, industrial lewisite is a dark brown liquid with a strong smell. Lewisite is a contact poison with practically no period of latent effect. Lewisite vapors cause irritation to the eyes and upper respiratory tract. According to the Center for Disease Control, lewisite would cause stinging and burning. Its smell, generally characterized as the strong smell of geraniums, could be confused with the smell of ammonia (the reaction to which is regulated by pain fibers rather than smell). Iraqi stores of lewisite were not located after the war according to the Department of Defense.

Cyanogen Chloride-The French first suggested the use of cyanogen chloride as a toxic agent. U.S. analysts have reported that it is capable of penetrating gas mask filters. Partially soluble in water, it dissolves well in organic solvents. It is absorbed easily into porous materials; its military state is a gas. Cyanogen chloride is a quick acting toxic agent. Upon contact with the eyes or respiratory organs, it injures immediately. Lethal exposures result in loss of consciousness, convulsions and paralysis.

Hydrogen Cyanide-A colorless liquid smelling of bitter almonds, hydrogen cyanide is a very strong, quick acting poison. Hydrogen cyanide affects unprotected humans through the respiratory organs and during the ingestion of contaminated food and water. It inhibits the enzymes which regulate the intra-cell oxidant-restorative process. As a result, the cells of the nervous system, especially those affecting breathing — are injured, which in turn leads to quick death. An important feature of hydrogen cyanide is the absence of a period of latent effect. The military state of hydrogen cyanide is a gas. The toxic and physiologic properties of hydrogen cyanide permit it to be used effectively in munitions— predominantly in rocket launched artillery. Death occurs after intoxication due to paralysis of the heart. Non-lethal doses do not cause intoxication.

Blister Agents

According to the material safety data sheet (MSDS) for sulfur mustard gas (HD) prepared by the U.S. Army Chemical

Research, Development and Engineering Center, Aberdeen Proving Ground, Maryland, "Chronic exposure to HD can cause skin sensitization, chronic lung impairment, cough, shortness of breath, chest pain, and cancer of the mouth, throat, respiratory tract, skin, and leukemia. It may also cause birth defects. (See appendix A for MSDS sheets on sulfur mustard agents HD and T.) The U.S. Army Chemical and Biological Defense Command lists the current detector sensitivity threshold for the M256A1 kits, a commonly used piece of chemical agent detection equipment in the Gulf War, as 2.0 mg/m3. According to the Material Data Safety Sheets for sulfur mustard, total weight average exposures of greater than.003mg/m3 over an 8 hr. period requires the use of protective equipment. (See appendix A.) Therefore, the detection kit would not detect the agent until the amount of agent present exceeded the safety threshold by a factor of over 660. The M8A1 automatic alarms do not detect blister agent.

Mustard Gas-This is a colorless, oily liquid which dissolves poorly in water, but relatively well in organic solvents, petroleum, luricant products, and other toxic agents. The injurious effect of mustard gas is associated with its ability to inhibit many enzyme systems of the body.

This, in turn, prevents the intra-cell exchange of chemicals and leads to necrosis of the tissue. Death is associated mainly with necrosis of the tissue of the central nervous system. Mustard gas has a period of latent effect (the first signs of injury appear after 2-12 hours), but does not act cumulatively. It does not have any known antidotes. In military use it can come in gas, aerosol, and droplet form. It therefore acts through inhalation, cutaneously, perorally and directly through the blood stream. The toxic and physico-chemical properties of mustard gas allow it to be used in all types of munitions.

RELATED CHEMICAL AGENT INFORMATION

Committee staff has learned that Iraq may have acquired any one of a number of the Soviet binary novachok ("newcomer") series of chemical warfare agent compounds or information relevant to the development of those compounds. This series of chemical warfare agents reportedly contains both lethal and debilitating agents. According to a confidential Committee source, if the Iraqis had obtained samples of these compounds they could be easily analyzed and produced with readily available materials. Several of these compounds are described as agents that even in microdoses can have long lasting effects.

These agents are described as inducing myosis, vomiting, memory loss, involuntary motions and internal organ dysfunction. Many of these materials are also described as having mutagenic effects. These materials are, according to the source, stored in the lipids (body fats) and have no known antidotes. In addition, according to the Committee source, the Soviets were believed to have conducted research in a number of dioxin-based chemical warfare agents, and on at least one agent that could be used to contaminate drinking water supplies. Committee staff is conducting further inquiries to determine if Iraq may have had access to any of these compounds.

Biotoxins

Biotoxins are natural poisons, chiefly of cellular structure. A distinction is made between exotoxins which are given off by an organism while it is alive, and endotoxins which are given off after a cell's death. The exotoxins cause the injurious effects of biological weapons, but endotoxins guarantee the effects of chemical weapons and do not cause the widespread disease outbreaks associated with biological warfare. Some examples of biotoxins include botulinus toxin and staphylococcic enterotoxin.

Biological Warfare Capability

According to the U.N., the Iraqi biological warfare program was initiated in mid-1986 at Salman Pak. UNSCOM inspectors discovered evidence of research into certain biological agents including botulinus toxin and anthrax — as well as organisms responsible for gas gangrene, tetanus and brucellosis, components of a biological weapons program which was not defensive in nature. In four years of work prior to the war, only 10 papers were published. These research programs focused on Iraqi efforts to isolate the most pathogenic spores.

They also did research on the aerosolization and on the environmental survivability of some of these biological materials according to the United Nations. While the Department of Defense maintains that the Iraqi military did not weaponize its biological warfare program, UNSCOM is less certain, reporting that their degree of confidence that weaponization did not occur is low.

In fact, readily high performance agricultural aerosol generators could easily be converted to both decontaminate areas in which chemicals are used and to aerosolize biological and chemical warfare agents.

Other ways in which biological materials could have been weaponized include the use of Iraqi 250-and 500lb bombs, aerial rockets, unmanned aerial vehicles, FAW ground-to-ground missiles, helicopters and Iraqi aircraft. The Committee has received several reports of Iraqi helicopters penetrating Saudi airspace during the war by flying at low levels through the wadis and of Iraqi aircraft penetrating the area over the northern Persian Gulf.

According to UNSCOM, indications that suggested that the program was offensive in nature include:

- No declared links between the BW defense program and medical corps research.
- No links between aerosolization research and research on defensive filters.

The United Nations said that the Biological Inspection was initiated on August 8, 1991 at Salman Pak. The inspection was delayed because of the need to extensively immunize the members of the inspection team. The Salman Pak facility was razed one week prior to the arrival of the inspection team.

The United States is aware of the Iraqi potential for using biological weapons. The employment of biological agents in a "cocktail" mix with chemical warfare agents is consistent with Soviet military doctrine.

It is clear that biological weapons are much more difficult than chemical weapons to detect and defend against. Some of the symptoms experienced by veterans suffering from Persian Gulf Syndrome are consistent with biological warfare agent use. Verification will require sophisticated medical diagnosis, which to date has not been publicly undertaken.

The question of whether U.S. forces were attacked with a biological agent is problematic. According to Chemical/ Biological Program: A Department of Defense Perspective, "it has been recognized that our biological defense program was inadequate. Creditble analysis indicated that optimal employment of biological agents could result in a significantly large hazard area."

It further cites a memo from the Chairman of the Joint Chiefs of Staff to the SECDEF (Secretary of Defense) noting: "inadequate ability to counter BW (biological warfare) attack/ BW defense is a priority requirement.

The inadequacy of the current biological defense and detection program was also supported by Deputy Secretary of Defense John Deutch in an unclassified May 6, 1994 address delivered at a Department of Defense sponsored counterproliferation conference at the Los Alamos National Laboratory. According to Deputy Secretary Deutch, the United States has "no biological detection capability deployed with any forces, anywhere."

Novel BW agents created by altering DNA plasmids and vectors are specifically intended to avoid detection. As noted below, several shipments of biological materials that might have been used to carry out such a program were licensed for export from the United States to the Iraq Atomic Energy Commission. In such a program, common intestinal flora such as e. coli could be altered to produce viral, bacterial, or other toxins and would be difficult to treat.

If Iraq was successful in developing such agents, diagnosis will continue to elude physicians testing for traditional illnesses. Novel BW agents would certainly elude biological detection devices. There is evidence, based on the nature of the materials imported, that this type of research was being conducted. Since the Iraqi government managed to dismantle much of its biological warfare program prior to the UNSCOM inspections, we can only speculate on how advanced this program might have been.

It has been suggested that if these problems the veterans are experiencing are Gulf War related, then we should be seeing even more serious problems among the Iraqis. Since beginning this investigation we have learned that many Iraqi enemy prisoners of war (EPW) suffered skin rashes, sores, nausea, vomiting, coughing and other medical problems while they were being detained in Saudi Arabia.

Many members of units who had close contact with these individuals are now reporting to the Committee symptoms consistent with those being suffered by other Gulf War veterans. In addition, Iraq has claimed a dramatic rise in reported cases of communicable diseases since the end of the Gulf War including typhoid, brucellosis, hepatitis and cholera.

Further, reports of Gulf War illnesses being reported are no longer limited to veterans of the Gulf War. Others reporting manifestation of these symptoms include:

- Department of Defense civilians who served in the Persian Gulf War.
- Department of Defense civilians working at the Anniston (AL) Army Depot and the Sharpsite (CA) Army Depot decontaminating equipment which was returned from the Persian Gulf.
- Spouses, particularly the spouses of male veterans, are reporting the following symptoms: chronic or recurring vaginal yeast infections, menstrual irregularities (excessive bleeding and severe cramping), rashes, fatigue, joint and muscle pain, and memory loss.
- Children born to veterans prior to the Gulf War. In many cases both male and female children born prior to the war have experienced symptoms similar to those of the veterans and their spouses.
- Children born following the Gulf war. Some reports have been published which suggest a high rate of miscarriages in the families of Gulf War veterans. Further, several reports have surfaced which suggest that there has been a high rate of physical abnormalities in children born to Gulf War veterans since the war.

5

FUNCTIONS OF THE MILITARY

INTRODUCTION

Upon India gaining independence in 1947, the British Indian Army was divided into two parts to serve the newly created nations of Union of India and Islamic Republic of Pakistan. Most units went to India; four Gurkha regiments were transferred to the British Army while the rest went to India. As the Indian Army derives from the British Indian Army, its structures, uniforms and traditions are essentially British in heritage. It is often said that the Indian Army is more British than the British. The Indian Army is the largest branch of the armed forces of India and has the responsibility for land-based military operations. Its primary objectives include defending India from external aggression, maintaining peace and security within the country, patrolling borders and conducting counter-terrorist operations.

It also conducts rescue and humanitarian operations during calamities and disturbances. Control and operation of the Army is administered by the Ministry of Defence. With more than 1,130,000 soldiers in active service and about 1,200,000 reserve troops, the Indian Army is the world's second largest. It is a completely voluntary service and though there is a provision for military draft in the Indian constitution, it has never been imposed. The Indian Army was formed soon after

India gained independence in 1947 and retained most of the regiments of the British Indian Army. The Army is deployed in many of the world's conflict zones as a part of the United Nations Peacekeeping forces. The force is currently headed by the Chief of Army Staff, General Deepak Kapoor. The Field Marshal is the highest attainable rank in the Indian Army and it is awarded by the President of India, on advise of the Union Government, only in exceptional circumstances

FIRST KASHMIR WAR (1947)

Almost immediately after independence, tensions between India and Pakistan began to boil over, and the first of three full-scale wars between the two nations broke out over the then princely state of Kashmir. Upon the Maharaja of Kashmir's reluctance to accede to either India or Pakistan, an impatient Pakistan sponsored a 'tribal' invasion of parts of Kashmir. The men are alleged by India to have also included Pakistan army regulars. Soon after, Pakistan sent in its troops to annex the state. The Maharaja, Hari Singh, appealed to India, and to Lord Mountbatten — the Governor General — for help, but it was pointed out to him that India saw no reason to do so. He signed the Instrument of Accession and Kashmir unilaterally acceded to India (a decision ratified by Britain but never accepted by Pakistan).

Immediately after, Indian troops were airlifted into Srinagar and repelled the invaders. This contingent included General Thimayya who distinguished himself in the operation and in years that followed, became a Chief of the Indian Army. An intense war was waged across the state and former comrades found themselves fighting each other. Both sides made some territorial gains and also suffered significant losses. An uneasy UN sponsored peace returned by the end of 1948 with Indian and Pakistani soldiers facing each other directly on the Line of Control, which has since divided Indian from Pakistani-held Kashmir. Tensions between India and Pakistan, largely over Kashmir, have never since been entirely eliminated.

Participation in UN peace-keeping operations

Presently, the Indian army has dedicated one brigade of troops to the UN's standby arrangements. The large number of sustained troop commitments made by India has been praised for taking part in long and difficult operations. The Indian Army has participated in several UN peace-keeping operations, including the ones in Angola, Cambodia, Cyprus, Congo, El Salvador, Namibia, Lebanon, Liberia, Mozambique, Rwanda, Somalia, Srilanka & Vietnam. The army had also provided a paramedical unit to facilitate the withdrawal of the sick and wounded in Korea.

Inclusion of Hyderabad (1948)

After the partition of India, the State of Hyderabad, a princely-state under the rule of a Nizam, chose to remain independent. The Nizam, refused to accede his state to the Union of India. The following stand-off between the Government of India and the Nizam ended on 12 September 1948 when India's then deputy-Prime Minister Sardar Vallabhai Patel ordered Indian troops to secure the state. Within 5 days of intense fighting, the Indian Army, backed by the Indian Air Force, successfully defeated Hyderabad State forces. The following day, the State of Hyderabad was proclaimed as a part of the Union of India. Major General Joyanto Nath Chaudhuri, who led the Operation Polo was appointed the Military Governor of Hyderabad (1948-1949) to restore law and order.

Goa, Daman and Diu Operation (1961)

Even though the British and French vacated all their colonial possessions in the Indian subcontinent, Goa, Daman and Diu remained under Portuguese control. On 12th December, 1961, after repeated Portuguese refusals to negotiate their leaving, New Delhi launched Operation Vijay and ordered a small contingent of its troops to invade the Portuguese territories and secure them. Unable to withstand the assault that lasted twenty-six hours, Goa, along with Daman and Diu (enclaves lying to the north of Maharashtra) joined India.

Sino-Indian Conflict (1962)

Since 1959, India followed a "forward policy" under which Indian border patrol units continuously pushed their posts forward deep into territory claimed by the People's Republic of China (PRC).

Small-scale clashes between the Indian and Chinese forces broke out as India insisted on the disputed McMahon Line being regarded as the international border between the two countries. Despite heavy casualties, Chinese troops did not retaliate the cross-border firing by Indian troops. China's misinterpretation of India's true intentions in Tibet created more rifts between the two countries.

Buoyed by the success of its military operations in Hyderabad and Goa, India took a more aggressive stance towards its border disputes with China. In 1962, the Indian Army was ordered to move to the Thag La ridge located near the border between Bhutan and Arunachal Pradesh and about three miles (5 km) north of the disputed McMahon Line. Meanwhile, Chinese troops too had made incursions into Indian-held territory and tensions between the two reached a new high when Indian forces discovered a road constructed by China in Aksai Chin.

After a series of failed negotiations, People's Liberation Army attacked Indian Army positions at the Thag La ridge. This move by China caught India by surprise and by October

12, Nehru gave orders for the Chinese to be expelled from Aksai Chin. However, poor coordination among various divisions of the Indian Army and the late decision to mobilize the Indian Air Force in vast numbers gave China a crucial tactical and strategic advantage over India. On October 20, Chinese soldiers attacked India in both the North-West and North-Eastern parts of the border and captured vast portions of Aksai Chin and Arunachal Pradesh.

As the fighting moved beyond disputed territories, China called on the Indian government to negotiate, however India remained determined to regain lost territory. With no peaceful agreement in sight, China unilaterally withdrew its forces from Arunachal Pradesh.

The reasons for the withdrawal are disputed with India claiming various logistical problems for China and diplomatic support from the United States while China stated that it still held territory that it had staked diplomatic claim upon. The dividing line between the Indian and Chinese forces was christened as the Line of Actual Control.

The poor decisions made by India's military commanders raised several questions. The Henderson-Brooks committee was soon set up by the Government of India to determine the causes of the poor performance of the Indian Army. The report of committee apparently faulted much of the command of Indian Armed Forces and severely criticized the executive government for its failures on several fronts.

The committee found that the major reason for the defeat was low deployment of troops on India's border with China even after hostilities began and also criticized the decision to not allow the Indian Air Force to target Chinese transport lines out of fear of Chinese aerial counter-attack on Indian civilian areas. Much of the blame was also targeted at the incompetence of then Defense Minister, Krishna Menon who resigned from his post soon after the war ended. Despite frequent calls for its release, the Henderson-Brooks report still remains classified.

Second Kashmir War (1965)

A second confrontation with Pakistan took place in 1965, largely over Kashmir. Pakistani President Ayub Khan launched *Operation Gibraltar* in August 1965 during which several Pakistani paramilitary troops infiltrated into Indian-administered Kashmir and tried to spark an anti-India rebellion. Pakistani leaders believed that India, which was still recovering from the disastrous Sino-Indian War, would be unable to deal with a military thrust and rebellion. However, the operation was a major failure since the Kashmiri people showed little support for such a rebellion and India quickly moved forces to drive the infiltrators out. Within a fortnight of the launch of the Indian counter-attack, most of the infiltrators had retreated back to Pakistan.

Battered by the failure of Operation Gibraltar and expecting a major invasion by Indian forces across the border, Pakistan launched Operation Grand Slam on September 1, invading India's Chamb-Jaurian sector. In retaliation, the India's Army launched major offensive throughout its border with Pakistan, with Lahore as its prime target. Though the Indian Army's break through of the final phases of Pakistani defense was considerably delayed due to logistical issues, the conflict was largely seen as a debacle for the Pakistani Army.

Initially, the Indian Army met with considerable success in the northern sector. After launching prolonged artillery barrages against Pakistan, India was able to capture three important mountain positions in Kashmir. By September 9, the Indian Army had made considerable in-roads into Pakistan. India had its largest haul of Pakistani tanks when the offensive of Pakistan's 1 Armoured Division was blunted at the Battle of Asal Uttar which took place on September 10th near

Khemkaran. Six Pakistani Armoured Regiments took part in the battle against three Indian Armoured Regiments with inferior tanks. By the time the battle had ended, the 4th Indian Division had captured about 97 Pakistani tanks in either destroyed, or damaged, or in intact condition.

This included 72 Patton tanks and 25 Chafees and Shermans. 32 of the 97 tanks, including 28 Pattons, were in running condition. In comparison, the Indians lost only 32 tanks at Khemkaran-Bhikkiwind. About fifteen of them were captured by the Pakistan Army, mostly Sherman tanks. Pakistan's overwhelming defeat at the decisive battle of Assal Uttar hastened the end of the conflict.

At the time of ceasefire declaration, India reported 12,500 casualties of whom about 3,000 were killed, 8,400 were wounded and 1,100 were either taken as prisoners of war or were missing. On the other hand, it was estimated that about 3,800 Pakistani soldiers were killed in the battle, 9,000 were wounded and about 2,000 were taken as prisoners of war.

About 200 Pakistani tanks were either destroyed or captured by India and an additional 150 were permanently put out of service. India lost a total of 190 tanks during the conflict and about 200 more had to undergo repair. In all, India lost about half as many tanks as Pakistan lost during the war.

Given India's advantageous position at the end of the war, the decision to return back to pre-war positions, following the Tashkent Declaration, caused an outcry among the polity in New Delhi. It was widely believed that India's decision to accept the ceasefire was due to political, and not military, factors since it was facing considerable pressure from the United States and the UN to stop hostilities. According to one independent analyst, continuation of the war would have led further losses and ultimately defeat for Pakistan.

BANGLADESH LIBERATION WAR (1971)

An independence movement broke out in East Pakistan which was brutally crushed by Pakistani forces. Due to large-scale atrocities against them, thousands of Bengalis took refuge in neighboring India causing a major refugee crisis there. In early 1971, India declared its full-support for the Bengali rebels, known as Mukti Bahini, and Indian agents were extensively involved in covert operations to aid them.

On November 20, 1971, Indian Army moved the 14 Punjab Battalion and 45 Cavalry into Garibpur, a strategically important town near India's border with East Pakistan, and successfully captured it. The following day, more clashes took place between Indian and Pakistani forces. Wary of India's growing involvement in the Bengali rebellion, the Pakistan Air Force (PAF) launched a pre-emptive strike on Indian military positions near its border with East Pakistan on December 3.

The aerial operation, however, failed to accomplish its stated objectives and caused India to declare a full-scale war against Pakistan the same day. By midnight, the Indian Army, accompanied by Indian Air Force, launched major military thrust into East Pakistan. The Indian Army won several battles on the eastern front including the decisive of battle of Hilli, which was the only front where the Pakistani Army was able to buildup considerable resistance.[17] India's massive early gains was largely attributed to the speed and flexibility with which Indian armored divisions moved across East Pakistan.

Pakistan launched a counter-attack against India on the western front. On December 4, 1971, the A company of the 23rd Battalion of India's Punjab Regiment detected and intercepted the movement of the 51st Infantry Division of the Pakistani Army near Ramgarh, Rajasthan. The battle of Longewala ensued during which the A company, though being outnumbered, thwarted the Pakistani advance until the Indian Air Force directed its fighters to engage the Pakistani tanks. By the time the battle had ended, 34 Pakistani tanks and 50 armored vehicles were either destroyed or abandoned. About 200 Pakistani troops were killed in action during the battle while only 2 Indian soldiers lost their lives. Pakistan suffered another major defeat on the western front during the battle of Basantar which was fought from December 4th to 16th.

By the end of the battle, about 66 Pakistani tanks were destroyed and 40 more were captured. In return, Pakistani forces were able to destroy only 11 Indian tanks. None of the numerous Pakistani offensives on the Western front materialized. By December 16th, Pakistan had lost sizable territory on both eastern and western fronts.

Under the command of Lt. General J.S Aurora, the three corps of the Indian Army, who had invaded East Pakistan, entered Dhaka and forced Pakistani forces to surrender on 16th December, 1971, one day after the conclusion of the battle of Basantar.

After Pakistan's Lt. General A.A.K. Niazi signed the Instrument of Surrender, India took more than 90,000 Pakistani prisoners of war, which included about 38,000 armed forces personnel and 52,000 militia and bureaucrats of West Pakistani origin. At the time of the signing of the Instrument of Surrender, 9,000 Pakistani soldiers were killed-in-action while India suffered only 2,500 battle-related deaths. In addition, Pakistan lost 200 tanks during the battle compared to India's 80.

In 1972, the Simla Agreement was signed between the two countries and tensions simmered. However, there were occasional spurts in diplomatic tensions which culminated into increased military vigilance on both sides.

Siachen Conflict (1984-)

The Siachen Glacier, though a part of the Kashmir region, is not officially demarcated. As a consequence, prior to the 1980s, neither India nor Pakistan maintained permanent military presence in the region. However, Pakistan started hosting a series of mountaineering expeditions to the glacier during the 1950s. By early 1980s, the government of Pakistan was granting special expedition permits to mountaineers and United States Army maps deliberately showed Siachen as a part of Pakistan. This practice gave rise to the contemporary meaning of the term *oropolitics*.

An irked India launched Operation Meghdoot in April 1984 during which the entire Kumaon Regiment of the Indian Army was airlifted to the glacier. Pakistani forces responded quickly and clashes between the two followed. Indian Army secured the strategic Sia La and Bilafond La mountain passes and by 1985, more than 1000 sq. miles of territory, claimed by Pakistan, was under Indian control.

The Indian Army continues to control more than 2/3rd of the glacier. Pakistan made several unsuccessful attempts to regain control over Siachen. In late 1987, Pakistan mobilized about 8,000 troops and garrisoned them near Khapalu, aiming to capture Bilafond La. However, they were thrown back after engaging the Indian Army personnel guarding Bilafond. During the battle, about 23 Indian soldiers lost their lives while more than 150 Pakistani troops perished. Further unsuccessful attempts to reclaim positions were launched by Pakistan in 1990, 1995, 1996 and 1999.

India continues to maintain a strong military presence in the region despite extremely inhospitable conditions and the conflict over Siachen is regularly cited as an example of mountain warfare. The highest peak in the Siachen glacier region, Siakangri, is strategically important for India because its immense altitude and proximity to the Karakoram Highway enables the Indian forces to keep check on any Pakistani or Chinese movement in the region.

Maintaining control over Siachen poses several logistical challenges for the Indian Army. Several infrastructure projects were constructed in the region, including a helipad 21,000 feet (6,400 m) above the sea level. In 2004, Indian Army was spending an estimated US$2 million a day to support its personnel stationed in the region.

Counter-insurgency Activities

The Indian Army has played a crucial role in the past, fighting insurgents and terrorists within the nation. The army launched Operation Bluestar and Operation Woodrose in the 1980s to combat Sikh insurgents. The army, along with some paramilitary forces, has the prime responsibility of maintaining law and order in the troubled Jammu and Kashmir region. The Indian Army also sent a contingent to Sri Lanka in 1987 as a part of the Indian Peace Keeping Force.

Kargil Conflict (1999)

In 1998, India carried out nuclear tests and a few days later, Pakistan responded by more nuclear tests giving both countries nuclear deterrence capability. Diplomatic tensions eased after the Lahore Summit was held in 1999. The sense of optimism was short-lived, however, since in mid-1999 Pakistani paramilitary forces and Kashmiri insurgents captured deserted, but strategic, Himalayan heights in the Kargil district of India.

These had been vacated by the Indian army during the onset of the inhospitable winter and were supposed to reoccupied in spring. The *mujahideen* who took control of these areas received important support, both in the form of arms and supplies, from Pakistan. Some of the heights under their control, which also included the *Tiger Hill*, overlooked the vital Srinagar-Leh Highway (NH 1A), Batalik and Dras.

Once the scale of the Pakistani incursion was realized, the Indian Army quickly mobilized about 200,000 troops and Operation Vijay was launched. However, since the heights were under Pakistani control, India was in a clear strategic disadvantage. From their observation posts, the Pakistani forces had a clear line-of-sight to lay down indirect artillery fire on NH 1A, inflicting heavy casualties on the Indians. This was a serious problem for the Indian Army as the highway was its main logistical and supply route. Thus, the Indian Army's first priority was to recapture peaks that were in the immediate vicinity of NH1a. This resulted in Indian troops first targeting the Tiger Hill and Tololing complex in Dras. This was soon followed by more attacks on the Batalik-Turtok sub-sector which provided access to Siachen Glacier. Point 4590, which had the nearest view of the NH1a, was successfully recaptured by Indian forces on June 14.

Though most of the posts in the vicinity of the highway were cleared by mid-June, some parts of the highway near Drass witnessed sporadic shelling until the end of the war. Once NH1a area was cleared, the Indian Army turned to driving the invading force back across the Line of Control.

The Battle of Tololing, among other assaults, slowly tilted the combat in India's favor. Nevertheless, some of the posts put up a stiff resistance, including Tiger Hill (Point 5140) that fell only later in the war. As the operation was fully underway, about 250 artillery guns were brought in to clear the infiltrators in the posts that were in the line-of-sight. In many vital points, neither artillery nor air power could dislodge the outposts manned by the Pakistan soldiers, who were out of visible range.

The Indian Army mounted some direct frontal ground assaults which were slow and took a heavy toll given the steep ascent that had to be made on peaks as high as 18,000 feet (5,500 m). Two months into the conflict, Indian troops had slowly retaken most of the ridges they had lost; according to official count, an estimated 75%–80% of the intruded area and nearly all high ground was back under Indian control.

Following the Washington accord on July 4, where Sharif agreed to withdraw Pakistani troops, most of the fighting came to a gradual halt, but some Pakistani forces remained in positions on the Indian side of the LOC. In addition, the United Jihad Council (an umbrella for all extremist groups) rejected Pakistan's plan for a climb-down, instead deciding to fight on. The Indian Army launched its final attacks in the last week of July; as soon as the Drass subsector had been cleared of Pakistani forces, the fighting ceased on July 26. The day has since been marked as *Kargil Vijay Diwas* (Kargil Victory Day) in India. By the end of the war, India had resumed control of all territory south and east of the Line of Control, as was established in July 1972 per the Shimla Accord.

By the time all hostilities had ended, the number of Indian soldiers killed during the conflict stood at 527 while more than 700 regular members of the Pakistani army were killed. The number of Islamist fighters, also known as *Mujahideen*, killed by Indian Armed Forces during the conflict stood at about 3,000.

MAJOR EXERCISES

Operation Parakram

After the December 13, 2001 attack on the Indian Parliament, Operation Parakram was launched in which tens of thousands of Indian troops were deployed along the Indo-Pakistan border. India blamed Pakistan for backing the attack.

The operation was the largest military exercise carried out by any Asian country. Its prime objective is still unclear but appears to have been to prepare the army for any future nuclear conflict with Pakistan, which seemed increasingly possible after the December attack on the Indian parliament.

Operation Sanghe Shakti

It has since been stated that the main goal of this exercise was to validate mobilisation strategies of the Ambala-based *II Strike* Corps. Air support was a part of this exercise, and an entire battalion of paratroops was paradropped during the conduct of the war games, with allied equipment. Some 20,000 soldiers took part in the exercise.

Exercise Ashwamedha

Indian Army tested its network centric warfare capabilities in the exercise Ashwamedha. The exercise was held in the Thar desert, in which over 30,000 troops participated. Asymmetric warfare capability was also tested by the Indian Army during the exercise.

Structure of the Indian Army

Initially, the army's main objective was to defend the nation's frontiers. However, over the years, the army has also taken up the responsibility of providing internal security, especially in insurgent-hit Kashmir and north-east. The army has a strength of about a million troops and fields 34 divisions. Its headquarters is located in the Indian capital New Delhi and it is under the overall command of the Chief of Army Staff (COAS), currently General Deepak Kapoor.

Regimental Organisation

In addition to this (not to be confused with the Field Corps mentioned above) are the Regiments or Corps or departments of the Indian Army. The corps mentioned below are the functional divisions entrusted with specific pan-Army tasks.

Arms

1. Indian Infantry Regiments
2. Armoured Corps Regiments - The Armoured Corps School and Centre is at Ahmednagar.
3. Regiment of Artillery - The School of Artillery is at Devlali near Nasik.
4. Corps of Engineers - The College of Military Engineering is at Dapodi, Pune. The Centers are located as follows- Madras Engineer Group at Bangalore, Bengal Engineer Group at Roorkee and Bombay Engineer Group at Khadki, Pune.
5. Corps of Army Air Defence-Center at Gopalpur in Orissa State.
6. Mechanised Infantry - Regimental Center at Ahmednagar.
7. Corps of Signals
8. Army Aviation Corps

Services

1. Army Dental Corps
2. Army Education Corps - Center at Pachmarhi.
3. Army Medical Corps - Center at Lucknow.
4. Army Ordnance Corps - Centers at Jabalpur andSecunderabad.
5. Army Postal Service Corps
6. Army Service Corps - Center at Bangalore
7. Corps of Electrical and Mechanical Engineers- Centers at Bhopal and Secunderabad .

8. Corps of Military Police [2] - Center at Bangalore
9. Intelligence Corps - Center at Pune.
10. Judge Advocate General's Deptt. - Institute of Military Law kamptee,Nagpur.
11. Military Farms Service
12. Military Nursing Service
13. Remount and Veterinary Corps
14. Pioneer Corps

Other Field Formations

- Division: An Army Division is an intermediate between a Corps and a Brigade. It is the largest striking force in the army. Each Division is headed by [General Officer Commanding] (GOC) in the rank of Major General. It usually consists of 15,000 combat troops and 8,000 support elements. Currently, the Indian Army has 34 Divisions including 4 RAPID (Re-organised Army Plains Infantry Divisions) Action Divisions, 18 Infantry Divisions, 10 Mountain Divisions, 3 Armoured Divisions and 2 Artillery Divisions. Each Division composes of several Brigades.
- Brigade: The Brigade is smaller than the Division and generally consists of 3 Infantry Battalions along with elements of various Combat & Support Arms & Services. It is headed by a Brigadier equivalent to a Brigadier General. The Indian Army also has 5 Independent Armoured Brigades, 15 Independent Artillery Brigades, 7 Independent Infantry Brigades, 1 Independent Parachute Brigade,3 Independent Air Defence Brigades, 2 Independent Air Defence Groups and 4 Independent Engineer Brigades. These Independent Brigades operate directly under the Corps Commander (GOC Corps).

- Battalion: A Battalion is commanded by a Colonel and is the Infantry's main fighting unit. It consists of more than 900 personnel.
- Company: Headed by the Major, a Company comprises 120 soldiers.
- Platoon: An intermediate between a Company and Section, a Platoon is headed by a Lieutenant or depending on the availability of Commissioned Officers, a Junior Commissioned Officer, with the rank of Subedar or Naib-Subedar. It has a total strength of about 32 troops.
- Section: Smallest military outfit with a strength of 10 personnel. Commanded by a Non-commissioned officer of the rank of Havildar Major or Sergeant Major.

Regiments

Infantry Regiments: There are several battalions or units under the same formation in a Regiment. The Gurkha Regiment, for instance, has several battalions. All formations under a Regiment are battalions of the same arms or Corps (i.e., Infantry or Engineers). Regiments are not exactly field formations; they mostly do not make a formation. All Regiments of the Gurkha's for instance would not fight together as one formation, but can be dispersed over various Brigades or Corps or even Commands.

Artillery Regiments

The Regiment of Artillery constitutes a formidable operational arm of Indian Army. Historically it takes its lineage from Moghul Emperor Babur who is popularly credited with introduction of Artillery in India, in the Battle of Panipat in 1526. However evidence of earlier use of gun by Bahmani Kings in the Battle of Adoni in 1368 and King Mohammed Shah of Gujrat in fifteenth century have been recorded.

INDIAN ARMY STAFF

Strength

Indian Army statistics	
Active Troops	1,300,000
Reserve Troops	1,200,000
Territorial Army	200,000**
Main Battle Tanks	4,500
Artillery	12,800
Ballistic missiles	100 (Agni-1,Agni-2)
Ballistic missiles	>500 (Prithvi-1)
Cruise missiles	BrahMos
Aircraft	10 squadrons of helicopters
Surface-to-air missiles	90000

* includes 300,000 1st line troops and 500,000 2nd line troops

** includes 40,000 1st line troops and 160,000 2nd line troops

Statistics

- 4 RAPID (Reorganised Army Plains Infantry Divisions)
- 18 Infantry Divisions
- 10 Mountain Divisions
- 3 Armoured Divisions
- 2 Artillery Divisions
- 13 Air Defence Brigades + 2 Surface-to-Air Missile Groups
- 5 Independent Armoured Brigades
- 15 Independent Artillery Brigades
- 7 Independent Infantry Brigades
- 1 Parachute Brigade
- 4 Engineer Brigades
- 14 Army Aviation Helicopter Units

Sub-Units

- 63 Tank Regiments
- 7 Airborne Battalions
- 200 Artillery Regiments
- 360 Infantry Battalions + 5 Para (SF) Battalions
- 40 Mechanised Infantry Battalions
- 20 Combat Helicopter Units
- 52 Air Defence Regiments

Rank Structure

The various rank of the Indian Army are listed below in descending order:

Commissioned Officers

- Field Marshal[1]
- General (the rank held by Chief of Army Staff)
- Lieutenant-General
- Major-General
- Brigadier
- Colonel
- Lieutenant-Colonel
- Major
- Captain
- Lieutenant

Junior Commissioned Officers (JCOs)

- Subedar Major/Honorary Captain[3]
- Subedar/Honorary Lieutenant[3]
- Subedar Major
- Subedar
- Naib Subedar

Non Commissioned Officers (NCOs)

- Regimental Havildar Major[2]
- Regimental Quarter Master Havildar[2]
- Company Havildar Major
- Company Quarter Master Havildar
- Havildar
- Naik
- Lance Naik
- Sepoy

Note:

1. Only two officers have been made Field Marshall so far: Field Marshal K M Cariappa – the first Indian Commander-in-Chief (a post since abolished) – and Field Marshal S H F J Manekshaw, the Chief of Army Staff during the Army in the 1971 war with Pakistan.
2. This has now been discontinued. Non-Commissioned Officers in the rank of Havildar are elible for Honorary JCO ranks.
3. Given to Outstanding JCO's Rank and pay of a Lieutenant, role continues to be of a JCO.

Combat Doctrine

The current combat doctrine of the Indian Army is based on effectively utilizing holding formations and strike formations. In the case of an attack, the holding formations would contain the enemy and strike formations would counterattack to neutralize enemy forces.

In the case of an Indian attack, the holding formations would pin enemy forces down whilst the strike formations attack at a point of Indian choosing. The Indian Army is large enough to devote several corps to the strike role. Currently, the army is also looking at enhancing its special forces capabilities.

Equipment

Most of the army equipment is imported, but efforts are being made to manufacture indigenous equipment. All Indian Military Firearms guns are manufactured under the umbrella administration of the Ordnance Factory Board, with principal Firearm manufacturing facilities in Ishapore, Cossipore, Kanpur, Jabalpur and Tiruchirapalli. Indian National Small Arms System (INSAS) rifle, which is successfully inducted by Indian Army since 1997 is a product of Rifle Factory, Ishapore. While ammunition is manufactured at Khadki and possibly at Bolangir.

Aircraft

The Indian Army operates more than 200 helicopters, plus additional unmanned aerial vehicles.

Aircraft	Origin	Type	Versions	In service[45]	Notes
HAL Dhruv	India	utility helicopter		36+	To acquire 73 more Dhruv in next 5 years.
Aérospatiale SA 316 Alouette III	France	utility helicopter	SA 316B Chetak	60	to be replaced by Dhruv
Aérospatiale SA 315 Lama	France	utility helicopter	SA 315B Cheetah	48	to be replaced by Dhruv
DRDO Nishant	India	reconnaissance UAV		12	Delivered 12 UAV's in 2008.
IAI Searcher II	Israel	reconnaissance UAV		100+	
IAI Heron II	Israel	reconnaissance UAV		50+	

The Indian army had projected a requirement for a helicopter that can carry loads of up to 75 kg heights of 23,000 feet (7,000 m) on the Siachen Glacier in Jammu and Kashmir. Flying at these heights poses unique challenges due to the rarefied atmosphere. The Indian Army chose the Eurocopter AS 550 for a $550 million contract for 197 light helicopters to replace its ageing fleet of Chetaks and Cheetahs, some of which were inducted more than three decades ago. The deal has however been scrapped amidst allegations of corruption during the bidding process.

Future Developments

India is currently reorganising their mechanised forces to achieve strategic mobility and high-volume firepower for rapid thrusts into enemy territory.

India has plans to progressively induct as many as 1,657 Russian-origin T-90S main-battle tanks (MBTs), apart from the ongoing upgradation of its T-72 fleet. the Indian Army has gone in for an urgent order of 4,100 French-origin Milan-2T anti-tank guided missiles (ATGMs). Defence ministry sources said the Rs 592-crore (USD 120 million approx.) order for 4,100 Milan-2T missiles was cleared after 26/11, with the government finally fast-tracking several military procurement plans.

6

CONSEQUENCES OF THE WAR

INTRODUCTION

India continued to increase its defense spending after the war. The Indian Military, which was already undergoing rapid expansions, made improvements in command and control to address some shortcomings. Partly as a result of the inefficient information gathering preceding the war, India established the Research and Analysis Wing for external espionage and intelligence. India viewed the American policy during the war as biased, since Pakistan had started the war but the US did little to restrain Pakistan. After the war, India slowly started aligning with the Soviet Union, both politically and militarily. This would be cemented formally years later before the Indo-Pakistani War of 1971.

In light of the failures of the previous war against the Chinese, the performance in this war was viewed as a "politico-strategic" victory in India. The Indian premier, Shastri was hailed as a hero in India. However, India was criticized in some quarters for not being able to defeat the much smaller Pakistani military. In its October 1, 1965 issue TIME magazine quoted a Western ambassador as saying 'It used to be you could feed the word 'India' into the machine and it would spit out 'Maharajahs, snakes, too many babies, too many cows, spindly-legged Hindus.' Now it's apparent to everybody that India is going to emerge as an Asian power in its own right.'

Pakistan

At the conclusion of the war, many Pakistanis considered the performance of their military to be positive. September 6 is celebrated as 'Defence Day' in Pakistan, in commemoration of the successful defence of Lahore against the Indian army. The performance of the Pakistani Air Force, in particular, was praised.

The myth of a mobile, hard hitting Pakistan Army, however, was badly dented in the war, as critical breakthroughs were not made. Several Pakistani writers criticized the military's ill-founded belief that their "Martial Race" of soldiers could defeat India in the war. Moreover, Pakistan had lost more ground than it had gained during the war and, more importantly, failed to achieve its goal of occupying Kashmir; this result has been viewed by many impartial observers as a defeat for Pakistan.

Many high ranking Pakistani officials and military experts later criticized the faulty planning of Operation Gibraltar that ultimately led to the war. The Tashkent declaration was also criticized in Pakistan, though few citizens realised the gravity of the situation that existed at the end of the war.

Political leaders were also criticized. Following the advice of Zulfikar Ali Bhutto, Pakistan's foreign minister, Ayub Khan had raised very high expectations among the people of Pakistan about the superiority - if not invincibility - of its armed forces, but Pakistan's inability to attain its military aims during the war, created a political liability for Ayub. The defeat of its Kashmiri ambitions in the war led to the army's invincibility being challenged by an increasingly vocal opposition. And with the war creating a huge financial burden, Pakistan's economy, which had witnessed rapid progress in the early 60s, took a severe beating.

Pakistan was surprised by the lack of support by the United States, an ally with whom the country had signed an Agreement of Cooperation. USA declared its neutrality in the war by cutting off military supplies to both sides, leading Islamabad to believe that they were "betrayed" by the United States. After the war, Pakistan would increasingly look towards China as a major source of military hardware and political support.

INDIAN ARMY IN THE WAR OF 1965

The Indo-Pakistani War of 1965 was a culmination of skirmishes that took place between April 1965 and September 1965 between India and Pakistan. This conflict became known as the Second Kashmir War fought by India and Pakistan over the disputed region of Kashmir, the first having been fought in 1947. The war began following the failure of Pakistan's Operation Gibraltar, which was designed to infiltrate forces into Jammu and Kashmir to precipitate an insurgency against rule by India. The five-week war caused thousands of casualties on both sides. It ended in a United Nations (UN) mandated ceasefire and the subsequent issuance of the Tashkent Declaration.

Much of the war was fought by the countries' land forces in Kashmir and along the International Border between India and Pakistan. This war saw the largest amassing of troops in Kashmir since the Partition of India in 1947, a number that was overshadowed only during the 2001-2002 military standoff between India and Pakistan.

Most of the battles were fought by opposing infantry and armored units, with substantial backing from air forces. Many details of this war, like those of other Indo-Pakistani Wars, remain unclear and many media reports have been riddled with media biases.

PRE-WAR ESCALATION

Since Partition of India in 1947, Pakistan and India remained in contention over several issues. Although the Kashmir conflict was the predominant issue dividing the nations, other border disputes existed, most notably over the Rann of Kutch, a barren region in the Indian state of Gujarat. When Junagadh, a former princely state, had been integrated into India, whose muslim prince wanted to join Pakistan.

On March 20, 1965, and again in April 1965, fighting broke out between India and Pakistan in the Rann of Kutch. Initially involving border police from both nations, the disputed area soon witnessed intermittent skirmishes between the countries' armed forces.

In June 1965, British Prime Minister Harold Wilson successfully persuaded both countries to end hostilities and set up a tribunal to resolve the dispute. The verdict, which came later in 1968, saw Pakistan awarded 350 square miles (900 km^2) of the Rann of Kutch, as against its original claim of 3500 square miles.

After its success in the Rann of Kutch, Pakistan, under the leadership of General Ayub Khan, believed the Indian Army would be unable to defend itself against a quick military campaign in the disputed territory of Kashmir as the Indian military had suffered a loss to China in 1962.

Pakistan believed that the population of Kashmir was generally discontented with Indian rule and that a resistance movement could be ignited by a few infiltrating saboteurs. Pakistan attempted to ignite the resistance movement by means of a covert infiltration, codenamed Operation Gibraltar. The Pakistani infiltrators were soon discovered, however, their presence reported by local Kashmiris, and the operation ended in a complete failure.

Pakistan claimed to have been concerned by attempts of India to absorb Kashmir - a state claimed by Pakistan as "disputed", into the Indian Union. The basis for this claim was the application of Articles 356 and 357 of the Indian Constitution that allow the President of India to declare President's Rule in the State.

THE WAR

On August 15, 1965, Indian forces crossed the ceasefire line and launched an attack on the region referred to by the disputants as either "Azad Kashmir" or "Pakistan-occupied Kashmir". Pakistani reports cite this attack as unprovoked, while Indian reports cite the attack as a response to massive armed infiltrations of Kashmir by Pakistan.

Initially, the Indian Army met with considerable success, capturing three important mountain positions after a prolonged artillery barrage. By the end of August, however, both sides had experienced successes; Pakistan had made progress in areas such as Tithwal, Uri and Punch and India had captured the Haji Pir Pass, eight kilometers inside Pakistani-occuppied territory.

On September 1, 1965, Pakistan launched a counterattack, called "Operation Grand Slam", with the objective to capture the vital town of Akhnoor in Jammu, which would sever communications and cut off supply routes to Indian troops. Attacking with an overwhelming ratio of troops and technically superior tanks, Pakistan initially progressed against Indian forces, who were caught unprepared and suffered heavy losses. India responded by calling in its air force to blunt the Pakistani attack. The next day, Pakistan retaliated, its air force attacked Indian forces and air bases in both Kashmir and Punjab. Although Operation Grand Slam ultimately failed, as the Pakistan Army was unable to capture Akhnoor, it became one of the turning points in the war when India decided to relieve pressure on its troops in Kashmir by attacking Pakistan further south.

India crossed the International Border on the Western front on September 6, marking an official beginning of the war. On September 6, the 15th Infantry Division of the Indian Army, under World War II veteran Major General Prasad, battled a massive counterattack by Pakistan near the west bank of the Ichogil Canal (BRB Canal), which was a *de facto* border of India and Pakistan. The General's entourage itself was ambushed and he was forced to flee his vehicle. A second, this time successful, attempt to cross the Ichhogil Canal was made over the bridge in the village of Barki, just east of Lahore.

These developments brought the Indian Army within the range of Lahore International Airport. As a result, the United States requested a temporary ceasefire to allow it to evacuate its citizens in Lahore.However,the Pakistani counter attack took Khem Karan from Indian forces which tried to divert the attention of Pakistanis from Khem Karan by an attack on Bedian and the adjacent villages.As said by Indian Lt. General Kaul,

"The C-in-C(Indian) got cold feet and decided, while the battle of Khem Karan was still in progress to take up an alternate position, several miles in the rear which would have meant giving up some well known and vital places and areas." (Kaul op. Cit. P478)

The thrust against Lahore consisted of the 1st Infantry Division supported by the three. tank regiments of the 2nd

Independent Armoured Brigade: they quickly advanced across the border, reaching the Ichhogil (BRB) Canal by 6 September.

The Pakistani Army held the bridges over the canal or blew up those it could not hold, effectively stalling any further advance by the Indians on Lahore.One unit of the Jat Regiment, 3 Jat, had also crossed the Ichogil canal and captured the town of Batapore (Jallo Mur to Pakistan) on the west side of the canal. The same day, a counter offensive consisting of an armored division and infantry division supported by Pakistan Air Force Sabres forced the Indian 15th Division to withdraw to its starting point.

Although 3 Jat suffered minimal casualties, the bulk of the damage being taken by ammunition and stores vehicles, the higher commanders had no information of 3 Jat's capture of Batapore and misleading information led to the command to withdraw from Batapore and Dograi to Ghosal-Dial. This move brought extreme disappointment to Lt-Col Desmond Hayde, CO of 3 Jat. Dograi was eventually recaptured by 3 Jat on 21 September, for the second time but after a much harder battle due to Pakistani reinforcements.

On the days following September 9, both nations' premiere formations were routed in unequal battles. India's 1st Armored Division, labelled the "pride of the Indian Army", launched an offensive towards Sialkot.

The Division divided itself into two prongs, was forced back by the 6th armoured division(an understrength formation of few armoured regiments) at Chawinda and was forced to withdraw after suffering heavy losses of nearly 100 tanks. Similarly, Pakistan's pride, the 1st Armored Division, pushed an offensive towards Khemkaran, with the intent to capture Amritsar (a major city in Punjab, India) and the bridge on River Beas to Jalandhar.

The Pakistani 1st Armored Division never made it past Khem Karan, however, and by the end of September 10 lay disintegrated by the defences of the Indian 4th Mountain Division at what is now known as the Battle of *Asal Uttar* (lit. meaning - "Real Answer", or more appropriate English equivalent - "Fitting Response"). The area became known as 'Patton Nagar' (Patton Town) as Pakistan lost or abandoned nearly 100 mostly US-made Patton tanks.The Pakistani 1st Armoured Division less 5th Armoured Brigade was next sent to Sialkot sector behind Pakistani 6th Armoured Division where it didnt see action as 6th Armoured Division was already in process of routing Indian 1st Armoured Division which was superior to it in strength.

The war was heading for a stalemate, with both nations holding territory of the other. The Indian army suffered 3,000 battlefield deaths, while Pakistan suffered no less than 3,800. The Indian army was in possession of 710 mile^2 (1,840 km^2) of Pakistani territory and the Pakistan army held 210 mile^2 (545 km^2) of Indian territory. The territory occupied by India was mainly in the fertile Sialkot, Lahore and Kashmir sectors, while Pakistani land gains were primarily in deserts opposite Sindh and in Chumb, in the northern sector.

Aerial Warfare

The war saw the Indian Air Force and the Pakistani Air Force engaged in full scale combat for the first time since independence. Though the two forces had previously faced off in the First Kashmir War during the late 1940s, that engagement was limited in scale compared to the 1965 conflict.

The two countries have made contradictory claims of combat losses during the war and hardly any neutral sources have verified the claims of either country. The Pakistan Air Force (PAF) claimed it shot down 104 IAF planes, losing only

19 in the process. The Indian Air Force (IAF) claimed it shot down 24 PAF planes, losing only 75 itself.[18] India also pointed out that, despite PAF claims of losing only a squadron of combat craft, Pakistan sought to acquire additional aircraft from Indonesia, Iraq, Iran, Turkey and China within 10 days of the beginning war.

Pakistan's strike force comprised the U.S. made F-86 Sabre jets, which claimed a fair share of Indian planes, though remaining vulnerable to the diminutive Folland Gnat, nicknamed "Sabre Slayer".[19] The F-104 Starfighter of the PAF was by far the fastest fighter plane operating in the subcontinent at that time. Unlike the PAF, whose planes largely consisted of American craft, the IAF flew an assortment of planes, from Vampires to Hawker Hunters, many of which were outdated in comparison to PAF planes.

Tank Battles

The 1965 war witnessed some of the largest tank battles since World War II. At the beginning of the war, the Pakistani Army had both a numerical advantage in tanks, as well as better equipment overall. Pakistani armour was largely American-made; it consisted mainly of Patton M-47 and M-48 tanks, but also included many M4 Sherman tanks, some M24 Chaffee light tanks and M36 Jackson tank destroyers, equipped with 90 mm guns. The bulk of India's tank fleet were older M4 Sherman tanks; some were up-gunned with the French high velocity CN 75 50 guns and could hold their own, whilst some older models were still equipped with the inferior 75 mm M3 L/40 gun. Besides the M4 tanks, India fielded the British-made Centurion Tank Mk 7, with the 105 mm Royal Ordnance L7 gun, and the AMX-13, PT-76, and M3 Stuart light tanks. Pakistan fielded a greater number and more modern artillery; its guns out-ranged those of the Indian artillery, according to Pakistan's Major General T.H. Malik.

At the outbreak of war in 1965, Pakistan had about 15 armoured cavalry regiments, each with about 45 tanks in three squadrons. Besides the Pattons, there were about 200 M4 Shermans re-armed with 76mm guns, 150 M24 Chaffee light tank and a few independent squadrons of M36B1 tank destroyers. Most of these regiments served in Pakistan's two armoured divisions, the 1st and 6th Armoured divisions - the latter being in the process of formation. The Indian Army of the time possessed 17 cavalry regiments, and in the 1950s had begun modernizing them by the acquisition of 164 AMX-13 light tanks and 188 Centurions. The remainder of the cavalry units were equipped with M4 Shermans and a small number of M3A3 Stuart light tanks. India had only a single armoured division, the 1st 'Black Elephant' Armoured Division, also called 'Fakhr I Hind' ('Pride of India'), which consisted of the 17th cavalry Poona Horse, the 4th Hodson's Horse, the 16th 'Black Elephant' Cavalry, the 7th Light Cavalry, the 2nd Royal Lancers, the 18th Cavalry and the 62nd Cavalry, the two first named being equipped with Centurions,. There was also the 2nd Independent Armoured Brigade, one of whose three regiments, the 3rd Cavalry, was also equipped with Centurions.

Despite the qualitative and numerical superiority of Pakistani armour, Pakistan was outfought on the battlefield by India, which made progress into the Lahore-Sialkot sector, whilst halting Pakistan's counteroffensive on Amritsar they were sometimes employed in a faulty manner, such as charging prepared defenses during the defeat of Pakistan's 1st Armored Division at Assal Uttar.

India's tank formations experienced same results. India's attack at the Battle of Chawinda, led by its 1st Armored Division and supporting units, was brought to a grinding halt by newly raised 6th Armoured Division(ex-100th indepedant brigade group) in the Chawinda sector. The Pakistanis pushed the Indians back farther after the Battle of Chawinda with Operation Windup. One true winner to emerge was India's Centurion battle tank, with its 105 mm gun and heavy armor, which proved superior to the overly complex Pattons and their exaggerated reputations..However, in the Sialkot sector outnumbered Pattons performed exceedingly well in the hands of the 25th Cavalry and other regiments of the 6th Armoured Division, which exacted a disproportionately heavy toll of Centurions from the Poona Horse and Hodson's Horse. The Indian Army has made much of the fact that some of its Centurions survived repeated hits; yet have failed to point out that the majority of tanks in the Sialkot sector were Shermans whose guns were inadequate even in 1944. Neither the Indian nor Pakistani Army showed any great facility in the use of armoured formations in offensive operations, whether the Pakistani 1st Armoured Division at Asal Uttar or the Indian 1st Armoured Division at Chawinda. In contrast, both proved adept with smaller forces in a defensive role such a the 2nd Armoured Brigade at Asal Uttar and the 25th Cavalry at Chawinda, where they defeated their better equipped but clumsier foes

Naval Hostilities

The navies of India and Pakistan did not play a prominent role in the war of 1965, although Pakistani accounts dispute this. On September 7, a flotilla of the Pakistani Navy carried out a small scale bombardment of the Indian coastal town and radar station of Dwarka, which was 200 miles (300 km) south of the Pakistani port of Karachi. Codenamed Operation Dwarka, it did not fulfill its primary objective of disabling the radar station and there was no immediate retaliatory response from India. Later, some of the Indian fleet sailed from Bombay to Dwarka to patrol the area and deter further bombardment. Foreign authors have noted that the "insignificant bombardment" of the town was a "limited engagement, with no strategic value."

According to some Pakistani sources, one submarine, PNS Ghazi, kept the Indian Navy's aircraft carrier INS Vikrant besieged in Bombay throughout the war. Indian sources claim that it was not their intention to get into a naval conflict with Pakistan, and wished to restrict the war to a land-based conflict. Moreover, they note that the Vikrant was in dry dock in the process of refitting. Some Pakistani defence writers have also discounted claims that the Indian Navy was bottled up in Bombay by a single submarine, instead stating that 75% of the Indian Navy was under maintenance in harbour. There were, however, unconfirmed reports of underwater attacks near Bombay by the Indian Navy against what they suspected were American-supplied Pakistani submarines.

Covert Operations

The Pakistan Army launched a number of covert operations to infiltrate and sabotage Indian airbases.[30] On September 7, 1965, the Special Services Group (SSG) commandos were parachuted into enemy territory. According to Chief of Army Staff General Musa Khan, about 135 commandos were airdropped at three Indian airfields(Halwara, Pathankot and Adampur). The daring attempt proved to be an "unmitigated disaster". Only 22 commandos returned to Pakistan as planned, 93 were taken prisoner (including one of the Commanders of the operations, Major Khalid Butt), and 20 were killed in encounters with the army, police or civilians The reason for the failure of the commando mission is attributed to the failure to provide maps, proper briefings and adequate planning or preparation.

Despite failing to sabotage the airfields, Pakistan sources claim that the commando mission affected some planned Indian operations. As the Indian 14th Division was diverted to hunt for paratroopers, the Pakistan Air Force found the road filled with transport, and destroyed many vehicles.

India responded to the covert activity by announcing rewards for captured Pakistani spies or paratroopers. Meanwhile, in Pakistan, rumors spread that India had retaliated with its own covert operations, sending commandos deep into Pakistan territory, but these rumors were later determined to be unfounded.

Losses

India and Pakistan make widely divergent claims about the damage they inflicted on each other and the amount of damage suffered by them. The following summarizes each nation's claims.

There have been few neutral assessments of the damages of the war; some of the neutral assessments are mentioned below:-

- According to the United States Library of Congress Country Studies:

The war was militarily inconclusive; each side held prisoners and some territory belonging to the other. Losses were relatively heavy—on the Pakistani side, twenty aircraft, 200 tanks, and 3,800 troops. Pakistan's army had been able to withstand Indian pressure, but a continuation of the fighting would only have led to further losses and ultimate defeat for Pakistan. Most Pakistanis, schooled in the belief of their own martial prowess, refused to accept the possibility of their country's military defeat by "Hindu India" and were, instead, quick to blame their failure to attain their military aims on what they considered to be the ineptitude of Ayub Khan and his government.

- TIME magazine analyzing the conflict, reported that India held 690 Mi^2 of Pakistan territory while Pakistan held 250 Mi^2 of Indian territory in Kashmir and Rajasthan, Pakistan had lost almost half its armour temporarily. The same article stated that 'severely mauled by the larger Indian armed forces,. Pakistan could continue the fight only by teaming up with Red China and turning its back on the U.N'.

- An excerpt from Stanley Wolpert's *India* summarizing the Indo-Pakistani War of 1965, is as follows:

In three weeks the second IndoPak War ended in what appeared to be a draw when the embargo placed by Washington on U.S. ammunition and replacements for both armies forced cessation of conflict before either side won a clear victory. India, however, was in a position to inflict grave damage to, if not capture, Pakistan's capital of the Punjab when the cease-fire was called, and controlled Kashmir's strategic Uri-Poonch bulge, much to Ayub's chagrin.

- Dennis Kux's *"India and the United States estranged democracies"* also provides a summary of the war.

Although both sides lost heavily in men and materiel, and neither gained a decisive military advantage, India had the better of the war. New Delhi achieved its basic goal of thwarting Pakistan's attempt to seize Kashmir by force. Pakistan gained nothing from a conflict which it had instigated.

- Newsweek magazine, however, praised the Pakistani military's ablility to hold of the much larger Indian Army.

"By just the end of the week, in fact, it was clear that the Pakistanis were more than holding their own."

Ceasefire

On September 22, the United Nations Security Council unanimously passed a resolution that called for an unconditional ceasefire from both nations. The war ended the following day.

The Soviet Union, led by Premier Alexey Kosygin, hosted ceasefire negotiations in Tashkent (now in Uzbekistan), where Indian Prime Minister Lal Bahadur Shastri and Pakistani President Ayub Khan signed the Tashkent Agreement, agreeing to withdraw to pre-August lines no later than February 25, 1966.

The ceasefire was criticized by many Pakistanis who, relying on official reports and the controlled Pakistani press, believed that the leadership had surrendered military gains. The protests led to student riots. Pakistan State's reports had suggested that their military was performing admirably in the war - which they incorrectly blamed as being initiated by India - and thus the Tashkent Declaration was seen as having forfeited the gains. Some recent books written by Pakistani authors, including one by ex-ISI chief titled "The Myth of 1965 Victory", allegedly exposed Pakistani fabrications about the war, but all copies of the book were bought by Pakistan Army to prevent publication because the topic was "too sensitive".

India and Pakistan accused each other of ceasefire violations; India charged Pakistan with 585 violations in 34 days, while Pakistan countered with accusations of 450 incidents by India. In addition to the expected exchange of small arms and artillery fire, India reported that Pakistan utilized the ceasefire to capture the Indian village of Chananwalla in the Fazilka sector. This village was recaptured by Indian troops on 25 December. On October 10, a B-57 Canberra on loan to the PAF was damaged by 3 SA-2 missiles fired from the IAF base at Ambala A Pakistani Army Auster was shot down on 16 December, killing one Pakistani army captain and on 2 February 1967, an AOP was shot down by IAF Hunters.

The ceasefire remained in effect until the start of the Indo-Pakistani War of 1971.

Intelligence Failures

Strategic miscalculations by both India and Pakistan ensured that the war ended in a stalemate.

Indian Miscalculations

Indian military intelligence gave no warning of the impending Pakistan invasion. The Indian Army failed to recognize the presence of heavy Pakistani artillery and armaments in Chumb and suffered significant losses as a result.

The "Official History of the 1965 War", drafted by the Ministry of Defence of India in 1992, was a long suppressed document that revealed other miscalculations. According to the document, on September 22 when the Security Council was pressing for a ceasefire, the Indian Prime Minister asked commanding Gen.

Chaudhuri if India could possibly win the war, were he to delay accepting the ceasefire. The general replied that most of India's frontline ammunition had been used up and the Indian Army had suffered considerable tank losses. It was determined later that only 14% of India's frontline ammunition had been fired and India held twice the number of tanks as Pakistan. By this time, the Pakistani Army had used close to 80% of its ammunition.

Air Chief Marshal (retd) P.C. Lal, who was the Vice Chief of Air Staff during the conflict, points to the lack of coordination between the IAF and the Indian army. Neither side revealed its battle plans to the other. The battle plans drafted by the Ministry of Defence and General Chaudhari, did not specify a role for the Indian Air Force in the order of battle. This attitude of Gen. Chaudhari was referred to by ACM Lal as the "Supremo Syndrome", a patronizing attitude sometimes held by the Indian army towards the other branches of the Indian Military.

Pakistani Miscalculations

The Pakistani Army's failures started with the supposition that a generally discontented Kashmiri people, given the opportunity provided by the Pakistani advance, would revolt against their Indian rulers, bringing about a swift and decisive surrender of Kashmir. The Kashmiri people, however, did not revolt. Instead, the Indian Army was provided with enough information to learn of Operation Gibraltar and the fact that the Army was battling not insurgents, as they had initially supposed, but Pakistani Army regulars.

The Pakistani Army also failed to recognize that the Indian policy makers would order an attack on the southern sector in order to open a second theater of conflict. Pakistan was forced to dedicate troops to the southern sector to protect Sialkot and Lahore instead using them to support penetrating into Kashmir.

"Operation Grand Slam", which was launched by Pakistan to capture Akhnoor, a town north-east of Jammu and a key region for communications between Kashmir and the rest of India, was also a failure. Many Pakistani commentators criticized the Ayub Khan administration for being indecisive during Operation Grand Slam. These critics claim that the operation failed because Ayub Khan knew the importance of Akhnur to India (having called it India's "jugular vein") and did not want to capture it and drive the two nations into an all-out war. Despite progress being made in Akhnur, General Ayub Khan relieved the commanding Major General Akhtar Hussain Malik and replaced him with Gen. Yahya Khan. A 24-hour lull ensued the replacement, which allowed the Indian army to regroup in Akhnur and successfully oppose a lackluster attack headed by General Yahya Khan. "The enemy came to our rescue", asserted the Indian Chief of Staff of the Western Command. Later, Akhtar Hussain Malik criticized Ayub Khan for planning

Operation Gibraltar, which was doomed to fail, and for relieving him of his command at a crucial moment in the war. Malik threatened to expose the truth about the war and the army's failure, but later dropped the idea for fear of being banned.

Some authors have noted that Pakistan might have been emboldened by a war game - conducted in March 1965, at the Institute of Defence Analysis, USA. The exercise concluded that, in the event of a war with India, Pakistan would win. Other authors like Stephen Philip Cohen, have consistently commented that the Pakistan Army had "acquired an exaggerated view of the weakness of both India and the Indian military... the 1965 war was a shock".

Pakistani Air Marshal and Commander-in-Chief of PAF during the war, Nur Khan, later said that the Pakistan Army, and not India, should be blamed for starting the war. However propaganda in Pakistan about the war continued; the war was not rationally analyzed in Pakistan, with most of the blame being heaped on the leadership and little importance given to intelligence failures that persisted until the debacle of the 1971 war, when Pakistan suffered a decisive defeat at the hands of India, leading to the creation of Bangladesh.

Involvement of other Nations

The United States of America, which had previously supplied military equipment to India and Pakistan, imposed an embargo against further supplies to both countries once the war had started. The US was apprehensive that military equipment that it had provided to be used in a battle against communism, would instead be used by the countries to fight one another. The American embargo especially affected Pakistan since the majority of its equipment was provided by America. This would cause Pakistan to believe that it could not continue the war beyond September.

Following imposition of the American embargo, other NATO allies (including the UK) discontinued providing military equipment to the nations.

Both before and during the war, China had been a major military associate of Pakistan and had invariably admonished India, with whom it had fought a war in 1962. There were also reports of Chinese troop movements on the Indian border to support Pakistan. As such, India agreed to the UN mandate in order to avoid a war on both borders.

India's participation in the Non-Aligned Movement yielded little support from its members. Pakistan, however, gained assistance from countries of Asia with large Islamic populations, including Turkey, Iran and Indonesia. The USSR was more neutral than most other nations during the war and even invited both nations to talks that it would host in Tashkent

Another negative consequence of the war was the growing resentment against the Pakistani government in East Pakistan(present day Bangladesh), particularly for West Pakistan's obsession with Kashmir. Bengali leaders accused the central government of not providing adequate security for East Pakistan during the conflict, even though large sums of money were taken from the east to finance the war for Kashmir.

In fact, despite some Pakistan Air Force attacks being launched from bases in East Pakistan during the war, India did not retaliate in that sector, although East Pakistan was defended only by an understrenghted infantry division (14 Division), sixteen planes and no tanks.[88]

Sheikh Mujibur Rahman was critical of the disparity in military resources deployed in East and West Pakistan, calling for greater autonomy for East Pakistan, which ultimately led to the Bangladesh Liberation war and another war between India and Pakistan in 1971.

INDIAN ARMY IN THE WAR 1971

On the 3rd of December 1971, the Pakistani Air Force (PAF) struck a number of Indian airfields in northern India. By midnight, India was officially at war with Pakistan. Two weeks later, the war was over. The Indian Army had overrun erstwhile East Pakistan (Bangladesh) and taken 93,000 POWs. It was one of the swiftest military campaigns in recent history.

The Setting

The partition of the Indian Subcontinent in 1947 created two independent countries: India and Pakistan. India, which became independent on 15 August 1947, stood for a secular, equitable polity based on the universally accepted idea that all men are created equal and should be treated as such. Pakistan, which officially came into existence a day earlier, was based on the premise that Hindus and Muslims of the Subcontinent constitute two different nationalities and cannot co-exist. The Partition created two different countries with most Muslim majority areas of undivided India going to the newly created nation, Pakistan (Land of the Pure). Pakistan was originally made up of two distinct and geographically unconnected parts termed West and East Pakistan. West Pakistan was made up of a number of races including the Punjabis (the most numerous), Sindhis, Pathans, Balochis, Mohajirs (Muslim refugees from India) and others. East Pakistan, on the other hand, was much more homogeneous and had an overwhelming Bengali-speaking population.

The Roots of Discord

Although the Eastern wing of Pakistan was more populous than than the Western one, political power since independence rested with the Western elite. This caused considerable resentment in East Pakistan and a charismatic Bengali leader called, Sheikh Mujibur Rehman, most forcefully articulated that resentment by forming an opposition political party called the Awami League and demanding more autonomy for East Pakistan within the Pakistani Federation. In the Pakistani general elections held in 1970, the Sheikh's party won the majority of seats, securing a complete majority in East Pakistan. In all fairness, the Sheikh should have been Prime Minister of Pakistan, or at least the ruler of his province. But West Pakistan's ruling elite were so dismayed by the turn of events and by the Sheikh's demands for autonomy that instead of allowing him to rule East Pakistan, they put him in jail.

ORIGINS OF THE CRISIS

The dawn of 1971 saw a great human tragedy unfolding in erstwhile East Pakistan. Entire East Pakistan was in revolt. In the West, General Yahya Khan, who had appointed himself President in 1969, had given the job of pacifying East Pakistan to his junior, General Tikka Khan. The crackdown of 25 March 1971 ordered by Tikka Khan, left thousands of Bengalis dead and Sheikh Mujibur Rehman was arrested the next day. The same day, the Pakistani Army began airlifting two of its divisions plus a brigade strength formation to its Eastern Wing. Attempts to dis-arm Bengali troops were not entirely successful and within weeks of the 25 March massacres, many former Bengali officers and troops of the Pakistani Army had joined Bengali resistance fighters in different parts of East Pakistan.

The Pakistani Army conducted several crackdowns in different parts of Bangladesh, leading to massive loss of civilian life. The details of those horrific massacres, in which defenceless people were trapped and machine-gunned, is part of Bangladeshi history. Survivors compare it to the Nazi extermination of Jews. At the same time, the Pakistani Administration in Dhaka thought it could pacify the Bengali peasantry by appropriating the land of the Hindu population and gifting it to Muslims. While this did not impress the peasantry, it led to the exodus of more than 8 million refugees (more than half of them Hindus) to neighbouring India. West Bengal was the worst affected by the refugee problem and the Indian government was left holding the enormous burden. Repeated appeals by the Indian government failed to elicit any response from the international community and by April 1971, the then Indian Prime Minister, Mrs. Indira Gandhi, decided that the only solution lay in helping Bengali freedom fighters, especially the Mukti Bahini, to liberate East Pakistan, which had already been re-christened Bangladesh by its people.

Pakistan felt it could dissuade India from helping the Mukti Bahini by being provocative. The Pakistan Air Force (PAF) in East Pakistan took to attacking suspected Mukti Bahini camps located inside Indian territory in the state of West Bengal. In the Western and Northern sectors too occasional clashes, some of them quite bloody, took place.

Pakistan was suggesting that should India continue with its plans it should expect total war as in 1965. Only this time, the Pakistanis would concentrate their forces in the West and thereby aim at capturing as much as Indian territory as possible. The Indians, on the other hand, would be fighting a war on two fronts (while at the same time keeping a fearful eye on the Chinese borders). Given this scenario, the Pakistanis felt that India at best would be able to capture some territory in East Pakistan and lose quite a bit in the West. In the end, the Pakistanis knew that the Western powers would intervene to stop the war and what would matter is who had the most of the other's territory.

Confident that another war would be as much of a stalemate as the 1965 Conflict, the Pakistanis got increasingly bold and finally on 3 December 1971 reacted with a massive co-ordinated air strike on several Indian Air Force stations in the West. At midnight, the Indian Prime Minister Mrs. Indira Gandhi in a broadcast to the nation declared that India was at war with Pakistan. As her words came on in million of Indian homes across the Subcontinent, the men at the front were already engaged in bitter combat...

PAF Strikes

For all practical purposes, the war started at about 5:40 pm on 3 December when Pakistan Air Force (PAF) combat aircraft struck nine Indian airfields along the Western borders. The air strikes were followed by a massive attack on the strategic Chhamb sector in the north. In the East, it was the Indian Army which went on the offensive. By late that night, artillery shells were raining down all along the Western and Eastern borders. India and Pakistan were locked in a two-front war.

In the West, the Indian Army had very limited offensive aims and was relegated more to a holding role. The initiative lay with Pakistan. In this theatre, Pakistan had near parity with India in armour and artillery while India had more infantry divisions. Pakistan's most successful thrust was in Chhamb where the 23rd Pakistani Division (along with two additional infantry brigades, one extra armoured brigade and Corps artillery units) under the able leadership of Major General Iftikhar Khan completely overwhelmed the forward defensive positions of the Indian 10 Division commanded by Major General Jaswant Singh.

Chhamb village was taken and the Pakistanis threatened to advance towards Jammu, the summer capital of the state of Jammu & Kashmir. Heavy fighting continued in this sector for a week until the indecisiveness of the Indian Divisional commander forced the Indian Corps Commander to intervene personally and launch heavy attacks to push the Pakistanis back to a non-threatening position. The Pakistanis surprisingly failed to take advantage of their initial successes in this sector and actually depleted the forces available to their commander, who was killed on 10 December in a helicopter crash.

Acting in accordance with its strategy to grab as much territory in the West as possible, Pakistan also launched a major attack on Punch in the state of Jammu & Kashmir. This attack, unlike the one on Chhamb, was completely repulsed, although here the Indian Army was at a locational disadvantage since the Pakistanis controlled the heights around the town. Smaller attacks were launched by Pakistan in Punjab at Fazilka and Hussainiwala.

Here the forward Indian defences were breached but the Pakistani Army could not sustain its attacks. A more ambitious armoured thrust in the deserts of Rajasthan was similarly stopped in the famous Battle of Longewal. In all, it appeared that the Pakistani military high command could not make up its mind as to where it should deliver its main punch and kept pulling back until it was too late.

The Indian Army chief, General Sam Maneckshaw, had a completely different set of problems. His strategy had to take into account the Chinese, with whom the Indian Army had fought a full blown war only nine years earlier. The Chinese were now firm Pakistani allies and had been making threatening noises ever since India resolved to intervene in the East Pakistan issue. General Maneckshaw, despite the disappointment of his Corps and divisional commanders, had to hold back his Army in the West, keep a watchful eye on the long and difficult Chinese borders and, at the same time, ensure that his Eastern Army secured its objective of grabbing a good chunk of East Pakistani territory within 2 to 3 weeks. The Indian aim was to install a Bangladeshi interim government in East Pakistani territory before the cessation of hostilities. It was not all clear in the beginning whether things would work out quite the way as planned.

MODEST AIMS, AMBITIOUS ACTION

One of the less remarked upon aspects of the 1971 war was the varied character of the key men who planned and executed the operations. Best known was of course the flamboyant Indian Army Chief, General Sam Maneckshaw, a Parsee who had won the Military Cross in WW II. To the Indian public, it was General Maneckshaw with his twirled moustache, Gorkha cap and baton, who was the symbolic hero. Yet, there were below him, an equally varied and extra-ordinary set of men, who planned and executed their own battles. The Western Army was commanded by an Anglo-Indian Lt. Gen. K.P.Candeth and the Eastern Army, headquartered at Calcutta, by a Sikh, Lt. Gen. J.S.Aurora. General Aurora's a brilliant Chief of Staff was Major. Gen. J.F.R.Jacob, the scion of an old Jewish family of Calcutta. Together these men planned and executed the lightning operations of December 1971.

The 4th morning saw Indian forces and Mukti Bahini guerrillas ready for battle with the Pakistanis, who were by now well dug in and waiting for the Indian assault. The Indian forces easily outnumbered the Pakistanis by a ratio of about 2:1. However, according to conventional infantry wisdom, an attacking Army requires a three-is-to-one superiority in numbers to attack. India did not have that. Besides, the Pakistani Army commander in the East, General A.A.K.Niazi, was determined merely to delay the Indian advance. For, in this war, the real battle was against time. The longer it took the Indian to secure their limited objectives, the greater the probability of the United Nations intervening to stop the war and effect a stalemate. Pakistan was confident that a stalemate was all that the Indians could get. Towards this strategy, General Niazi, had fortified the towns and approaches to the East Pakistani heartland and had boasted before the war began that should hostilities begin, he would take the battle inside India.

The brief given by the Indian Army chief, General Maneckshaw, to the Eastern Command was very limited. The aim was to occupy only two areas of East Pakistan - Chittagong and Khulna - so that an interim Bangladeshi government could be established. The capture of the whole of East Pakistan was not even conceived. A major problem was the geography and terrain of East Pakistan. Three major rivers - the Brahmaputra, the Ganga and the Meghna - divided East Pakistan into four natural regions. Each of the rivers were major ones - all of them wider than any European river. Each sub-region was further divided into several pockets cut by smaller rivers and their tributaries. The idea that an attacking army could bridge these, fight the enemy and then take territory, all within a couple of weeks, was ludicrous.

Lt. General Aurora's Chief of Staff, Major General Jacob, however, did not entirely agree with the Indian Army top brass. "I think the aim of the government was to take as much territory as possible in East Pakistan so as to establish an Bangladeshi government in their own territory," he recalled in an interview with SAPRA INDIA. "Army Headquarters issued an operations instruction according to which our main objectives were to take Chittagong and Khulna ports, which were termed the entry ports. But we at Eastern Command felt differently. We felt that Dhaka was the geo-political centre of Bangladesh and therefore any campaign to be successful had to capture Dhaka."

The Eastern Command went ahead with its own plans, although Army Headquarters felt it was too ambitious and could not be achieved. Jacob's commander, Lt. Gen. Aurora, provided full support for his Army's own plans and allowed

Jacob to pull down troops kept in reserve for a possible attack by the Chinese. Some of these troops had to be brought into battle so hurriedly that the only way was to paradrop them. This was accomplished with the help of the IAF and soon soldiers geared to fight the Chinese in the high mountains found themselves in the tropical riverine areas of Tangail in East Pakistan.

"We realised that any campaign to be successful had to be swift. The United Nations was putting great pressure on us and also the Russians had indicated that they did not want to exercise their veto any more," Jacob explained. "Therefore any campaign had to be quick. We realised that Niazi (the Pakistani Army commander in East Pakistan) was going to fortify the towns and defend them in strength. We therefore decided not attack any towns but bypass them using subsidiary tracks to get to our objective: Dhaka."

The immense practical problem of moving thousands of troops and tonnes of equipment across rivers and marshes was accomplished largely due to the efforts of the Army Corps of Engineers, and with a lot of local help.

The IAF chipped in by using helicopters to lift entire battalions across larger rivers that could not be quickly bridged by the Engineers. In most places, the swiftly moving contingents quickly overcame enemy resistance and moved forward. The Pakistanis for the most part, were completely taken by surprise.

Within 6 days of the war, Indian troops were deep inside East Pakistani territory and moving fast. The Mukti Bahini section of the advancing forces played a crucial role in guiding the Indian Army through the treacherous riverine areas and providing critical intelligence. It is doubtful whether the Indian Army could have moved so fast and decisively without the help of the Bangladeshis. At any rate, by the seventh day of the war, the Pakistani Army High Command, headquartered in Rawalpindi, was in a complete panic.

Using Sea Power

The 1971 war was the first, and only, occasion when the Indian political leadership exhibited a proper understanding of the use of military power for achieving a clear national aim. In past conflicts, Indian leaders either had no clear aim in mind and were merely reacting to events or they were confused about how best to use the military power available to them. During the 1962 India-China war, for instance, the Indian government ordered the Indian Air Force to withdraw its fighter bomber squadrons from the north east and not to hit the invading Chinese.

IAF bombers could have changed the course of the 1962 war had it been allowed to hit the thin and tenuous Chinese logistics lines. Similarly, in the 1965 India-Pakistan conflict, the Navy was ordered to keep its ships in port and not engage in any offensive action against Pakistan. The Pakistani Navy was given a free hand and it managed to lob a few shells at one point in the Western Coast. The Indian Navy's chance to see some action came only in 1971 December.

Since East and West Pakistan were two separate geographical entities more than 1,600 miles apart, the only way Pakistani forces in East Pakistan could be sustained was through the sea. The Indian Prime Minister, Mrs. Indira Gandhi, decided that the Navy would be given the strategic task of denying both East and West Pakistan access to war supplies. The aim in short was a complete naval blockade of both parts of Pakistan. The bigger aim was of course to ensure that the conflict was not perpetuated beyond the time required to capture a chunk of East Pakistani territory.

The Indian Navy's best and biggest warship at that time was its sole aircraft carrier, INS Vikrant, a carefully preserved World War II vintage carrier built in Britain. Ideally, a task force centred around the Vikrant should have been used to block Karachi, which at that time was West Pakistan's sole deep water port. However, one of Vikrant's main boilers was out of operation and the ship could not maintain the kind of speed required for manoeuvring in a situation where the air threat would be considerable. It was decided that the Vikrant would be used to blockade the ports in East Pakistan, and destroy the riverine craft used by the Pakistanis there.

Vikrant in Action

The day war was declared, the Vikrant, which had been anchored off the northern-most tip of the Andaman & Nicobar chain of islands, moved towards the principal East Pakistani port, Chittagong. The Pakistanis, having learnt that Vikrant was positioned in the Bay of Bengal, despatched one of their submarines, PNS Ghazi, to the east. The Pakistani submarine thought it could sneak into Vizag harbour, the principal naval port in the Indian east coast. It was, however, detected and sunk before it could cause any damage. The Vikrant continued unhindered. Rear Admiral (retired) P.D.Sharma, who was then an aviator aboard the Vikrant, recalls what it was like:

"Fighter pilots practice for years and when they finally get an opportunity to see real action, it is thrilling - it is the moment one has been waiting for all one's life. And it was so for us aboard the Vikrant on 4th December 1971...

"The first sortie was mounted against Cox's Bazaar. Eight Sea Hawks went in led by the squadron commander. I was in the second sortie which attacked Chittagong. This was in the afternoon of the 4th because it took some time for the Vikrant to close in the range to Chittagong.

"We went in low level, pulled up and carried out repeated attacks on the airfield. In the first attack itself we inflicted considerable damage. We withdrew for the night and sailed towards the Mangla-Khulna area. Our next attacks were on those harbours. Then we came back to Chittagong. And by the time we were through with that area, especially Chittagong harbour, Chittagong airfield and the approaches to Chittagong, the scene was something to be seen. The place had been devastated. There were ships that had turned turtle, there were half-sunk ships by the quay side, the airfield was pockmarked with craters and no ship could even think of approaching the place."

THE ATTACK ON KARACHI

The most dramatic naval plan was drawn up by the Western Naval Command. It was decided that the main attack on Karachi harbour would be launched by tiny PT-15 missile boats instead of regular warships. There were several reasons for this decision. Regular ships without air cover would be vulnerable whereas the tiny missile boats would present difficult, fast-moving targets. Moreover, the Navy wanted to try out the missiles to see how effective they could be in real action, although this kind of use of missile boats, which were designed for coastal defence and not for long range offensive action of any kind, was highly unorthodox. At any rate, three missile boats were chosen for the mission and despatched in the dead of night from Bombay harbour.

Leading the missile boat squadron was Commodore (Retired) Babru Bahan Yadav:"The task given to us was not easy. Our ships were little more than boats and did not have the range to go all the way to Karachi on their own steam. So an oiler was placed about half-way to the target and we were able to refuel and carry on.

"As we neared their coast, we found some of their ships patrolling the area. The boat on my left was detailed to engage the contact. That boat was the first Indian warship to fire a missile in anger. Two missiles were fired and both were direct hits. It is interesting to recall that the radar contact which was on our screen slowly diminished and then suddenly disappeared. We were very jubilant at that time. Later, we found that this has been a Pakistani destroyer.

Very soon another ship was located right in front of my boat. We fired a couple of missiles as well but did not sink it. The boat on our right was ordered to attack the ship. It did so and managed to cripple it completely. We thought we had sunk it but later the Pakistanis claimed that the ship had been badly crippled and put out of action but not sunk. Anyway, as we continued, both the other boats could not keep up and had to turn back.

Only Nipat, the boat I was on, could proceed towards Karachi harbour. We pressed on and fired missiles on Karachi which hit the oil installations there. The attack took place just 1 minute before midnight and we could see the flames from the oil installations lighting up the sea. It looked like Diwali (Indian festival of lights and firecrackers)."

It took a few more days for Commodore Yadav's boat to return to harbour as they had to take evasive action and ran out of fuel. In the meanwhile, the Pakistanis who were hunting for the boat put out a message that an Indian vessel had been sunk. Nipat, the only boat not accounted for at that time, was presumed sunk. But Nipat returned, thanks to the ingenuity of its engineers who managed to take out pump oil and use it to run the engines.

The Indian Navy accomplished the task assigned to it within the first few days of the war. No enemy shipping could move in or out of its harbours. Merchant ships did not dare approach Karachi. Control of the seas around both wings of Pakistan was with the Indian Navy.

BATTLE OF LONGEWAL

An Audacious Plan

The Battle of Longewal, fought in the deserts of the Indian state of Rajasthan, merits inclusion in any account of the 1971 India-Pakistan war because of the sheer audacity of the Pakistani generals who had planned it. Had it succeeded, India would have lost thousands of kilometres of a vast expanse of desert. But there is a fine line between the daring and the foolhardy. Did Pakistani generals cross that dividing line?

The Rajasthan sector was rather thinly held by both the Indians and by the Pakistanis for the simple reason that the Thar desert is not conducive to vehicular movement. Unlike in North Africa where the desert surface is relatively hard and the coastal areas allow for easy movement of traffic, the loose shifting sands of the Thar cannot be crossed by wheeled vehicles and even tracked vehicles are liable to get bogged down.

The region also has very few dirt tracks and even fewer paved roads. On the Pakistani side, the principal town is Rahimiyar Khan which is also an important railway junction connecting prosperous Pakistani Punjab in the north with the barren province of Sindh and its capital, Karachi, in the south. On the Indian side, the four principal towns are Jaisalmir, Barmer, Bikaner and Jodhpur. The major portion of Indian forces in 1971 were concentrated near the border towns of Barmer and Jaisalmir, both of which are supported by a forward air force base. The original Indian plan was to attack Rahimiyar Khan from Jaisalmir with a view to cutting off the main railway artery in West Pakistan.

The Pakistani plan was no less ambitious and a surprise attack was launched along the Gabbar-Longewal axis. The main axis lay to the north, connecting the Indian town of Jaisalmir with the Pakistani town of Islamgarh and Rahimiyar Khan beyond it. The intruding Pakistani armoured column and accompanying towed artillery was spotted by an Indian patrol on 4th December after it had come 16 km into Indian territory. The first reports were dismissed, until the enemy took up position just 300 metres away from the isolated Indian Army company located at Longewal.

The unit had no anti-tank weapons or mines. The Pakistanis could have overrun the post within hours. But the Indian company commander, Major Kuldip Singh Chandpuri, showed presence of mind by bringing in the company's recoilless guns and heavy machine guns and directing concentrated and sustained fire at the enemy positions. The Pakistanis were taken aback by the extent of the fire and felt that the Indians must have a much larger force at Longewal than reported by their Intelligence. Instead of storming the post and carrying on to Jaisalmir as was the plan, the Pakistanis encircled the post and decided to set up their artillery to soften it up before attacking.

By this time, the GOC of 12 Indian Infantry Division based at Tanot north of Jaisalmir was fully in the picture and realised that the Pakistanis had launched a full-scale armoured thrust to take Jaisalmir by outflanking 12 Division's main forces concentrated in the Tanot-Kishengarh area. Later it was discovered that the commanding officer of 18 Pakistani Army Division had planned to breakfast at Ramgarh and have dinner at Jaisalmir before proceeding on to Jodhpur. In complete contrast to the Pakistani divisional commander's audacity was over-cautiousness of the Indian generals. Confronted by the surprise attack, both the Indian divisional commander and his senior in charge of Southern Command dithered. They neither continued with their planned attack on Rahimiyar Khan nor did they send a large enough force to engage the Pakistani intruders. The job of relieving pressure on the beleaguered Indian company was left to the Indian Air Force.

The IAF at that time had only two oldish Hawker Hunter aircraft positioned at Jaisalmir and that too mainly for reconnaissance purposes. Among the two pilots posted there was Squadron Leader R.N.Bali:"It was on the 4/5th night that we learnt of a change in plans and that we had to take on the enemy tank thrust at Longewal. It was sometime after midnight when we received our orders and it took 2 to 3 hours to change the role of our aircraft from air defence to ground attack. But we had to wait till first light to launch our mission...

"We saw enemy tanks strewn around in an area in a radius of more than 30 kilometres since the enemy tanks had started taking evasive action. We had to split our basic two-level missions into one level so that each aircraft could go in turn by turn. We were lucky in the sense that there was no enemy air opposition in the first phase and we could afford to put in more time over the target and see what we were destroying."

Squadron Leader Bali and his colleague flew sortie after sortie all through 5th December and completely broke up the enemy formation. The second contingent of Pakistani armour following the spearhead too got bogged down and was shot up. On 6 December, the two Hunters were joined by another two Hunters and the air to ground battle continued. By 7 December the Pakistani column was in full retreat and the PAF had started flying sorties to cover them. The Indian Army should have pursued and destroyed the enemy force but it failed to do so because of the lack of initiative of the Indian generals.

But the Hunters had done their job well. Of the 54 or so Pakistani T-59 and Sherman tanks that had come in, as many as forty were destroyed or abandoned. Another 138 vehicles of all types were destroyed along with 5 field guns and three anti-aircraft guns. The desert around Longewal was a smouldering graveyard of tanks and vehicles. The Pakistanis replaced the commander of their 18 Division based at Rahimiyar Khan, well before the retreat probably because it was clear that he had not considered co-ordinating air support or even arranging for adequate air defence guns before launching his attack. The pity is that the Indian generals in that sector too failed to take advantage of the rout and in the end started the campaign far too late. 12 Division ultimately managed only to advance cautiously to the town of Islamgarh. In contrast, 11 Indian Army Division, operating from near Barmer about 240 km away towards the south, did a much better job and continued its advance across difficult terrain, which required the laying of duckboard before tanks or vehicles could advance. 11 Division was active throughout the war despite enemy air action, stiff enemy opposition and lack of water. At the cessation of hostilities, 11 Division was poised to take the town of Naya Chor about 50 kilometres inside Pakistan.

The lessons of Longewal are clear: success in any endeavour requires balancing caution with courage. The Indian commander in the Jaisalmir sector lost out because he was too cautious while his Pakistani counterpart lost his job because he threw caution to the desert winds. And war can at times be brutally unforgiving..

The scene of action was in the eastern sector, a few minutes flying time away from Calcutta, the largest Indian metropolis in the east. The provocation was the repeated intrusion by groups of PAF F-86 Sabres into a salient inside Indian territory. This salient called Boyra was being used by Bangladeshi Mukti Bahini guerrillas to launch attacks inside East Pakistan. The Pakistani Army in the east had reacted angrily by launching a full scale attack in that sector but had had to beat a retreat after losing 13 tanks and many men. The job of messing up the Mukti Bahini was given to the PAF Sabres which began crossing into Indian territory, strafing the area and slipping back into Pakistani air space. The IAF had to get them while they were in Indian air space. The window was small: barely a couple of minutes wide, and the PAF fighters had to be intercepted over a 3 km wide corridor surrounded on three sides by Pakistani territory.

Four IAF Gnats were ordered to scramble at about 2:49 on 22 November afternoon to take on four Sabres strafing the Indian salient. The Gnats got three Sabres. The IAF formation leader, Flight Lieutenant R. Massey; Flight Lieutenant M. A. Ganapathy and Flying Officer D.Lazarus each got one Sabre. One Sabre crashed into a pond in Chaugacha on the East Pakistani side of the border, while the other two went down over Indian territory.

Flt. Lt. Parvez Mehdi Qureshi and Fg Offr Khalil Ahmed, the two PAF pilots who ejected over India were captured and produced before a crowded press conference the next day. The action was splashed in newspaper front pages all over the country and the three pilots who scored hits became national heroes overnight. This encounter set the tone of the air battles that were to follow. News of the incident and the famous gun camera shots were splashed across newspaper headlines the world over and the tiny Gnat acquired a reputation of being the Sabre killer. Conversations picked up in the air suggested that PAF fighters were instructed not to engage with Gnats, although this small aircraft could easily be out flown by Sabres and Starfighters. The PAf also subsequently withdrew some its aircraft from East Pakistan leaving a sole squadron of Sabres to grapple with the eleven IAF squadrons positioned in the east.

Protecting the Skies

A major reason for India's rapid successes in the 1971 conflict was the excellent co-ordination effected between the Indian Air Force (IAF) and the Army. Air Chief Marshal P.C.Lal, the IAF's low profile chief, appreciated that the IAF's primary role would be to fly in support of the Army. Achieving complete air superiority was not the primary aim, especially on the western front where the Pakistani Air Force (PAF) had massed its squadrons, leaving only one squadron of F-86 Sabres for the defence of the east.

The Indians had more aircraft but most of them were generally much older than the aircraft in the PAF's inventory. The IAF's pride and the most advanced aircraft of the time was the MiG-21. But the MiG-21 required long runways not always available in many of the frontline air bases and required expert handling. The IAF's primary interceptor continued to be the Folland Gnat, a tiny but highly maneuverable aircraft that had been passed over by its British manufacturers. The Gnats flew the highest number of sorties during the war. The IAF's primary ground attack aircraft were the old British built Hunters, the positively ancient Canberras and the spanking new Sukhoi-7s (acquired in 1968). The IAF also operated the indigenous Marut HF-24 fighters, which were somewhat under powered and difficult to manoeuvre, and a number of other obsolete types including the Harvard IIR's, the Vampires and Mysteres.

The PAF's mainstay was the F-86F Sabre, which was in service with many NATO countries although it belonged to a line that had been in production since the time of the Korean War. The Sabre was an excellent aircraft and had been substantially modified over the years to keep up with evolving Soviet combat aircraft. In 1971, the PAF Sabres included the ones upgraded to '40s' standards and newer Mk.6s from Canada. Pakistan also had the F-104 Starfighter, touted as the most sophisticated aircraft of the day. The rest of PAF's inventory was made up of Mirage-IIIs, newer Chinese variants of the MiG-19 (F-6s) and American B-57 bombers. A few IAF pilots had flown Sabres in the United States and knew the fine handling properties of their enemy's main combat fighter. The Indians rated the Mirage-III as the best PAF fighter but that aircraft was not seen as much as it was hoped. The IAF, despite its superiority in numbers, knew it would be a tough fight but was fully prepared for a no-holds barred contest.

Air Superiority in the East

The IAF's strength in the east was made up of 4 squadrons of Hunters, one of Su-7s, 3 of Gnats and 3 of the newer MiG-21s. The IAF also was prepared to hit any Chinese incursions into Indian territory in the eastern Himalayas. As it turned out, the Chinese did not stir and the IAF managed to knock out the PAF squadron within 2 days of the outbreak of war.

The IAF had gone into action within hours of Pakistan's pre-emptive strikes of 3/4 December 1971. Counter air sorties in the east were so successful that the PAF was neutralized within hours of the outbreak of war. In their first raid on the 4th of December a four ship formation of MiG-21FLs from the No.28 Squadron took out the runways at Tezgaon air base near Dhaka. Three Sabers attempting to intercept the MiGs were taken out by a combination of cannon fire and K-13 missiles. For the remainder of the war, round the clock attacks on the Kurmitola and Tezgaon air bases kept them, and the PAF non-operational.

Meanwhile, later that day Hunters from No.14 Squadron struck Chittagong Harbour as a prelude to strikes from the carrier INS Vikrant. The Hunters were to continue flying interdiction missions for the remainder of the war in, shooting up ammunition dumps and other fixed installations. Gnats and Sukhoi Su-7s flew many missions in support of army units as they moved swiftly towards Dhaka, delivering ordnance such as iron bombs to take out enemy bunkers which occasionally posed an obstacle to advancing infantry.

Canberras repeatedly struck Jessore forcing the enemy to abandon this strategic city. On the 11th of December three converted An-12s from the No.44 Squadron struck the Jaydebpur Ordnance factory in East Pakistan. Once Kurmitola and Tezgaon were put out of action the IAF had gained complete air superiority over East Pakistan.

The story of the old Caribou transporters speaks a lot about the mood of the times. Two of these old Canadian transporters were posted at Hashimara during the war and were used during the Tangail air drop and for minor missions. The Caribou air crew were getting restless.

They wanted a piece of the action. Finally, Eastern Air Command agreed by allowing them to bomb Dhaka by night. The PAF had been knocked out by then but the Pakistanis still had plenty of Chinese made multi-barrel anti-aircraft guns, which could be pretty devastating.

The Caribous were fitted with old World War II bombs and told to circle Dhaka for as long as they could during the night. While the pilots droned over Dhaka along with the occasional AN-12 keeping the Pakistanis awake, an airman aboard the Caribou once in a while pushed out a bomb from the open back. None of the bombs caused significant damage but they kept the Pakistani generals getting much sleep. After the surrender, one Pakistani general was to angrily remark about the damned aircraft which did not allow any of them to sleep for a week or more.

The Western Air Situation

Pakistani military analysts writing after the War tried to make out that the Pakistani Air Force (PAF) was heavily outnumbered even in the West. One writer claims that Pakistan had just 10 squadrons against 44 fielded by India. Such absurd assertions notwithstanding, fact is in 1971 the Indian Air Force (IAF) had a total of about 34 effective combat squadrons plus three under strength Canberra bomber squadrons and one AN-12 transporter squadron, which as it turned out played a remarkable role as modified bombers during the War. Of these Indian squadrons, ten were in the East (plus one Canberra squadron) and four were kept as reserves for protecting the inner cities. This meant the IAf had about 20 front-line combat squadrons in the West. Some of the front-line Indian squadrons were broken up and posted at different stations. This could be one reason for confusion on the Pakistani air intelligence side - and considerable exaggeration.

The Pakistanis, according to the IISS (International Institute of Strategic Studies) Military Balance 1971, had 19 squadrons including two B-57B light bomber and one recce squadron. According to our studies, the Pakistanis had about 14 effective combat squadrons in the West excluding the B-57B bombers and recce aircraft. However, PAF squadrons tended to have more aircraft per squadron than the IAF. This was further bolstered by the acquisition of an unspecified number of F-86 Sabres, Mirage IIIs, Starfighters (from Jordan) and about 15 Chinese F-6s in the months prior to the war.

These aircraft were not accounted for the IISS in its 1971 Military balance or in any other report. Also, the serviceability of PAF Sabres was much higher - meaning more aircraft could be fielded. The Indians had 16 aircraft per combat squadron but the effective availability during the war was 12 per squadron. Bomber and transporter squadron had 10 aircraft each of which about 6 to 8 were serviceable at any given time. Many PAF squadrons, in contrast, had as many as 25 aircraft. Thus, while the PAf was outnumbered in the West, at no point was it ever fighting against overwhelming odds.

More important, the PAF on the whole was far better equipped to fight a modern air war than the IAF. The Pakistanis, for instance, had very effective air-to-air missiles which the Indians lacked. American made Sidewinder missiles were fitted on Chinese-made F-6 aircraft, on Sabres and on Starfighters. These were accurate missiles and accounted for at least three kills by PAF fighters in air-to-air combat. The Indians had only their guns and cannons to rely on. The Soviet-made MiG-21 was the only aircraft in the IAF's inventory fitted with missiles. But the missiles - the infamous K-13 - were a poor copy of the American Sidewinders and were so useless that they were scrapped after the war.

The other major advantage, and a critical one, the Pakistanis had was their radar and communication system built by the Americans. In most parts, particularly Punjab, the PAF had a real time radar surveillance system, the ability to track low flying aircraft coming over Pakistan and the means to guide their aircraft right to intruding enemy aircraft. India had nothing in comparison. Instead of low level radar, the IAF had to rely on men posted near the borders.

Every time a suspected enemy aircraft flew over, the observation post had to call in on their high frequency radio sets to warn the sector controllers. Even the medium and high level radar cover available to the IAF was poor with the result that each forward base had to earmark between one to two combat squadrons just for air defence. It was a primitive and wasteful system - and the Pakistanis knew it. The technologically inferior but numerically superior Indian Air Force could be tackled quite easily by a smaller but more modern force. This is what prompted the PAF to launch pre-emptive strikes against forward Indian air bases on 3 December 1971.

IAF Counter Strike

Within 30 minutes of the Pakistani President General Yahya Yahya Khan's declaration of war against India at 1630 hours on 3rd December 1971, Pakistani fighter bombers struck five Indian airfields - Srinagar, Avantipur, Pathankot, Amritsar and the advanced landing ground at Faridkot. More strikes by PAF B-57 bombers followed at night against Ambala, Agra, Halwara, Amritsar, Pathankot, Srinagar, Sirsa, Adampur, Nal, Jodhpur and Jamnagar. Not a single aircraft was destroyed in these raids and runways damaged were repaired within a matter of hours.

The IAF's counter strike in the west was mounted on much greater scale than in the east. Within hours of the first PAF strike, converted An-12s from No.44 Squadron (led by Wg Cmdr Vashist) struck ammunition dumps in the Changa Manga forests. In one of the first counter air sorties of the war, Sukhois from No.222 Squadron struck Risalwala air field, while aircraft from the No.101 attacked Pasrur.

The No.101 was to later become involved in providing support to the 10 Infantry Division in the Sialkot Sector,. eventually destroying over 60 enemy tanks. Keamri oil installations near Karachi harbour were struck twice on the 4th by a three ship Hunter formations. And No.27 Squadron's Hunters continuously strafed enemy positions around Poonch and Chhamb. The four antiquated Harvard/Texans of the IAF also joined in ground support missions, their slow speed being particularly useful in hitting enemy gun emplacements in the valleys and gorges of Kashmir. Three counter air strikes were mounted on the 4th by Hunters of No.20 Squadron against

PAF airfields at Peshawar, Chaklala and Kohat. The raids left 8 aircraft destroyed on the ground, including at least 1 Mirage III. Maruts from No.10 Squadron were heavily involved in counter air operations, hitting targets upto 200 miles inside Pakistani territory.

The second day of the war began with a Canberra strike against Masroor air base and other strategic installations around Karachi. A force of eight Canberras flying lo-lo over the Arabian sea set strategic and military installations around Karachi alight. A similar raid was mounted on the 6th. The success of these missions being confirmed by Photo Recon. Canberras reporting "the biggest blaze ever seen over South Asia".

On the 5th , one four-ship formation from No.20 struck Chaklala for a second time in as many days destroying a C-130 and an Twin Otter on the ground. A second four-ship formation went for radar installation around Lahore and Walton. And a third raid by No.20 was mounted against the radar site at Sakesar, unfortunately two Hunters were lost during this mission. Later that day Maruts from the Nos. 10 and 220 Squadrons, and their MiG escorts moved against rail heads at Sundra, Rohri and Mirpur Khas. Between the 5th and the 12th , two Sukhoi squadrons flying form Halwara and Adampur repeatedly struck railway marshalling yards around Lahore.

One of the most celebrated actions of the 5th and 6th December is contribution of four Hunters from the ATW in the defeat of a Pakistani armoured force at Longewala. A previous section covers this in great detail. The AN-12s were also quite busy on the 6th. A bombing raid by the AN-12s early in the day destroyed a Pakistani brigade in the Haji Pir salient. Later that day HQ 18 (Pakistan) Division at Fort Abbas was bombed, as were areas around Bhawalpur.

The 7th of December got off to a rather bizarre start; a Marut from the No.220 Squadron, on its way back from a bombing raid against Rohri, actually engaged and brought down with cannon fire an F-86 sent up to intercept it. Surprisingly no Maruts were ever lost to enemy aircraft, although four were downed by ground fire. Two days later an enemy Shenyang F-6 was to be brought down by a ground attack aircraft - this time a Su-7 from No.32 Squadron. Between the 7th and the 12th, Sukhoi and Mystere Squadrons were engaged in support of I and XI Corps in the Fazilka-Ferozepur sector. The Indian Army's efforts in the Fazilka area were also assisted by bombing raids by No.44 Squadron's AN-12s. A four-ship formation flying at 180 ft above sea level struck Pakistani installations across from Fazilka on the 9th. As fighting in the west intensified, the Pakistanis launched an offensive against Poonch on the 10th. To break up this offensive Canberras dropped 28,000 lbs. of ordnance on the enemy. On the 11th, in even larger interdiction sorties the Canberras delivered 36,000 lbs. of ordnance against enemy emplacements and tank farms. Despite the damage, the Canberras inflicted on the enemy, four of the force were lost to ground fire.

The war in 1971 revealed the true air-ait combat capabilities of the MiG-21, altering perceptions held about it as an outcome of its disappointing performance in the Arab-Israeli war of 1967. The MiGs on both fronts had ample opportunity to engage the enemy in aerial combat.

The five squadrons that served on the western front conducted frequent armed reconnaissance missions deep into enemy territory to lure out PAF fighters. All Su-7 and Marut raids were given MiG-21 cover. Unfortunately for the Indian pilots who flew in the northern sector (Western Air Command) there was little by way of aerial engagements. On the 11th a Gnat of the No.23 Squadron engaged and severely damaged a Mirage over Pathankot. Those who flew with the South Western Air Command were luckier. On the 12th a Jordanian

F-104A Starfighter, on loan to the PAF was shot down by cannon fire by a MiG-21FL of No.47 Squadron flying from Jamnagar.

A Marut strike against Naya Chor on the 16th was intercepted by three PAF Shenyang F-6s. In the ensuing dogfight one of the F-6's was brought down by cannon fire from one of the two MiG escorts from the No.29 Squadron. No Indian aircraft were lost in the engagement and the Maruts were able to hit their targets. The following morning a low flying Starfighter was destroyed by a MiG-21 scrambled from Utterlai. A few hours later MiG-21 escorts of a Marut mission near Umarkot destroyed a pair of Starfighters. While the hi performance MiGs were shooting down enemy fighters, the lumbering Antonovs were contributing more than their share to victory in the West. The Rohri railway yards which had remained under attack from day one of the war were hit by a pair of An-12s at dusk on the 13th. The following day the Antonovs delivered their coup-de-main against the enemy's fighting capabilities. On the evening of the 14th a three-ship formation of the Antonovs flying from Jodhpur struck the Sui Gas Plant. The damage caused by these aircraft was so extensive that it took six months to restore gas production at Sui to even 50% of capacity. Happily all three aircraft taking part in the mission were recovered safely, landing at Utterlai. Sadly however, that very night, Fg Offr N.S.Sekhon of the No.18 Squadron lost his life as he gallantly engaged 6 enemy Sabres over Srinagar by himself. Before being shot down Sekhon's Gnat managed to score hits on two of the enemy for which he was awarded the Param Vir Chakra posthumously.

The An-12s flew in the bombing role for the last time on the 17th. A mixed formation of Canberras and Antonovs commanded by Vashist sortied against Skardu air field in Pakistani occupied Kashmir. Of the thirty six bombs dropped on the runway by the Antonovs, twenty eight hit the target while two fell within yards of it (this was confirmed by a PR sortie later the same day). On the way back, Vashist's aircraft was chased by two Mirages. In order to evade them he climbed down into a valley and kept circling for twenty minutes until the Mirages gave up and left.

The most astonishing thing about the An-12 bombing raids is that none of the eleven (ten bombers and one flying command post) converted aircraft were lost, although many were peppered by ack ack. The ease with which these rather slow aircraft could strike deep into enemy territory is testimony to the ineffectiveness of the Pakistani Air Force during the winter of 1971. Only the absence of modern weapons delivery systems for its air-to-surface weapons prevented the Indian Air Force from causing more damage than it did.

Who Won the Air War?

One of the last enduring debates on the 1971 War is the outcome of the air war. Both sides continue to claim that it won the air war. This debate continues because victory in the air is more difficult to quantify than victory on land or sea. In the land and sea wars, India emerged as the clear victor both in terms of objectives attained and losses/gains versus the enemy. In the air war, even estimates of losses on both sides are widely divergent.

Immediately after the war, the official Indian Government figures given out were 86 Pakistan Air Force (PAF) aircraft destroyed as against 42 Indian Air Force (IAF) lost. The Pakistanis later claimed that they had actually won the air war by destroying over a 100 Indian aircraft while losing only 36 of their own. The truth, as usual, is somewhere in between.

Unlike in 1965, the Indian Air Force in 1971 handled claims of aerial victories by its pilots with great maturity. No "kills" were awarded until all claims could be verified, preferably by photo reconnaissance missions. Almost immediately after the War was over, the Air Chief asked the Halwara station commander, Air Marshal C.V.Gole, to visit every IAF station in the West to ascertain the performance of various squadrons. "Later, we had access to other information as well and we worked out a pretty accurate picture of losses on both sides", he explains. But discrepancies could well remain.

For instance, Gole recalls that one SAM battery had fired missiles at a couple of attacking Pakistani B-57 bombers. One was hit and streaming smoke. A few hours later, some villagers called to say that they had found the debris of the Pakistani aircraft.

On investigation it was found that what remained was not the debris of an aircraft but that of a missile. The hit was not taken into account. It was only much after the war that some Pakistani report spoke about a B-57 pilot who had become "Shaheed" after he tried to bail out his burning aircraft but could not make it.

Pakistani claims of their own losses are less than reliable. The main cause of this confusion has to do with various "Official" histories of the PAF quoting different figures. It has been estimated by some observers, based on signal intercepts from the PAF, that the PAF lost at least seventy-two aircraft (including at least fifty-five combat types). Pakistan itself admits to the loss of twenty-nine combat aircraft on the ground. Only 16 were claimed to have been shot down over India. Add to this the 13 Sabres destroyed by the PAF itself at Dhaka. Even then the figure comes to 58. However, a lot of this is inaccurate.

After almost a year's of research, we at SAPRA INDIA believe that the losses of combat aircraft on both sides were as follows:

Combat Aircraft Losses

Description	Pakistan	India
Air to Air	19	19
Ground Fire	15	35
On Ground	29	2
Total	63	56

* Combat aircraft and bomber losses only. Transporters and Recce PAF aircraft shot down or destroyed on the ground not included.

** PAF losses include 13 aircraft destroyed by PAF on the ground at Dhaka.

The PAF lost many more aircraft on the ground not only because the Indians launched many more counter air operations than the Pakistanis but also because the PAF itself destroyed 13 of its Sabres in Dhaka within a few days of the war. PAF's No. 14 squadron with about 18 aircraft felt it had been abandoned by its higher command and left to face the onslaught of ten full Indian squadrons. After a couple of gallant actions by Pakistani pilots, the PAF commanders in East Pakistan appear to have decided that the game was not worth the effort. The last aerial engagement in East Pakistan took place on 4 December.

Even if the Pakistani claim that the Indians lost more aircraft is accepted, does it suggest that the Pakistanis won the air war? The answer is a clear no. Because war, in the ultimate analysis, is not a numbers game. Winning a war has to do with achieving clear objectives. For the IAF, the aim was twofold: first, to prevent the PAF from messing with the Indian Army's advances, logistics and launching points; and second, to seriously impair Pakistan's capacity to wage war. The PAF's job was to do the opposite. The pre-emptive air strikes on 3rd December were aimed at knocking out a good part of the IAF while it was on the ground. This failed for the simple reason that the

Indians had learnt their lessons of the 1965 war and had constructed fortified pens and bunkers to store their aircraft. More important, young IAF fliers proved they had the grit to go out and fight, even if it meant losing one's life.

By the end of the first week of the war, PAF fighters in the West appeared to have lost their will to fight. By this time, the IAF was repeatedly hitting secondary targets including railway yards, cantonments, bridges and other installations as well as providing close air support to the Army wherever it was required. The most dangerous were the close air support missions which involved flying low and exposing aircraft to intense ground fire. The IAF lost the most aircraft on these missions as is proved by the high losses suffered by IAF Sukhoi-7 and Hunter squadrons. But their pilots flew sortie after sortie keeping up with the Army and disrupting enemy troop and tank concentrations.

Once it was known that the Indian Army was knocking at the gates of Dhaka, the PAF in the West virtually gave up flying. During the last few days of the war, the IAF brass ordered attacks on PAF airfields with the sole purpose of drawing out their aircraft. But that rarely succeeded as the PAF aircraft for the most part remained secured inside their pens, refusing to come out and fight. The strongest indictment of the Pakistani Air Force was made not by an Indian but by the Pakistani leader, Zulfiqar Ali Bhutto, who took over from General Yahya Yahya Khan after the 1971 defeat. On taking over, he made a speech in which he castigated the PAF chief Air Marshal Rahim Khan and several other officers by name.

A better analysis of effectiveness of the two air forces is provided by the losses per sortie figure. The IAF flew at least double the number of combat sorties per day than the PAF, thereby exposing itself to ground fire and enemy interdiction Despite this, the IAF's attrition rate of 0.86 per 100 sorties during the 1971 War compares favourably with the Israeli rate of 1.1 in the Yom Kippur War. The PAF's overall attrition rate works out to 2.47 (including transporters and recce aircraft lost on the ground). If aircraft destroyed on the ground are not taken into account, the rate works out to 1.12, which is still very high given that PAF aircraft never really stood back to fight.

The question of loss is important but, in the ultimate analysis, secondary. Achieving air superiority cost the IAF dearly in 1971 but in the end it managed to achieve complete dominance over the skies in both East and West Pakistan.

DEFENDING THE WEST

Limited Plans

The Indian Army HQ's plans on the western front clearly demonstrate that India's aim was not the destruction of Pakistan. Operations instructions issued to commanders on the western front were quite limited and the larger aim was to ensure that the Indian Army took as much as territory from the Pakistanis and conceded as little of Indian territory as possible. India felt that whoever held the most territory would end up as the winner because the final word on the war would only be spelt out during the post-war negotiations that were expected to follow.

Pakistani commanders were aware of this basic dynamic and had concentrated virtually all their forces in the West. Their Air Force was equipped with Starfighters, new Chinese F-6s and newer versions of the F-86 Sabre. Their Army had a lot of fire power in the form of heavy artillery, new Chinese built T-59 tanks, and US-built Patton tanks. India had been preparing for war for some months but the Pakistanis were not perturbed. They felt that any Indian advance in the East could be held up for a while during which their concentrated forces in the West would seize strategically important Indian territory. In the end, India would be forced to negotiate and, the Pakistanis hoped, India's strategic designs would be frustrated. Bangladesh would never come into being.

The First Blow

Pakistan struck the first blow by attacking nine Indian air bases on 3 December 1971 and followed up by a massive attack on Chhamb (see "War is declared"). The Chhamb attack was stopped - but at a cost. Many of the major battle plans drawn up before the outbreak of war had to be hastily changed - even abandoned in some cases. One very disappointed soldier was Major. General. Z.C.Bakshi, commanding thc 26 Indian Infantry Division. "I toured the front-lines in my jeep, flying my flag, and there was no problem," recalls the General. "At one or two places, Pakistani soldiers even saluted my jeep. And I knew we could break through these lines and threaten Sialkot town, which was the objective given to my Division."

Major. General. Bakshi had a reputation of being a fighter and had done brilliantly in the previous war. When he took over 26 Division, in the southern part of the state of Jammu & Kashmir, a major worry was a dagger-shaped strip of territory measuring 170 square kilometres under Pakistani control that protruded into the Indian side. This "dagger" threatened an important link town called Akhnur.

After studying the map a few times, Bakshi told his subordinates that this was no "dagger" but a chicken's neck:"We shall squeeze this part like a chicken's neck as soon as the war begins." And he did just that. Within two days of the outbreak of the war, the "chicken's neck" had been wrung by one brigade under 26 Division. But the more ambitious plan to move towards Sialkot was never effected. "After the Pakistani thrust at Chhamb, headquarters was in a in flap and they took away one of my brigades and told me to not to attack," says Bakshi. "All those brilliant plans prepared before the war went to waste all because people could not keep their cool in the heat of battle and let one temporary reverse cloud their judgement."

The Indians had prepared just two other offensive plans for the entire western sector, which stretches from Ladakh (Jammu & Kashmir) in the north to the salt water marshes of the Runn of Kutch (Gujarat) in the south. The terrain in this sector is highly varied and begins with tall snow covered mountains in the north, then turns into riverine flats before moving to scrub covered stretches and rich farmland further south in the plains of Indian Punjab. Below Punjab, is the state of Rajasthan, made up mostly of desert. The desert stops short of the state of Gujarat and gives way to vast dry flat lands ending with the marshes of Kutch, which eventually merge into the Arabian Sea.

The western border is long - more than the distance between Paris and Moscow - and many an army has perished in the past in these areas. Taking territory here is a costly enterprise and the Indians knew it. This is why the overwhelming majority of its Army divisions were (and continue to be) termed as 'holding" formations as opposed to "strike" formations. The emphasis traditionally has been on defence rather than offense. The responsibility of defending the entire western sector was the responsibility of two Indian Army commands - the Western Command and the Southern Command. In 1971, India had just one strike formation, the 1 Corps. The other divisions under the Western and Southern commands were all designated holding formations. Though the holding corps also engaged in offensive action, these were all limited and not geared to carry the battle deep into enemy territory.

The three offensive missions drawn up by Indian Army Headquarters included the aborted 26 Division plan to move towards Sialkot, a major thrust by 1 Corps to capture the 30 km thick Shakargarh bulge which juts into the region between north Punjab and south Jammu & Kashmir, and a plan to move across the deserts to cut off the rail link between Pakistan's Punjab and Sindh provinces. The first two of these actions were to be carried out by Western Command, the largest of the two commands. The other command - Southern Command - was responsible for the borders south of Anupgarh at the northernmost edge of Rajasthan right down to the Arabian Sea. Due to the difficult terrain in the south, only two Indian Army divisions from Southern Command took part in the fighting and their battles is part of the story of Longewala (see section on "Battle of Longewala").

All the battles that took place in the Western sector are two numerous to be recounted here but the fight for Shakargarh deserves mention. For, here the fighting was particularly bitter with the most lives lost on both sides. As for the Pakistanis, despite grandiose pre-war plans, their only notable success was in Chhamb. In other areas, Pakistani units fought tenaciously but got nowhere because of the failure of their higher command.

Attack by 1 Corps

The Shakargarh Bulge points to the north Punjab town of Pathankot, which is squeezed between the mountains rising in the east and the Pakistani border on the west. Pathankot is strategically important for the defence of Jammu & Kashmir and the northern parts of Himachal Pradesh. This was also the Headquarters of India's only strike corps, commanded at that time by Lt. General. K.K.Singh. His forces included three infantry divisions, two independent armoured brigades, two independent artillery brigades and the equivalent of about two engineers brigades. The corps was, however, tied down due to defensive commitments that took up more than a division's worth of troops. The Pakistanis too had a formation designated 1 Corps opposite its Indian counterpart. This too was a heavy formation possessing considerable strike force. It was made up of two infantry divisions and four independent armoured brigades, apart from artillery and other support units. The Pakistanis also had committed considerable reserves for this sector, which they were able to bring in with surprising agility.

The Indian corps commander decided to attack the bulge from three sides: one division (54 Div) was to attack from Samba, a town in the north of the bulge where he had shifted his HQ; another (39 Div) was deployed more towards the western tip of the bulge; and the other (36 Div) was to commence from the southern part of the bulge. All these divisions had far less than their full complement of units and in practice had to operate at the brigade level. The fighting showed that in the end it is not only plans but hard fighting that decides the course of battles.

The advances of 39 Division under Major General B.R. Prabhu was a series of disasters right from the beginning. Although his units crossed the enemy lines easily enough, they got bogged down in minefileds and could not secure their objectives. To be fair, the Div commander had none of his brigades and had to make do with one brigade and two independent armoured brigades less a regiment. This made him a little cautious and somewhat disinclined to rally his forces forward. This caused major problems for the other two depleted divisions which were pressing ahead only to find their flanks exposed because of 39 Div's lack of progress.

54 Div attacking from the north was the most active although during the initial days of the war two of its three brigades had been taken away for the protection of Chhamb.

Nevertheless Major General W.A.G.Pinto, commanding the Div, and his able armoured brigade commander, Brigadier A.S.Vaidya (later General Vaidya, who became Chief of Army Staff), made tremendous progress. By 15 December 1971, the Div had control of all the points overlooking the Shakargarh-Zafarwal road. The big test was the crossing of the Basantar river, which had been mined by the Pakistanis and the minefield continued for 1,400 metres. The Pakistanis also had more than four independent armoured brigades worth of armour to throw at the Indians, which was far more than what the attackers had. The most formidable task was the river crossing.

By this time, the Pakistanis had got wind of the plan and had thrown in two infantry brigades and one armoured brigade to prevent the formation of a successful bridgehead. The Pakistani Air Force too was called in to fly relentless sorties against the Indian build-up. The Indian battalions and the brave engineers literally had to run through a wall of fire to establish crossing points and move across. The bridgehead was secured but the enemy was not dispersed. One Indian battalion had its commanding officer shot by Pakistanis infiltrating the bridgehead. Other units suffered horrendous losses in the concentrated artillery fire and aerial bombing. The Indian units pressed on regardless and by 15 December had established a bridgehead. The Pakistanis tried to destroy the bridgehead by launching a series of counter-attacks headed by tanks of Pakistan's 8 Independent Armoured Brigade. Indian tanks were rushed in to stop the Pakistanis from breaking through.

Two Indian tank regiments tried and were virtually decimated. Finally, the third Indian armoured regiment (17 Horse) held the Pakistanis with the help of three Indian infantry battalions. The fighting here was easily the most desperate in the war with the Pakistanis losing as many as 46 tanks in less than a days of fighting. The Pakistanis counter-attack was eventually stopped by nothing less than sheer grit. If anybody could tell the story best, it was Major Nisar, squadron commander of Pakistan's 13 Cavalry. The Pakistani armoured counter-attacks were stopped by 17 Horse and in the end it was just 3 tanks of a troop commanded by Captain V.Malhotra that ultimately took on one of the final Pakistani assaults from an entire squadron of tanks.

Leading the Pakistani squadron was Major Nisar. He was amazed to find his advance stopped by just three tanks. But before he could get over his surprise, he found most of his tanks hit. One of the Indian tanks, commanded by young Second Lieutenant Arun Khetarpal was responsible for most of the damage.

Even after both the other tanks or their commanders were put out of action, Khetarpal continued to fight until his tank was hit by Major Nisar's tank and caught fire. He was ordered to abandon his tank but he refused. He kept engaging the Pakistani tanks and stopped Major Nisar's tank with a hit. Although Nisar's tank ground to a halt it managed to fire one last shot at Khetarpal's stricken tank, killing the Second Lieutenant instantly. Major Nisar escaped by leaping out of his burning tank. The attack was stopped but out of the three squadron commanders only one lived to tell the tale- Captain Malhotra. After the cease fire, Major Nisar paid a courtesy calls across the lines to pay his complements.

He only found Captain Malhotra. Khetarpal was one of the few Indians in the country's 50 year history to have received the highest award for gallantry, the Param Vir Chakra. His posthumous citation read:"His calculated and deliberate decision to fight from a burning tank was an act of valour and self-sacrifice beyond the call of duty." But that is just what thousands of other soldiers did in the fighting in the Shakargarh bulge. The Pakistanis too fought to the man and in many areas, the fighting often ended up in hand-to-hand combat. From all accounts, this is the area where the Pakistanis fought for every inch of soil and the Indian shed blood for every yard they captured. The Indians clung on to every inch of territory they had conquered and the Indian Army's third Param Vir Chakra was won on these very killing fields. Major Hoshiar Singh led the forward company of the 3 Grenadiers into battle into the bridgehead and took a village called Jarpal. The Pakistanis counter-attacked later the same day.

Hoshiar Singh undaunted went from trench to trench to rally his men disregarding the bullets flying all around him. His behaviour so encouraged the men that they took on a battalion sized attack the next morning even after being pounded by artillery in which Hoshiar Singh was seriously wounded.

He continued to move amongst his men and kept up the fire against the enemy. When one of his machine gun crews was knocked out by a shell, he personally took over and shot a number of Pakistanis. At the end of the days fighting, over 85 Pakistani soldiers were found dead in front of their trenches.

That was the end of the Pakistani counter-attacks but the Indians could get no further as the cease-fire came into effect on the same evening. The Indians had halted their advance just 7 kilometres short of Zafarwal.

Some Indian military historians have been critical of 1 Corps' actions, arguing that much more could have been achieved had the corps commander not dispersed his resources and had not been forced to tie down a major chunk of his assets for defensive purposes.

But this is not quite fair considering that the actual offensive was late in starting and the Indians had actually less than a week to gain their objectives. Besides, this area was traversed by numerous rivers, ditches and defended embankments. The enemy had re-inforced the area in depth and laid extensive minefields all over the place. They also had significant artillery fire and were supported by the PAF. Making headway under such conditions in so limited a time was difficult.

Soldiers on both sides fought hard and if, in the end, the whole affair was a stalemate, it was justly so. Had the war dragged for even a week more, things would certainly have been very different.

That is why the Pakistani high command despite having lost all its strategic objectives readily agreed to a cease-fire. The Indian Army in the west proved that the regimental colours its men carried were still a matter of honour. The stories of the 1971 War ensured that those traditions would be carried on by many generations of fighting men in the years to come. Most of all, Indian troops had learnt that after all was said and done, honour in battle meant standing one's ground and fighting - even to the last man or tank if necessary.

THE SURRENDER

Modest Aims, Ambitious Action

Dhaka's fall was imminent. Everybody concerned including the Pakistani generals holed up in that city knew it was only a matter of time before the Indian Army and the Mukti Bahaini would get in. General Tikka Khan after killing a few million East Pakistanis had fled to Rawalpindi, leaving a professional soldier Lt. General A.A.K. Niazi in charge. He wanted to avoid a carnage but could not disobey the orders from Rawalpindi asking him to hold on. For the Indians, it was simply a question of how to speed up the surrender process.

The Indians got just the break they were looking for thanks to the Mukti Bahini intelligence. "Early on 14 December, the IAF got a message through the Mukti Bahini that an important meeting was scheduled in the Governor House (now 'Banga Bhaban') that morning.

Four MiG-21s of No. 28 Sqn from Gauhati were tasked to attack the Governor House. As Dr. Malek, the puppet Governor of the then East Pakistan, along with his cabinet and high officials were in session, the MiGs came screaming down and accurately fired salvos of rockets into the Darbar Hall.

The Governor was so traumatised that he resigned then and there, and rushed to the Hotel Intercontinental (now Sheraton), to seek shelter under the UN Flag. The Pakistani civil administration in the East ceased to exist. Of and on, between 12-14 December, the IAF transport planes came over Dhaka and dropped leaflets urging the Pak forces to surrender...By 15 December, at the request of the Pakistani Commander in the East, all air operations ceased and the negotiation for the surrender of the Pak forces started.

On 16 December morning, the IAF helicopter carrying the Indian negotiating team landed in Tejgaon", wrote Air Cdre Ishfaq Ilahi Choudhury (Retd).

On the morning of 16th December, Major General Jacob flew into Dhaka to persuade the East Pakistani Army commander, Lt. General A.A.K.Niazi, to accept an unconditional surrender.

The Pakistanis still had about 24,000 troops to defend Dhaka. He could have held on and some military eperts in Pakistan have criticsed him severely for accepting what is considered a "shameful surrender".

But Niazi needs to be applauded for saving the lives of thousands more and effectively rescuing the 94,000 Pakistani armed men who became POW and later returned unharmed to Pakistan. Had the Pakistanis decided to fight on, they would have been massacred to the man.

For, General Niazi had been offered, and had accepted, fair treatment from the Indians. The Indians had promised to protect him and his soldiers. The Mukti Bahini wanted the Indians to hand over the Pakistanis to them for trial and reprisals. If left to the Mukti Bahini and the general populace, the Pakistanis would have been butchered. Not surprisingly, General Niazi accepted the surrender terms and signed the unconditional surrender document at a public ceremony in Dhaka on 16 December 1971.

The act of surrender marked the birth of a new nation: Bangladesh. Sheikh Mujibur Rehman was released and returned triumphant to Dhaka after a brief stop-over at New Delhi where he was warmly embraced by Indian leaders.

In Dhaka, a grand ceremony was held with the Indian Eastern Army commander, Lt. General J.S.Aurora, in attendance with Sheikh Mujib. This was the Indian armed forces' finest hour. From a rag-tag, left over colonial remnaint, the three services had evolved into a new and formidable fighting force.

The East Pakistan campaign would always be remembered as a model in innovation and would serve to inspire generations of soldiers of the future.

The country's hero was Chief of Army Staff, General Sam Maneckshaw, who later went on to become the country's first Field Marshall. Indian had also won a great moral victory, for it had fought what was basically a liberation war. And as the Bangladeshi crowds and guerilla fighters rejoiced in the streets of Dhaka, it was clear that yet another round in the battle for liberty and justice had just been won.

7

INDIA DISCOVERS INFILTRATION AND MOBILIZES

INTRODUCTION

Initially, these incursions were not detected for a number of reasons: Indian patrols were not sent into some of the areas infiltrated by the Pakistani forces and heavy artillery fire by Pakistan in some areas provided cover for the infiltrators. But by the second week of May, the ambushing of an Indian patrol team, acting on a tip-off by a local shepherd in the Batalik sector, led to the exposure of the infiltration.

Initially with little knowledge of the nature or extent of the encroachment, the Indian troops in the area assumed that the infiltrators were jihadis and claimed that they would evict them within a few days.

Subsequent discovery of infiltration elsewhere along the LoC, and the difference in tactics employed by the infiltrators, caused the Indian army to realize that the entire plan of attack was on a much bigger scale. The total area seized by the ingress is generally accepted to between 130 km^2 - 200 km^2; Musharraf however, stated that 500 square miles (1,300 km^2) of Indian territory was occupied.

The Government of India responded with Operation Vijay, a mobilisation of 200,000 Indian troops.

However, because of the nature of the terrain, division and corps operations could not be mounted; the scale of the subsequent fighting was mostly at the regimental or battalion level. In effect, two divisions of the Indian Army, numbering 20,000, plus several thousand from the Paramilitary forces of India and the air force were deployed in the conflict zone.

The total number of Indian soldiers that were involved in the military operation on the Kargil-Drass sector was thus close to 30,000. The number of infiltrators, including those providing logistical backup, has been put at approximately 5,000 at the height of the conflict. This figure includes troops from Pakistan-administered Kashmir that were involved in the war providing additional artillery support.

The Indian Air Force launched Operation Safed Sagar in support of the mobilization of Indian land forces, but its effectiveness during the war was limited by the high altitude, which in turn limited bomb loads and the number of airstrips that could be used.

The Indian Navy also readied itself for an attempted blockade of Pakistani ports (primarily Karachi port) to cut off supply routes. Later, the then-Prime Minister of Pakistan Nawaz Sharif disclosed that Pakistan was left with just six days of fuel to sustain itself if a full-fledged war had broken out.

INDIA ATTACKS PAKISTANI POSITIONS

The terrain of Kashmir is mountainous and at high altitudes; even the best roads, such as National Highway No. 1 (NH 1) from Leh to Srinagar, are only two lanes. The rough terrain and narrow roads slowed traffic, and the high altitude, which affected the ability of aircraft to carry loads, made control of NH 1A (the actual stretch of the highway which was under Pakistani fire) a priority for India.

From their observation posts, the Pakistani forces had a clear line-of-sight to lay down indirect artillery fire on NH 1A, inflicting heavy casualties on the Indians. This was a serious problem for the Indian Army as the highway was its main logistical and supply route. The Pakistani shelling of the arterial road posed the threat of Leh being cut off, though an alternative (and longer) road to Leh existed via Himachal Pradesh.

The infiltrators, apart from being equipped with small arms and grenade launchers, were also armed with mortars, artillery and anti-aircraft guns. Many posts were also heavily mined, with India later stating to having recovered more than 8,000 anti-personnel mines according to an ICBL report. Pakistan's reconnaissance was done through unmanned aerial vehicles and AN/TPQ-36 Firefinder radars supplied by the US.

The initial Indian attacks were aimed at controlling the hills overlooking NH 1A, with high priority being given to the stretches of the highway near the town of Kargil. The majority of posts along the Line of Control were adjacent to the highway, and therefore the recapture of nearly every infiltrated post increased both the territorial gains and the security of the highway. The protection of this route and the recapture of the forward posts were thus *ongoing objectives* throughout the war. The Indian Army's first priority was to recapture peaks that were in the immediate vicinity of NH1a. This resulted in Indian troops first targeting the Tiger Hill and Tololing complex in Dras, which dominated the Srinagar-Leh route. This was soon followed by the Batalik-Turtok sub-sector which provided access to Siachen Glacier.

Some of the peaks that was of vital strategic importance to the Pakistani defensive troops were Point 4590 and Point 5353. While 4590 was the nearest point that had a view of

NH1a, point 5353 was the highest feature in the Dras sector, allowing the Pakistani troops to observe NH1A. The recapture of Point 4590 by Indian troops on June 14 was significant, notwithstanding the fact that Point 4590 resulting in the Indian Army suffering the most casualties in a single battle during the conflict. Though most of the posts in the vicinity of the highway were cleared by mid-June, some parts of the highway near Dräss witnessed sporadic shelling until the end of the war.

Once India regained control of the hills overlooking NH 1A, the Indian Army turned to driving the invading force back across the Line of Control. The Battle of Tololing, among other assaults, slowly tilted the combat in India's favor. Nevertheless, some of the posts put up a stiff resistance, including Tiger Hill (Point 5140) that fell only later in the war. A few of the assaults occurred atop hitherto unheard of peaks – most of them unnamed with only Point numbers to differentiate them – which witnessed fierce hand to hand combat.

As the operation was fully underway, about 250 artillery guns were brought in to clear the infiltrators in the posts that were in the line-of-sight. The Bofors field howitzer (infamous in India due to the Bofors scandal) played a vital role, with Indian gunners making maximum use of the terrain that assisted such an attack. However, its success was limited elsewhere due to the lack of space and depth to deploy the Bofors gun.

It was in this type of terrain that aerial attacks were used with limited effectiveness. The IAF lost a MiG-27 strike aircraft which it attributed to an engine failure as well as a MiG-21 fighter which was shot down by Pakistan; Pakistan said it shot down both jets after they crossed into its territory and one Mi-8 helicopter to Stinger SAMs. During attacks the IAF used laser-guided bombs to destroy well-entrenched positions of the Pakistani forces.

In many vital points, neither artillery nor air power could dislodge the outposts manned by the Pakistan soldiers, who were out of visible range. The Indian Army mounted some direct frontal ground assaults which were slow and took a heavy toll given the steep ascent that had to be made on peaks as high as 18,000 feet (5,500 m). Since any daylight attack would be suicidal, all the advances had to be made under the cover of darkness, escalating the risk of freezing.

Accounting for the wind chill factor, the temperatures were often as low as “11 °C to “15 °C (12 °F to 5 °F) near the mountain tops. Based on military tactics, much of the costly frontal assaults by the Indians could have been avoided if the Indian Military had chosen to blockade the supply route of the opposing force, virtually creating a siege. Such a move would have involved the Indian troops crossing the LoC as well as initiating aerial attacks on Pakistan soil, a manoeuvre India was not willing to exercise fearing an expansion of the theatre of war and reducing international support for its cause.

Two months into the conflict, Indian troops had slowly retaken most of the ridges they had lost; according to official count, an estimated 75%–80% of the intruded area and nearly all high ground was back under Indian control.

WITHDRAWAL AND FINAL BATTLES

As Pakistan found itself struggling, the army had covertly planned a nuclear strike on India, the news of which alarmed U.S. President Bill Clinton, resulting in a stern warning to Nawaz Sharif. Following the Washington accord on July 4, where Sharif agreed to withdraw Pakistani troops, most of the fighting came to a gradual halt, but some Pakistani forces remained in positions on the Indian side of the LOC. In addition, the United Jihad Council (an umbrella for all extremist groups) rejected Pakistan's plan for a climb-down, instead deciding to fight on. The Indian army launched its final attacks in the last week of July; as soon as the Drass subsector had been cleared of Pakistani forces, the fighting ceased on July 26. The day has since been marked as *Kargil Vijay Diwas* (Kargil Victory Day) in India. By the end of the war, India had resumed control of all territory south and east of the Line of Control, as was established in July 1972 as per the Shimla Accord.

World Opinion

Pakistan was criticised by other countries for allowing its paramilitary forces and insurgents to cross the Line of Control. Pakistan's primary diplomatic response, one of plausible deniability linking the incursion to what it officially termed as "Kashmiri freedom fighters", was in the end not successful. Veteran analysts argued that the battle was fought at heights where only seasoned troops could survive, so poorly equipped freedom fighters would neither have the ability nor the wherewithal to seize land and defend it.

Moreover, while the army had initially denied the involvement of its troops in the intrusion, two soldiers were awarded the Nishan-E-Haider (Pakistan's highest military honour). Another 90 soldiers were also given gallantry awards, most of them posthumously, confirming Pakistan's role in the episode.

India also released taped phone conversations between the Army Chief and a senior Pakistani general where the latter is recorded saying: "the scruff of the militants necks is in our hands," although Pakistan dismissed it as a "total fabrication". Concurrently, Pakistan made several contradicting statements, confirming its role in Kargil, when it defended the incursions saying that the LOC itself was disputed. Pakistan also attempted to internationalize the Kashmir issue, by linking the crisis in

Kargil to the larger Kashmir conflict but, such a diplomatic stance found few backers on the world stage. As the Indian counter-attacks picked up momentum, Pakistani prime minister Nawaz Sharif flew to meet U.S. president Bill Clinton on July 4 to obtain support from the United States. Clinton rebuked Sharif, however, and asked him to use his contacts to rein in the militants and withdraw Pakistani soldiers from Indian territory.

Clinton would later reveal in his autobiography that "*Sharif's moves were perplexing*" since the Indian prime minister had travelled to Lahore to promote bilateral talks aimed at resolving the Kashmir problem and "*by crossing the Line of Control, Pakistan had wrecked the bilateral talks.*" On the other hand, he applauded Indian restraint for not crossing the LoC and escalating the conflict into an all-out war.

G8 nations supported India and condemned the Pakistani violation of the LOC at the Cologne summit. The European Union also opposed Pakistan's violation of the LOC. China, a long-time ally of Pakistan, did not intervene in Pakistan's favour, insisting on a pullout of forces to the LoC and settling border issues peacefully. Other organizations like the ASEAN Regional Forum too supported India's stand on the inviolability of the LOC.

Faced with growing international pressure, Sharif managed to pull back the remaining soldiers from Indian territory. The joint statement issued by Clinton and Sharif conveyed the need to respect the Line of Control and resume bilateral talks as the best forum to resolve all disputes.

Impact and Influence of Media

The Kargil War was significant for the impact and influence of the mass media on public opinion in both nations. Coming at a time of exploding growth in electronic journalism in India, the Kargil news stories and war footage were often telecast live on TV, and many websites provided in-depth analysis of the war. The conflict became the first "live" war in South Asia; it was given such detailed media coverage that one effect was the drumming up of jingoistic feelings.

The conflict soon turned into a news propaganda war. Press briefings by government officials of each nation produced such conflicting claims and counterclaims that an outside observer listening to both Indian and Pakistani coverage would wonder whether they were describing the same conflict.

The Indian government placed a temporary news embargo on information from Pakistan, banning the telecast of the state-run Pakistani channel PTV and blocking access to online editions of the *Dawn* newspaper.

The Pakistani media criticized this apparent curbing of freedom of the press in India, while India media claimed it was in the interest of national security.

The Indian government ran advertisements in foreign publications including *The Times* and *The Washington Post* detailing Pakistan's role in supporting extremists in Kashmir in an attempt to garner political support for its position.

As the war progressed, media coverage of the conflict was more intense in India than in Pakistan. Many Indian channels showed images from the battle zone in a style reminiscent of CNN's coverage of the Gulf War (one of the shells fired by Pakistan troops even hit a Doordarshan transmission centre in Kargil while coverage continued).

Reasons for India's increased coverage included the greater number of privately owned electronic media in India compared to Pakistan and relatively greater transparency in the Indian media. At a seminar in Karachi, Pakistani journalists agreed that while the Indian government had taken the press and the people into its confidence, Pakistan had not. The print media in India and abroad was largely sympathetic to the Indian cause, with editorials in newspapers based in the west and other neutral countries observing that Pakistan was largely responsible for the conflict.

Some analysts believe that Indian media, which was both larger in number and more credible, may have acted as a force multiplier for the Indian military operation in Kargil and served as a morale booster. As the fighting intensified, the Pakistani version of events found little backing on the world stage.

This helped India gain valuable diplomatic recognition for its position.

WMDs and the Nuclear Factor

Since Pakistan and India each had weapons of mass destruction, many in the international community were concerned that if the Kargil conflict intensified, it could lead to nuclear war. Both countries had tested their nuclear capability in 1998 (India conducted its first test in 1974 while it was Pakistan's first-ever nuclear test).

Many pundits believed the tests to be an indication of the escalating stakes in the scenario in South Asia. When the Kargil conflict started just a year after the nuclear tests, many nations desired to end it before it intensified.

International concerns increased when Pakistani foreign secretary Shamshad Ahmad made a statement on May 31 warning that an escalation of the limited conflict could lead Pakistan to use "any weapon" in its arsenal. This was immediately interpreted as a threat of nuclear retaliation by Pakistan in the event of an extended war, and the belief was reinforced when the leader of Pakistan's senate noted, "The purpose of developing weapons becomes meaningless if they are not used when they are needed."

Many such ambiguous statements from officials of both countries were viewed as warnings of an impending nuclear crisis where the combatants would consider use of their limited nuclear arsenals in 'tactical' nuclear warfare in the belief that it would not have ended in mutual assured destruction, as could have occurred in a nuclear conflict between the United States and the USSR.

Some experts believe that following nuclear tests in 1998, the Pakistani military was emboldened by its nuclear deterrent to markedly increase coercion against India.

The nature of the India-Pakistan conflict took a more sinister turn when the U.S. received intelligence that Pakistani nuclear warheads were being moved towards the border.

Bill Clinton tried to dissuade Pakistan prime minister Nawaz Sharif from nuclear brinkmanship, even threatening Pakistan of dire consequences. According to a White House official, Sharif seemed to be genuinely surprised by this supposed missile movement and responded that India was probably planning the same.

In an article in May 2000 Dr Sanjay Badri-Maharaj claimed that India too had readied at least five nuclear-tipped ballistic missiles, but could not back up this claim with any official proof.

Sensing a deteriorating military scenario, diplomatic isolation, and the risks of a larger conventional and nuclear war, Sharif ordered the Pakistani army to vacate the Kargil heights. He later claimed in his official biography that General Pervez Musharraf had moved nuclear warheads without informing him.

Recently however, Pervez Musharraf revealed in his memoirs that Pakistan's nuclear delivery system was not operational during the Kargil war; something that would have put Pakistan under serious disadvantage if the conflict went nuclear.

The threat of WMD included chemical and even biological weapons. Pakistan accused India of using chemical weapons and incendiary weapons such as napalm against the Kashmiri fighters.

India, on the other hand, showcased a cache of gas masks, among other firearms, as proof that Pakistan may have been prepared to use non-conventional weapons. US official and the OPCW determined that Pakistani allegations of India using banned chemicals in its bombs were unfounded.

AFTERMATH

India

From the end of the war until February 2000, the Indian stock market rose by over 30%. The next Indian national budget included major increases in military spending. There was a surge in patriotism, with many celebrities expressing their support for the Kargil cause. Indians were angered by media reports of the death of pilot Ajay Ahuja, especially after Indian authorities reported that Ahuja had been murdered and his body mutilated by Pakistani troops.

The war had produced higher than expected fatalities for the Indian military, with a sizeable percentage of them including newly commissioned officers. One month after conclusion of the Kargil war, the Atlantique Incident - where a Pakistan Navy plane was shot down by India - briefly reignited fears of a conflict between the two countries.

After the war, the Indian government severed ties with Pakistan and increased defence preparedness. India increased its defence budget as it sought to acquire more state of the art equipment.

Media reported about military procurement irregularities and criticism of intelligence agencies like RAW, which failed to predict the intrusions or the identity/number of infiltrators during the war.

An internal assessment report by the armed forces, published in an Indian magazine, showed several other failings, including "a sense of complacency" and being "unprepared for a conventional war" on the presumption that nuclearism would sustain peace.

It also highlighted the lapses in command and control, the insufficient troop levels and the dearth of large-calibre guns like the Bofors.

In 2006, retired Air Chief Marshal, A.Y. Tipnis, alleged that the Indian Army did not fully inform the government about the intrusions, adding that the army chief Ved Prakash Malik, was initially reluctant to use the full strike capability of the Indian Air Force, instead requesting only helicopter gunship support. Soon after the conflict, India also decided to complete the project- previously stalled by Pakistan - to fence the entire LOC.

The end of the Kargil conflict was followed by the 13th Indian General Elections to the Lok Sabha, which gave a decisive mandate to the NDA government. It was re-elected to power in September–October 1999 with a majority of 303 seats out of 545 in the Lok Sabha.

On the diplomatic front, Indo-U.S. relations improved, as the United States appreciated Indian attempts to restrict the conflict to a limited geographic area.

Relations with Israel – which had discreetly aided India with ordnance supply and matériel such as unmanned aerial vehicles and laser-guided bombs, as well as satellite imagery – also were bolstered.

Pakistan

Faced with the possibility of international isolation, the already fragile Pakistani economy was weakened further. The morale of Pakistani forces after the withdrawal declined as many units of the Northern Light Infantry suffered heavy casualties, and the government refused to acknowledge the dead bodies of its soldiers, an issue that provoked outrage and protests in the Northern Areas.

Pakistan initially did not acknowledge many of its casualties, but Sharif later said that over 4,000 Pakistani troops were killed in the operation and that Pakistan had lost the conflict. Responding to this, Pakistan President Pervez Musharraf said, "It hurts me when an ex-premier undermines his own forces," and claimed that Indian casualties were more than that of Pakistan.

Many in Pakistan had expected a victory over the Indian military based on Pakistani official reports on the war, but were dismayed by the turn of events and questioned the eventual retreat. The military leadership is believed to have felt let down by the prime minister's decision to withdraw the remaining fighters.

However, some authors, including ex-CENTCOM Commander Anthony Zinni, and ex-PM Nawaz Sharif, state that it was General Musharraf who requested Sharif to withdraw the Pakistani troops.

With Sharif placing the onus of the Kargil attacks squarely on the army chief Pervez Musharraf, there was an atmosphere of uneasiness between the two. On October 12, 1999, General Musharraf staged a bloodless *coup d'état*, ousting Nawaz Sharif.

Benazir Bhutto, an opposition leader and former prime minister, called the Kargil War "Pakistan's greatest blunder". Many ex-officials of the military and the ISI (Pakistan's principal intelligence agency) also believed that "Kargil was a waste of time" and "could not have resulted in any advantage" on the larger issue of Kashmir.

A retired Pakistani Army General, Lt Gen Ali Kuli Khan, lambasted the war as "a disaster bigger than the East Pakistan tragedy", adding that the plan was "flawed in terms of its conception, tactical planning and execution" that ended in "sacrificing so many soldiers."

The Pakistani media criticized the whole plan and the eventual climbdown from the Kargil heights since there were no gains to show for the loss of lives and it only resulted in international condemnation.

Despite calls by many, no public commission of inquiry was set up in Pakistan to investigate the people responsible for initiating the conflict. The PML(N) published a white paper in 2006, which stated that Nawaz Sharif constituted an inquiry committee that recommended a court martial for General Pervez Musharraf, but Musharraf "stole the report" after toppling the government, to save himself.

The report also claims that India knew about the plan 11 months before its launch, enabling a complete victory for India on military, diplomatic and economic fronts. A statement in June, 2008 by a former army corps commander of Pakistan that Sharif "was never briefed by the army" on the Kargil attack, reignited the demand for a probe of the episode by legal and political groups.

Though the Kargil conflict had brought the Kashmir dispute into international focus – which was one of the aims of Pakistan– it had done so in negative circumstances that eroded its credibility, since the infiltration came just after a peace process between the two countries was underway. The sanctity of the LOC too received international recognition.

President Clinton's move to ask Islamabad to withdraw hundreds of armed militants from Indian-administered Kashmir was viewed by many in Pakistan as indicative of a clear shift in US policy against Pakistan. After the war, a few changes were made to the Pakistan army. In recognition of the Northern Light Infantry's performance in the war - which even drew praise from a retired Indian Lt.

General - the regiment was incorporated into the regular army. The war showed, that despite a tactically sound plan that had the element of surprise, little groundwork had been done to gauge the politico-diplomatic ramifications.

And like previous unsuccessful infiltrations attempts, such as *Operation Gibraltar*, which sparked the 1965 war, there was little coordination or information sharing among the branches of the Pakistan military. One U.S. Intelligence study is reported to have stated that Kargil was yet another example of Pakistan's (lack of) grand strategy, repeating the follies of the previous wars.

Significant Notes

Note (I): Names for the conflict: There have been various names for the conflict. During the actual fighting in Kargil, the Indian Government was careful not to use the term "war", calling it a "war-like situation", even though both nations indicated that they were in a "state of war". Terms like Kargil "conflict", Kargil "incident" or the official military assault, "Operation Vijay", were thus preferred.

After the end of the war however, the Indian Government increasingly called it the "Kargil War", even though there had been no official declaration of war. Other less popularly used names included "Third Kashmir War" and Pakistan's codename given to the infiltration: "Operation Badr".

Note (II): Casualties: Pakistan army losses have been difficult to determin, partly because Pakistan has not published an official casualties list. The US Department of State had made an early, partial estimate of close to 700 fatalities. According to numbers stated by Nawaz Sharif there were 4,000+ fatalities. His party Pakistan Muslim League (N) in its "white paper" on the war mentioned that more than 3,000 Mujahideens, officers and soldiers were killed. Another major Pakistani political party, the PPP, assesses the casualties to be three thousand soldiers and irregulars.

Indian estimates, as stated by the country's Army Chief mention 1,042 Pakistani soldiers were killed Musharraf, in his hindi version of his memoirs, titled "Agnipath", differs from all the estimates stating that 357 troops were killed with a further 665 wounded. Apart from General Musharraf's figure on the number of Pakistanis wounded, the number of people injured in the Pakistan camp is not yet fully known. One Indian Pilot was officially captured during the fighting, while there were eight Pakistani soldiers who were captured during the fighting, and were repatriated on 13 August 1999.

CASUALITIES IN KARGIL WAR

"Battalions of Northern Light Infantry (NLI) were wiped out by the Indian Forces in Kargil", the deposed Prime Minister of Pakistan Nawaz Sharief told newsmen while in detention testifying to the ferocious counter attack launched by the Indian Army and Indian Air Force to evict the regular Pakistani intruders from Indian soil in the Drass, Batalik, Mushkoh sectors in June-July last year.

The nation gratefully commemorates the sacrifices made by 527 brave soldiers and airmen for the success of "Operation Vijay", which is being observed as *Kargil Vijay Diwas* on July 26, 2000.

Indian forces had thus foiled Pakistan's politico-strategic motives to internationalise Kashmir as a nuclear flash point requiring urgent third party intervention, to alter the Line of Control (LOC) and disrupt its sanctity by capturing unheld areas in Kargil and to achieve a better bargaining position for a possible trade off against the positions held by India in Siachen.

Another tactical move on the part of enemy, was to interdict the Srinagar-Leh road by disrupting the vital NH-1A and to give fillip to militancy in J&K. The Indian political leadership and the various Ministries of Government of India worked in perfect synergy to meet the challenge.

The media coverage on the Kargil war, especially the electronic media, served as a force multiplier leading to a national upsurge of giant proportions and a feeling of oneness with our courageous *jawans*. Significantly, as the *15 Corps* mobilised its forces for the counter attack and elements of the *18 Mountain Division* poured into the various sectors of Kargil, the people of Jammu & Kashmir were steadfast against the enemy forces.

The gallantry displayed by *'Ladakh Scouts'* and *'J&K Light Infantry'* is testimony to that. The rapid Indian deployment was not reckoned by the Pakistanis.

The use of the Indian Air Force in support of the Army in Kargil had a strong impact on the course of the tactical battle in terms of the interdiction of Pakistani supply lines within Indian territory, the damage inflicted on the Pakistani defences and the lowering of the morale of the intruders.

In a skilful use of naval power in the form of *'Operation Talwar'*, the *'Eastern Fleet'* joined the *'Western Naval Fleet'* and blocked the Arabian sea routes of Pakistan. Apart from a deterrent, the former Prime Minister Nawaz Sharief later disclosed that Pakistan was left with just six days of fuel (POL) to sustain itself if a full fledged war broke out.

At the end of the day, it was the courageous deeds of soldiers from the *Jat Regiment, Rajputana Rifles,* the *Grenadiers, Madras Regiment, Sikh Regiment* and *Mahar Regiment* at the icy heights of Kargil mountains that overwhelmed the enemy.

The *'Artillery Regiments'* performed a splendid job by destroying enemy positions and pinning them down by continuous barrage of fire from 155 mm Bofors howitzers and 130 mm field guns. When the strategic Tiger Hill fell on account of a brilliantly executed tactical plan, the Prime Minister of Pakistan Nawaz Sharief was blissfully unaware of the development. His wife Kulsoom Sharief heard the news on ZEE TV and rushed to inform Nawaz Sharief, who was then enjoying golf at his residence near Lahore.

Apart from sheer courage of forces fighting in very hostile and inclement weather conditions, the military leadership has to be given due credit for keeping up the great traditions of Indian Army namely, obedience to the civilian authority in letter and spirit. The situation was such and militarily so compelling that the Army Chief would have felt it absolutely necessary to violate the LOC and get behind the enemy and threaten its lines of withdrawal.

In doing so, the Indian side would have succeeded in driving out the enemy much earlier. While the Army considered this option, it also restrained itself to go by the Central Government decision, i.e. to avoid the escalation of the conflict. It is precisely because of this reason that the eviction of the enemy took a little over two months and resulted in heavy loss of life.

Strangely, a war limited to a small area like Kargil sector had gone to highlight the Indian Foreign Policy that is principally directed towards world peace. By deciding not to take the war with Pakistan, by deciding not to violate the LOC, by deciding to wily-nily accept high rate of casualties on its side and thus limiting the conflict on its side and in determining that these are small sacrifices in the larger cause of world peace – all this reflects India's innate love for peace and good neighbourly relations even if it meant at some cost.

This exemplary demonstration of restraint, in the face of provocations, India was able to project itself to the international community that it stood for peace and not war. This peaceful assertion turned the tables on Pakistan to the extent that America, once Pakistan's most dependable ally, not only chose to condemn it as an aggressor but build up fresh solid relations between India and itself.

The result is Pakistan's isolation and General Musharaaf's regime left in lurch. For, this is the first military regime in Pakistan that has been disapproved by America and P-5 countries. Kargil war brought into sharp focus India's commitment to peace. While remembering the martyrs of Kargil war, let us also imagine what these martyrs were saying while dying, "go back and tell them that we are giving up our today for their tomorrow."

INDIAN ARMY IN THE WAR OF KARGIL

Before the Partition of India in 1947, Kargil was part of the Baltistan district of Ladakh, a sparsely populated region with diverse linguistic, ethnic and religious groups, living in isolated valleys separated by some of the world's highest mountains. The First Kashmir War (1947–48) concluded with the Line of Control (LOC) bisecting the Baltistan district, with the town and district of Kargil lying on the Indian side in the Ladakh subdivision of the Indian state of Jammu and Kashmir. After Pakistan's defeat in the Indo-Pakistani War of 1971, the two nations signed the Simla Agreement promising not to engage in armed conflict with respect to that boundary. The town of Kargil is located 205 km (120 miles) from Srinagar, facing the Northern Areas across the LOC. Like other areas in the Himalayas, Kargil has a temperate climate. Summers are cool with frigid nights, while winters are long and chilly with temperatures often dropping to “48 °C (“54 °F).

An Indian national highway (NH 1) connecting Srinagar to Leh cuts through Kargil. The area that witnessed the infiltration and fighting is a 160 km long stretch of ridges overlooking this highway. The military outposts on the ridges above the highway were generally around 5,000 metres (16,000 ft) high, with a few as high as 5,485 metres (18,000 ft). Apart from the district capital, Kargil, the populated areas near the front line in the conflict included the Mushko Valley and the tiny town of Drass, southwest of Kargil, as well as the Batalik sector and other areas, northeast of Kargil.

One of the reasons why Kargil was targeted was that the terrain surrounding it, lent itself to pre-emptive seizure of unoccupied military positions. With tactically vital features and well-prepared defensive posts atop the peaks, a defender of the high ground would enjoy advantages akin to a fortress. Any attack to dislodge a defender from high ground in mountain warfare requires a far higher ratio of attackers to defenders, and the difficulties would be exacerbated by the high altitude and freezing temperatures.

Kargil was also just 173 km (108 mi) from the Pakistani-controlled town of Skardu, which was capable of providing logistical and artillery support to Pakistani combatants. In addition to these tactical advantages, the Kargil district had a Muslim majority, which may have led Pakistani forces to expect local support for the infiltration as it had been expected in Operation Gibraltar.

BACKGROUND

After the Indo-Pakistani War of 1971, there had been a long period with relatively few direct armed conflicts involving the military forces of the two neighbors - notwithstanding the efforts of both nations to control the Siachen Glacier by establishing military outposts on the surrounding mountains ridges and the resulting military skirmishes in the 1980s.

During the 1990s, however, escalating tensions and conflict due to separatist activities in Kashmir, some of which were supported by Pakistan, as well as the conducting of nuclear tests by both countries in 1998, led to an increasingly belligerent atmosphere. In an attempt to defuse the situation, both countries signed the Lahore Declaration in February 1999, promising to provide a peaceful and bilateral solution to the Kashmir conflict.

During the winter of 1998 -1999, some elements of the Military of Pakistan were covertly training and sending Pakistani troops and paramilitary forces, some allegedly in the guise of mujahideen, into territory on the Indian side of the LOC. The infiltration was code named "Operation Badr"; its aim was to sever the link between Kashmir and Ladakh, and cause Indian forces to withdraw from the Siachen Glacier, thus forcing India to negotiate a settlement of the broader Kashmir dispute. Pakistan also believed that any tension in the region would internationalise the Kashmir issue, helping it to secure a speedy resolution.

Yet another goal may have been to boost the morale of the decade-long rebellion in Indian Administered Kashmir by taking a proactive role. Some writers have speculated that the operation's objective may also have been as a retaliation for India's Operation Meghdoot in 1984 that seized much of Siachen Glacier. According to India's then army chief Ved Prakash Malik, and many other scholars, much of the background planning, including construction of logistical supply routes, had been undertaken much earlier. On several occasions during the 1980s and 1990s, the army had given Pakistani leaders (namely Zia ul Haq and Benazir Bhutto) similar proposals for infiltration into the Kargil region, but the plans had been shelved for fear of drawing the nations into all-out war.

Some analysts believe that the blueprint of attack was reactivated soon after Pervez Musharraf was appointed chief of army staff in October 1998. After the war, Nawaz Sharif, Prime Minister of Pakistan during the Kargil conflict, claimed that he was unaware of the plans, and that he first learned about the situation when he received an urgent phone call from Atal Bihari Vajpayee, his counterpart in India. Sharif attributed the plan to Musharraf and "just two or three of his cronies"., a view shared by some Pakistani writers who have stated that only four generals, including Musharraf, knew of the plan. Musharraf, however, asserted that Sharif had been briefed on the Kargil operation 15 days ahead of Vajpayee's journey to Lahore on February 20.

War Progress

There were three major phases to the Kargil War. First, Pakistan infiltrated forces into the Indian-controlled section of Kashmir and occupied strategic locations enabling it to control NH1. The next stage consisted of India discovering the infiltration and mobilizing forces to respond to it. The final stage involved major battles by Indian and Pakistani forces resulting in India capturing positions held by Pakistani forces and the withdrawal of Pakistani forces back across the Line of Control.

OCCUPATION BY PAKISTAN

During the winter season, due to extreme cold in the mountainous areas of Kashmir, it was a common practice for both the Indian and Pakistan Armies to abandon some forward posts on their respective sides of the LOC and to reduce patrolling of areas that may be avenues of infiltration. When weather conditions became less severe, forward posts would be reoccupied and patrolling resumed.

During February 1999, the Pakistan Army began to re-occupy the posts it had abandoned on its side of the LOC in the Kargil region, but also sent forces to occupy some posts on the Indian side of the LOC.

Troops from the elite Special Services Group as well as four to seven battalions of the Northern Light Infantry (a paramilitary regiment not part of the regular Pakistani army at that time) covertly and overtly set up bases on the vantage points of the Indian-controlled region. According to some reports, these Pakistani forces were backed by Kashmiri guerrillas and Afghan mercenaries.

Pakistani intrusions took place in the heights of the lower Mushkoh valley, along the Marpo La ridgeline in Dras, in Kaksar near Kargil, in the Batalik sector east of the Indus river, the heights above of the Chorbatla sector where the LC turns North as well in the Turtok sector south of the Siachen area.

INDIAN PEACE KEEPING FORCE

Indian Peace Keeping Force was the Indian military contingent performing a peacekeeping operation in Sri Lanka between 1987 and 1990. It was formed under the mandate of the Indo-Sri Lankan Accord signed between India and Sri Lanka in 1987 that aimed to end the Sri Lankan Civil War between militant Sri Lankan Tamil nationalists such as the Liberation Tigers of Tamil Eelam (LTTE) and the Sri Lankan military. Its task was to enforce the terms of the accord, and maintain peace. and was inducted into Sri Lanka on the request of then-Sri Lankan president J. R. Jayewardene under the terms of the Indo-Sri Lanka Accord. Currently LTTE is proscribed as a terrorist organization by the United States and European Union.

The force was initially not expected to be involved in any significant combat by the Indian High Command. However, within a few months, the IPKF became embroiled in battle with the LTTE to enforce peace. Then a couple months after that the IPKF began to engage the LTTE militarily. In the two years it was in northern Sri Lanka, the IPKF launched a number of combat operations aimed at destroying the LTTE-led insurgency. In the process, IPKF was also accused of number of Human Rights violations against the civilian population. The IPKF began withdrawing from Sri Lanka in 1989, following the election of the Vishwanath Pratap Singh government in India and on the request of the newly-elected Sri Lankan President Ranasinghe Premadasa. The last IPKF contingents left Sri Lanka in March 1990.

BACKGROUND

Sri Lanka, from the early 1980s, was facing increasingly violent ethnic strife in the Sri Lankan Civil War. The origins of the Sri Lankan Civil War can be traced to the independence of Sri Lanka in 1948, after the end of British rule. At the time, a Sinhalese majority government was instituted. This government passed legislation deemed discriminatory against the substantial Tamil minority in Sri Lanka.

In the 1970s, two major Tamil parties united to form the Tamil United Liberation Front (TULF), a separatist Tamil nationalist group that agitated for a separate state of Tamil Eelam in north and eastern Sri Lanka that would grant the Tamils greater autonomy within the federal structure.

However, the Sixth Amendment to the Constitution of Sri Lanka, enacted in August 1983, classified all separatist movements as unconstitutional, Outside the TULF, Tamil factions advocating more militant courses of action soon emerged, and the ethnic divisions eventually led to violent civil war.

INDIAN INVOLVEMENT AND INTERVENTION

India had initially, under Indira Gandhi and later under Rajiv Gandhi, began to sympathize with the Tamil insurrection in Sri Lanka due to the strong support for the Tamil cause within the Indian state of Tamil Nadu. However, this emboldened the domestic support within Tamil Nadu to included providing sanctuary to the separatists, as well as help them smuggle arms and ammunition through which the LTTE emerged as the strongest force on the island. This activity was left unchecked as India's regional and domestic interests wanted to limit foreign intervention on what was deemed as a racial issue between the Tamils and the Sinhalese. To this end, the Indira Gandhi government sought to make it clear to Sri Lankan President Junius Richard Jayewardene that armed intervention in support of the Tamil movement was an option India would consider if diplomatic solutions should fail.

The first round of civil violence flared in 1983 when the killing of 13 soldiers of the Sri Lanka Army sparked anti-Tamil pogroms-the Black July riots-in which over 3000 Tamils were killed. The riots only aided in the deterioration of the ethnic relations. Militant factions, including the LTTE, at this time recruited in large numbers and continued building on popular Tamil dissent and stepped up the guerrilla war. By May 1985, the guerrillas were strong enough to launch an attack on Anuradhapura, attacking the Bodhi Tree shrine-a sacred site for Buddhist Sinhalese-followed by a rampage through the town. At least 150 civilians died in the hour long attack. However, after Gandhi's assassination, the Indian support for the militant movement waned at the very time the violence escalated. Rajiv Gandhi's government attempted to re-establish friendly relations with the various factions in Sri Lanka while maintaining diplomatic efforts to find a solution to the conflict as well as limiting overt aid to the Tamil fighters.

The Sri Lankan government, deducing a decline in support for the Tamil rebels from India, tried to rearming itself extensively for its anti-insurgent role with support from Pakistan, Israel, Singapore, and South Africa. In 1986, the campaign against the insurgency was stepped up. In 1987, retaliating against an increasingly bloody insurgent movement, the Vadamarachchi Operation (Operation Liberation) was launched against LTTE strongholds in Jaffna Peninsula. The operation involved nearly 4,000 troops, supported by helicopter gunships as well as ground-attack aircraft. In June 1987, the Sri Lankan Army laid siege on the town of Jaffna.

This resulted in large-scale civilian casualties and created a condition of humanitarian crisis. India, which had a substantial Tamil population in South India faced the prospect of a Tamil backlash at home, called on the Sri Lankan government to halt the offensive in an attempt to negotiate a political settlement. However, the Indian efforts were unheeded. Added to this, in the growing involvement of Pakistani advisers, it was necessary for Indian interest to mount a show of force. Failing to negotiate an end to the crisis with Sri Lanka, India announced on 2 June 1987 that it wound send a convoy of unarmed ships to northern Sri Lanka to provide humanitarian assistance but this was intercepted by the Sri Lankan Navy and forced to turned back.

Following the failure of the naval mission the decision was made by the Indian government to mount an airdrop of relief supplies in aid of the beleaguered civilians over the besieged city of Jaffna. On 4 June 1987, in a bid to provide relief, the Indian Air Force mounted Operation Poomalai. Five Antonov

An-32s under fighter cover flew over Jaffna to airdrop 25 tons of supplies, all the time keeping well within the range of Sri Lankan radar coverage. At the same time the Sri Lankan Ambassador to New Delhi was summoned to the Foreign Office to be informed by the Minister of State, External Affairs, K. Natwar Singh, of the ongoing operation and also indicated that the operation was expected not to be hindered by the Sri Lankan Air Force. The ultimate aim of the operation was both to demonstrate the seriousness of the domestic Tamil concern for the civilian Tamil population and reaffirming the Indian option of active intervention to the Sri Lankan government.

THE INDO-SRI LANKA ACCORD

Following Operation Poomalai, faced with the possibility of an active Indian intervention and lacking any possible ally, the President, J. R. Jayewardene, offered to hold talks with the Rajiv Gandhi government on future moves. The siege of Jaffna was soon lifted, followed by a round of negotiations that led to the signing of the Indo-Sri Lankan Accord on July 29, 1987 that brought a temporary truce. Crucially however, the negotiations did not include the LTTE as a party to the talks.

The signing of the Indo-Sri Lankan Accord on 29 July 1987 brought a temporary truce to the Sri Lankan Civil War. Under the terms of the agreement, Colombo agreed to a devolution of power to the provinces the Sri Lankan troops were withdrawn to their barracks in the north, the Tamil rebels were to disarm.

THE MANDATE FOR THE IPKF

Among the provisions undersigned by the Indo-Sri Lanka Accord was the commitment of Indian military assistance should this be requested for by the Sri Lankan Government, as well as the provision of an Indian Peace Keeping Force that would "guarantee and enforce the cessation of hostilities".

It was on these grounds, and on the request of President J. R. Jayewardene, that Indian troops were inducted to Northern Sri Lanka. J N Dixit, the then Indian ambassador to Colombo, in an interview to rediff.com in 2000 described that ostensibly, Jayawardene's decision to request Indian assistance came in the face of increasing civil riots and violence within the southern Sinhala majority areas, including the capital Colombo that were initiated by the Janatha Vimukthi Peramuna and the Sri Lanka Freedom Party that necessitated the withdrawal of the Sri Lankan Army from the Tamil areas of northern Sri Lanka to maintain order.

THE INDIAN PEACE KEEPING FORCE

Originally a reinforced division with small naval and air elements, the IPKF at its peak deployed four divisions and nearly 20,000 men with one mountain (4th) and three Infantry Divisions (36th, 54th, 57th) as well as supporting arms and services. At the peak of its operational deployment, IPKF operations also included a large Indian Paramilitary Force and Indian Special Forces elements. Indeed Sri Lanka was first theatre of active operation for the Indian Navy Commandos.

The main deployment of the IPKF was in northern and eastern Sri Lanka. Upon its withdrawal from Sri Lanka the IPKF was renamed the 21st Corps and was headquartered near Bhopal and became a quick reaction force for the Indian army.

IPKF ORDER OF BATTLE

The first Indian Army troops to be inducted into Sri Lanka were a ten thousand strong force from the 54th Infantry division, composed of elements of the Sikh Light Infantry, the Maratha Light Infantry and the Mahar Regiment which flew into Palay airbase , from July 30 onwards. This was followed later by the 36th Infantry division. By August, the 54th Infantry Division under the command of Maj Gen Harkirat Singh and the 340th Indian Inf Bde had landed in Sri Lanka. By 1987, the IPKF consisted of :

- 54th Air Assault Division. (Major General Harkirat Singh (General Officer Commanding), Brigadier Kulwant Singh, Dy GOC):- Became an infantry division later duie to lack of airlift capacity within the Indian armed forces.
    - o 10 Para Commando. (Jaffna) - an attached unit
    - o 65 Armoured Regiment (originally with T-54 tanks and later with T-72s). - an attached unit, it was later determined that the T55 was a better vehicle for counterinsurgency operations. Listed by some sources as an independent unit.
    - o 91 Infantry Brigade (Jaffna)
- 5 Madras Bn
- 8 Mahar Bn
- 1 Maratha Light Infantry Bn
    - o 76 Infantry Brigade (Brigadier I.M. Dhar) (Munnar, Vavuniya, Mulliativu)
    - o 47 Infantry Brigade (Trincomalee-Batticoloa-Amparai)
- 36 Infantry Division.
    - o 115 Infantry Brigade.(Jaffna)
- 5th Bn The First Gorkha Rifles.(5/1 GR).(Battle Of Urumparai,Battle Of Nallur Temple Jaffana,Battle Of Manipai)
- 72 Infantry Brigade.(Jaffna)
- 4 Bn./5 Gorkha Regiment.

- 13 Sikh LI Bn.
  - o 41 Infantry Brigade. (Jaffna)
- 5 Rajputana Rifles
- 57th Infantry Division, trained in jungle warfare,
- 4th Mountain division, only two brigades used.
- Independent Units
  - o 340 Independent Infantry Brigade (Amphibious). (Trincomalee) The Indian Marines
  - o 18 Infantry Brigade. (Jaffna)
  - o 5 Para Battalion.

Indian Air Force

Soon after its intervention in Sri Lanka and especially after the confrontation with the LTTE, the IPKF received a substantial commitment from the Indian Air Force, mainly transport and helicopter squadrons, including:

- No. 19 Squadron- Antonov An-32s
- No 109 and No. 119 Helicopter Units - Mil Mi-8 helicopters.
- No. 125 HU - Mil Mi-24s.
- No. 664 AOP Squadron Chetak and Cheetah

Indian Navy

The Indian Navy regularly rotated naval vessels thru Sri Lanka waters, mostly smaller vessels such as patrol boats.

- Indian Naval Air Arm
  - o No. 321 Squadron of the Indian Navy- HAL Chetaks
  - o No. 310 Squadron of the Indian Navy- Breguet Alizé
- MARCOS (also the Marine Commando Force or MCF) - Took part in Operation Pawan (Hindi, "wind") in 1988

and in the raid on an LTTE base at Guru Nagar. MARCOS operators (including Lt Singh) boarded two Gemini rafts off the coast of Jaffna City and towed two wooden rafts of explosives into a channel leading to the city's Guru Nagar Jetty. Avoiding mines, eight men and two officers shifted to the wooden rafts and paddled to the jetty then fixed demolition charges to the jetty and LTTE speedboats. The commandos were detected but laid down suppressive fire and detonated the explosives before retreating to the Geminis without taking casualties. Two nights later, commandos swam back into the harbour amidst heavy patrolling by the LTTE to destroy the remaining speedboats. They were again detected and sustained minor injuries. These actions helped recapture Trincomalee and Jaffna harbours from the LTTE. For leading these actions the 30 year old Lt. Singh became the youngest officer to receive the Maha Vir Chakra Award.

Indian paramilitary forces

Central Reserve Police Force

The Central Reserve Police Force (CRPF) is a paramilitary security agency/Force functioning under the aegis of Ministry of Home Affairs(MHA), Government of India. The CRPF's primary role lies in assisting the State/Union Territories in police operations to maintain law and order and contain insurgency. It came into existence as the Crown Representative's Police on 27 July 1939. After Indian Independence, it became the Central Reserve Police Force on enactment of the CRPF Act on 28 December 1949.

The Director General of CRPF is Mr.SIS Ahmed of 1970 IPS batch,appointed on 1 March 2007 who was earlier the Director General of CISF since 6 May 2005.

Besides Law and Order and counter insurgency duties, the role of CRPF in the General Elections, held repeatedly during the past few years, has been very significant and vital.

This is especially true for the trouble torn states of J&K, Bihar and in the North East. During the Parliamentary elections of September 1999, the CRPF played a major role in the security arrangements. The CRPF is one of the largest paramilitary force in the world with 200 battalions besides various establishments. Of late, CRPF contingents are also being deployed in UN missions.

History

CRPF was originally created as CRP(Crown Representative Police) on 27 July 1939, with 2 Battalions. Its primary duty at that time was to protect the British residents in sensitive states. In 1949, Sardar Patel had it renamed as CRPF under the CRPF Act. The Sixties saw major expansion of CRPF in which many State Reserve Police Battalions were merged with CRPF. Today, the force has 200 Battalions.

CRPF has been active against foreign invasion and domestic insurgency. On 21 October 1959, Dy.S.P. Karam Singh and his 20 soldiers were attacked by the Chinese Army, at Hot Springs in Ladakh. 10 were killed and the rest were taken prisoners. 21 October is now remembered across the country as POLICE COMMEMORATION DAY.In the 1965 India-Pakistan war, two companies (approx. 150 men) of the 2nd Battalion of CRPF defeated an infantry brigade (approx. 1600 men) of Pakistan Army at Kanjar Kot in Gujarat.

The CRPF guarded the India-Pakistan border until 1965, at which point the Border Security Force was created for that purpose. On 13 December 2001, the CRPF troopers killed all five terrorists who had entered the premises of the Indian Parliament at New Delhi.

In 2005, the CRPF troops killed all terrorists who had stormed the Ram Temple at Ayodhya.

In recent years, the Central Government has decided to follow up on recommendations of the Cabinet to use each security agency for its mandated purpose. Therefore, the counterinsurgency operations in India has been entrusted to the CRPF. The CRPF is currently charged with securing the Kashmir valley. Recently CRPF have completely relieved the Border Security Force in the Kashmir Valley of its Internal Security duties.

Organization

The CRPF is headed by Director general and is divided into ten administrative sectors headed each by an Inspector General .Each Sector consists of one or more administrative and/or Operational Ranges ,headed by an officer of the rank of Deputy Inspector General of Police.Group Centres are headed by Addl DIGs. There are 200 CRPF battalions of 720 constables approximately each and commanded by an officer designated as Commandant and consists of seven CRPF companies.The Companies are in charge of Assistant Commandants.

The Rapid Action Force

The Rapid Action Force (RAF) is a specialised 10 battalion wing of the Indian Central Reserve Police Force. It was formed in October 1992, to deal with communal riots and related civil unrest. The battalions are numbered from 99 to 108.

Weapons

CRPF uses basic Infantry weapons such as:

1. FN 35 and Glock 17 9 mm pistols
2. Heckler & Koch MP5 replacing the Carbine 1A 9 mm sub-machine guns

3. INSAS 5.56 mm assault rifles replacing the FN FAL, 1A1, 1C, AKM and V.58 7.62 mm assault rifles
4. INSAS 5.56 mm light machine guns replacing the 7.62 mm FN MAG, Bren L4 and the .50 cal Browning M2HB machine guns
5. Dragunov, Mauser SP66 and Heckler & Koch MSG-90 7.62 mm sniper rifles
6. AGS-17 Plamya 30 mm automatic grenade launcher
7. M40 RCL 106 mm and Carl Gustav 84 mm recoilless rifles . CRPF also uses landmine detectors ; Light Machine-Guns and Heavy-Machine-Guns.strling carbine9mm

Women in the CPRF

The CRPF is the only Paramilitary Force in the world to have two battalions staffed entirely by women. The first battalion was raised in 1986 with its headquarters at New Delhi. The second battalion came into existence in 1996 at Gandhinagar, Gujarat.

The Green Force

Another specialised outfit of the CRPF is the Green Force. The force has been able to effectively check environmental degradation and sustain the regeneration of local flora and fauna. Every year Green Force personnel plant lakhs (hundreds of thousands) of trees in various parts of the country.

Indian Coast Guard

The Indian Coast Guard is a part of Armed forces (under Navy) of India created to guard Republic of India's vast coastline. Many people confuse the Indian Coast Guard as an Armed Force (akin to the Indian Army, Navy and Air Force) since it is placed under the Ministry of Defence. The Indian Coast Guard's structure is similar to the other Para Military Forces of India such as the Border Security Force (BSF) and the Central Industrial Security Force (CISF) which are all constituted as 'Armed Forces' of India (so is the Indian Coast Guard), wherein the 'Armed Force' means a Force which is authorised by the Government to Handle and use Arms in the legal discharge of their duties. It was created on 18 August 1978 as an independent entity as per the Coast Guard Act. It's primary objective is to guard India's vast coastline and operates under the effective control of the Ministry of Defense.

The coast guard works closely with the Indian Navy and the Indian Customs Department, and is generally headed by a naval officer of the rank of Vice-Admiral. India's coast guard has a large number of fast craft including hovercrafts and hydrofoils. They patrol the seas and river mouths. The coast guard has performed a number of commendable tasks of rescuing distressed personnel. It has also apprehended pirates on high seas and cleaned up oil spills. Heavy patrolling of sensitive areas such as Gujarat, West Bengal and Mumbai have resulted in the nabbing of a large number of smugglers and illegal immigrants.

Unfortunately, the Indian Coast Guard was unable to intercept the heavily armed terrorists who came ashore from small boats during the seaborne November 2008 Mumbai attacks. After hijacking a fishing trawler to provide cover and avoid detection by the Indian Coast Guard, terrorists showed fake identification papers to Indian Coast Guard boarding officers and were allowed to continue on their way. Terrorist teams then sailed close to the Mumbai coast and deployed in small boats laden with arms and explosives. Once ashore, they killed and wounded hundreds in a standoff battle that went on for four days. After this attack decision was taken to improve the service by providing more assets and setting up nine more stations.

It's Responsibilities Include:

- Enforcing the provisions of enactment in force in the maritime zones.
- Assisting the Customs and other authorities in anti-smuggling operations.
- To preserve & protect the marine environment and control marine pollution.
- Measures for safety of life and property at sea including aid to mariners in distress.
- Ensuring the safety & protection of artificial islands, offshore terminals and other installations in MR zones
- Assist the Indian Navy in times of war

Motto: Vayam Rakshaamah -- "We Protect" in Sanskrit. (It is seen in Devanagari script on the coat of arms.)

The Coast Guard is responsible for the policing of over 2.01 million square kilometres of ocean. The area under its control includes nearly 1,200 islands and a coastline of 7517 kilometres.

History

In 1974, the Government of India set out to create an autonomous coast guard to protect the nation's long coast line. This coast guard was modelled on the lines of the British (HMCG) and American (USCG) coast guards. Like many coast guards around the world, the Indian Coast Guard has borrowed the white paint scheme and "racing stripe" from the U.S. service. The dress uniforms are similar to those of their counterparts from the Indian Navy. An interim Indian Coast Guard was set up on February 1, 1977 equipped with modern weaponry and quick sea craft with the help of the Indian Navy.

The duties and functions of the service were formally defined in the Coast Guard Act, which was passed on 18 August 1978, and came into effect the next day. The Indian Coast Guard conducts exercises with the other coast guards of the world. In 2006, the Indian Coast Guard conducted exercises with Japanese and Korean counterparts. In May 2005, the Indian Coast Guard agreed to set up liaison links with Pakistan Coast Guard.

RANK STRUCTURE

Coast Guard Rank Structure Equivalent Indian Navy Rank Structure

Coast Guard	Indian Navy
Director General	Vice Admiral
Inspector General	Rear Admiral
Deputy Inspector General +	Commodore
Deputy Inspector General	Captain
Commandant	Commander
Commandant (Junior Grade)	Commander
Deputy Commandant	Lieutenant Commander
Assistant Commandant	Lieutenant
Assistant Commandant †	Acting Lieutenant
Assistant Commandant ?	Midshipman

+ With three years seniority † Under training after completion of Phase III afloat training and during sub courses ? Under training after completion of Phase II afloat training

Bases

The Coast Guard is headed by a Director General from the Navy, of the rank of Vice Admiral. Coast Guard is presently headed by Vice Admiral Anil Chopra, AVSM. Although Coast Guard officers have previously headed the force (in the alternative rank of Director General), these have been naval officers on permanent deputation to the force. The force has a strength of 5440, including 633 officers. Its headquarters is based in the capital, New Delhi. It has:

- three Regional Headquarters at Mumbai, Chennai, and Port Blair
- one District headquarters in each of the nine coastal states and 2 in the Union territories of Andaman and Nicobar Islands and Lakshadweep Islands.
- Twenty nine Coast Guard stations[3] at places like Vadinar, Haldia, Kakinada, Okha, Tuticorin and Mandapam.
- two air bases, in Daman and Chennai
- Air enclaves at Goa, Kolkata and Port Blair.
- A new station has been recently commissioned in Pondicherry patrol vessels, aircraft and helicoptes into service.

Aircraft inventory

Aircraft	Origin	Type	Versions	In service	Notes
HAL Dhruv	India	Utility helicopter		4	
Aérospatiale SA 316 Alouette III	France	Utility helicopter	SA 316B	17	
Dornier Do 228	Germany India	transport search and rescue patrol	Do 228-101	24	18 built by HAL

COMBAT OPERATIONS

Indian Intervention in the Sri Lankan Civil War

The Indian intervention in the Sri Lankan Civil War (1987 - 1990) was deployment of the Indian military contingent Indian Peace Keeping Force intended to perform a peacekeeping operation in Sri Lanka. It was formed under the mandate of the Indo-Sri Lankan Accord signed between India and Sri Lanka in 1987 that aimed to end the Sri Lankan Civil War between militant Sri Lankan Tamil nationalists Liberation Tigers of Tamil Eelam (LTTE) and the Sri Lankan military.

The force was initially not expected to be involved in any significant combat by the Indian High Command. However, within a few months, the IPKF became embroiled in battle with the LTTE to enforce peace. In the two years it was in northern Sri Lanka, the IPKF launched a number of combat operations aimed at destroying the LTTE-led insurgency. The IPKF began withdrawing from Sri Lanka in 1989, following its military fiasco and the election of the Vishwanath Pratap Singh government in India and on the request of the newly-elected Sri Lankan President Ranasinghe Premadasa. The last IPKF contingents left Sri Lanka in March 1990.

The Indian Intervention

The LTTE had enjoyed support from India till the IPKF started getting inducted. However, not having been party to the negotiations leading up to the accord, it agreed to the truce only reluctantly. The Tigers had rejected the Provincial Council framework as inadequate and Prabhakaran had protested against the Indian military intervention. The Tigers resisted the spread what was deemed India's self-serving aim of binding Sri Lanka into India's geo political sphere of influence, as well as a symapthy for Sri Lanka's ruling Sinhala community in India outside the support-base in Tamil Nadu. With the induction of the Indian troops, the Tigers initially complied by surrendering arms along the terms of the truce. However, the opposition to the induction of Indian troops soon flared into active confrontation. Along with this, there developed an increasingly brutal confrontation within Tamil factions, with allegations that the LTTE, predominantly a Northern Tamil powerbase, was attempting to destroy both the PLOTE and the EPRLF, which represented more of the Eastern provinces. The LTTE boycotted the elections that were held in October and November 1988 along the lines outlined in the accord. The Indian administration had not expected opposition from the Tigers and was initially taken unaware.

The support for Tamil Nationalism in India also raised the spectre to the Indian Govt. of a possible situation of Tamil secessionist movement in Tamil Nadu. However, faced with growing diligence from her erst-while partner, India adopted a strategy of aiding alternative Tamil power bases, including the Eelam People's Revolutionary Liberation Front, which ultimately emerged strongly in the November 1988 elections, and at the same time continue negotiations with the LTTE. At the same time, however, Sinhalese nationalists, led by the JVP loathed the foreign presence on their soil.

Conflict with the LTTE

Two incidences that occurred in September-October 1987 marked the turning point of Indo-LTTE relationship. The first of these was the hunger strike and subsequent death of Lt. Col. Thileepan, a popular political wing leader of the LTTE, on 26 September 1987. Thileepan had begun his fast in protest against what was termed the failures of the Indian forces to satisfy the political demands of the Tamils, and his death was mourned throughout the Tamil community and fuelled a growing dissatisfaction and impatience with the pace of promised reforms. In addition it was a huge propaganda victory for the LTTE, which started taking an increasingly hard line in the negotiations for the Interim Provincial Council. The talks broke down. However, on 4 October 1988, the Sri Lankan Navy captured an LTTE boat off Point Pedro with seventeen

Tigers, including some high-profile leaders of the movement, onboard. The Colombo government alleged the boat was involved in smuggling arms across the Palk Straits and on the grounds denied immunity to these captured Tiger rebels.

The LTTE denied this claiming the rebels' movements were in accordance with the truce, being in the process of transferring documents for shifting the Tigers Headquarters from Madras to Jaffna. The Sinhalese government intended to bring a number of the rebels captured, including Pulendran, Kumarappa and others, to trial in Colombo for allegedly masterminding the massacre of a hundred and fifty civilians.

The Tigers, who were at the time still in negotiation with the Indian authorities, appealed for enforcement of protection by the IPKF. The rebels were at this time in IPKF custody at Palay Airbase pending transfer to Sinhalese authorities. Although the Indian authorities insist that they had explained the possible repercussions of such an action on the fragile truce and exerted considerable pressure on the Sinhalese authorities to desist from proceeding, ultimately the IPKF withdrew allowing the Sri Lankan forces to proceed with transferring the captured rebels to Colombo.

The detainees however, attempted mass suicide by swallowing cyanide- a common LTTE practice when faced imminent capture. This singular event marked a total break-down of the truce. The night of 5 October saw large scale slaughter of Sinhalese people who had returned to Jaffna, including eight soldiers of the Sri Lankan Army who were at the time being held hostages by the LTTE. These coincided with armed confrontations between the Tiger Cadres and the Indian Troops in and around Jaffna. On 8 October, the LTTE carried out a number of mortar attacks and ambushes on the IPKF.

In the face of this deteriorating situation, President Jayawardene threatened the visiting Indian Defence Minister and the Chief of Army Staff to re-induct the Sri Lankan Army to protect Sinhala interests if the IPKF did not take actions against the LTTE. The Indian government, already accused of inaction in the face of a failing accord, was forced into a position of having to enforce peace in Jaffna by force. By 7 October, the COAS had issued directives to the IPKF, laying down its operations parameters in the directive as:

- Seize/destroy the LTTE radio/TV transmission equipment in the Jaffna Peninsula;
- Seize or jam LTTE communication network;
- Carry out raids on LTTE camps, caches and strong points;
- Personnel manning LTTE offices in the East be detained and interrogated to gain information. In case of resistance,force to be used;
- Actions to further consolidate hold of IPKF in the region.

It was declared on 9 October that the IPKF was to launch a final campaign against the LTTE. This was the point of no return.

Operation Pawan

The first of the major IPKF operation was launched on 9 October 1987. Codenamed Operation Pawan (Hindi: Wind), it was expected to neutralise the LTTE operations capability in and around Jaffna. This included the capture or neutralisation of the LTTE's chain of command. which was expected to leave the rebel movement directionless in the face of the impending assault on the LTTE strongholds by the IPKF. On the nights of October 9 and October 10, the IPKF raided and captured the LTTE radio station at Tavadi and TV station at Kokkuvil, while the printing presses of two LTTE sponsored newspapers were destroyed. These operations also led to the capture of nearly two hundred Tiger rebels. In retaliation, the LTTE ambushed a CRPF convoy near Tellipallai, killing four jawans, as well as an IPKF post at Tellipallai with automatic and mortar fire on IPKF post. Later that day, the Tigers hijacked a 10 Para Commando jeep on patrol, killing all five occupants.

On October 10, the Indian 91st Brigade, consisting of three battalions and led by Brigadier J. Ralli, began its push into the city of Jaffna.

The Jaffna University Helidrop

The first battle signalling the real beginning of Operation Pawan was the Heliborne assault on Jaffna University headquarters of the LTTE by a detachment of Indian Para Commandos and the Sikh LI on the night of 12 October. Jaffna University was the tactical headquarters of the LTTE. This was planned as a quick commando raid to capture the top LTTE leadership and local commanders who, based on Indian Intelligence, were supposed to be in the building at the time. and was thus expected to cut short the Battle for Jaffna. The plan was to land a company of 70 men from 10 Para Cdo. to secure the football field. A second wave was to follow with a company of the 13th Sikh LI. The heliborne troops were to link up with 4/5 Gorkhas of 72 Brigade and the Sikh LI troops advancing on the ground. However, the operation ended in disaster as the LTTE, having intercepted IPKF radio transmissions, set up an ambush. The helidropped troops came under intense LTTE fire as they were inserted which, while increasingly vicious fire from LTTE positions hit and crippled the Mi-8s enough to force the insertion to be terminated midway through operation. Over the battle that lasted through the night, twenty nine of the entire Sikh LI contingent of thirty troops and six of the one hundred and twenty commandos were killed before detachments of the 65th armoured regiments were able to extract the Paras from their defensive positions. The Sikh LI radioman was shot by LTTE snipers early on, with the unit losing contact with the Indian High Command at Palay Air base and the lone survivor of the Sikh LI detachment, Sepoy Gora Singh was taken prisoner by the Tigers. It was not until his release later during the conflict that the fate of the unit was known.

Battle for Jaffna

As the battle for Jaffna proggressed, the IPKF advance came under intense and vicious opposition from the Tigers. Fighting in built-up and an as-yet unevacuated Jaffna, the Indian High command insists that the slow advance was, in addition to Tiger resistance, more a result of reluctance on the part of the IPKF to use heavy weaponry to clear LTTE defences. Furthermore all the approach roads had been armed with Claymore mines or explosives by the Tigers in its years of fighting with the Sri Lankan army. The Tigers also made extensive use of IED which could be remotely detonated from over a kilometre away. During this time, the Indian Navy, supported by the Coast Guards was key in establishing a 300-mile long blockade around the Northern Sri Lanka from October 1987 to disrupt the Tigers' supply and communications routes. In addition, it was around this time the MARCOS commandos of the Navy first went into action. Detachments of the IMSF (Indian Marine Special Forces, as the MARCOS was then known), along with a battalion of the 340th Independent Brigade of the Indian Army, provided beach reconnaissance around Jaffna and Batticaloa. The 340th Brigade was one of the first IPKF units to be deployed, and served until operations in the Trincomalee area were complete. The IMSF, at this time, also provided security patrols along the coastal road west of Jaffna until the 41st Brigade took charge later in November.

On October 15/16, the IPKF advance stopped its advance to stabilize the front. In addition, Palay, the major operations headquarters for the 54th Infantry Division, was secured from Tiger attacks. At this time the Indian Air Force undertook a massive airlift to reinforce the 91st with three brigades and heavy equipments including T-72 Tanks s and BMP-1 fighting vehicles. The improvised controllers worked round the clock to fly in troops and equipment. In addition, the Indian Airlines is said to have contributed, with its Boeing 737s transporting troops. In addition, this short interval saw the induction of the Mi-8s and the first induction of the Mi-25s of the No. 125 Sqn, along with the HAL Cheetahs. By end of October the IAF flew 2200 tactical transport and 800 helicopter sorties.

Now reinforced, the IPKF resumed the battle for Jaffna town. The tanks and armoured fighting vehicles are said to have been an effective protection against the anti-personnel mines. However, even with this protection, the IPKF advance was torturous in the face of the Tigers' sniper fire.

BIBLIOGRAPHY

Bellamy, C.: *Knights in White Armour: The New Art of War and Peace*, London, Random House, 1997.

Chandra, R.: *Judicial System in India*, Lucknow, Print House (India), 1992.

Davies .A.: *Telecommunications and Politics. The Secentralised Alternative*, London, Pinter, 1994.

Friedman, G.: *The Future of War: Power, Technology and Indian Army*, N.Y., Random House, 1996.

Heimanson, Rudolph: *Dictionary of Political Science and Law*, N.Y.: Oceana Publications, 1967.

Huntington, S.P.: *The Soldier and the Indian Army*, N.Y., Vintage Books, 1964.

Jones, W.H.: *The Government and Politics of Indian Army*, London, Hutchinson, 1971.

Kelly, John B.: *India and the Pakistan War*, Oxford, Clarendon Press, 1968.

Mary, W.: *Asian Power and Politics: the Cultural Dimensions of Authority*, Cambridge, Belknap Press, 1985.

Nair, A. M.: *Role of Indian Army in Kargir War*, Bombay, Orient Longman, 1983.

Posen, B.R.: *The Sources of Indian Military*, Cornell Univ. Press.

Rosen, P.: *Societies and Military Power: India and its Armies*, Ithaca, Cornell University Press, 1996.

Simon, D. : *Public Administration*, New York, Knopf, 1950.

INDEX

□□□